A little book learning is so ~~~~~~~~~~ n
actual experience.

Love (and a little banana
bread)

Richard

5⁰⁰

Jxx/h

·HOME·
·COMFORT·

·LIFE ON TOTAL LOSS FARM·

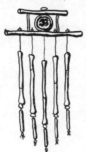

Saturday Review Press

·Home·Comfort·
·Stories and Scenes·
·of·
·Life on Total Loss Farm·

by

Hugh Beame

Pete Gould

Marty Jezer

Alicia Bay Laurel

Joan Marr

Raymond Mungo

Doug Parker

Robert Payne

Jeanne Pepper

Verandah Porche

Connie Silver

Ellen Snyder

Edited by

Richard Wizansky

With additional contributions by

Josiah Adams

Vicki Goucher

Fritz Hewitt

Frank Kebbell

Sandra Marr

Andrew Mungo

David Mylin

Pip Rice

Bill Root

Harry Saxman

Peter Simon

Ron Squires

Published simultaneously in Canada by Doubleday Canada Ltd., Toronto

Library of Congress Catalog Card Number: 72-91186

ISBN 0-8415-0228-5

Saturday Review Press
380 Madison Avenue
New York, New York 10017

Printed in the United States of America

·FOR ALL EXILES AND WANDERERS·

"IF YOU COULD
ONLY TELL THEM
that living and spending isn't the same thing!
But it's no good. If only they were educated to
live instead of earn and spend, they could manage
very happily on twenty-five shillings.
If the men wore scarlet trousers, as I said,
they wouldn't think so much of money:
if they could dance and hop and skip, and sing
and swagger and be handsome, they could do
with very little cash. And amuse the women
themselves, and be amused by the women.
They ought to learn to be naked and handsome,
and to sing in a mass and dance the old group
dances, and carve the stools they sit on, and
embroider their own emblems. Then they
wouldn't need money. And that's the only way to
solve the industrial problem: train the people
to be able to live, and live in handsomeness,
without needing to spend. But you can't do it.
They're all one-track minds nowadays. Whereas
the mass of people oughtn't even to try to think,
because they can't! They should be alive and
frisky, and acknowledge the great god Pan.
He's the only god for the masses, forever.
The few can go in for higher cults if they like.
But let the mass be forever pagan."

from D. H. LAWRENCE'S LADY CHATTERLEY'S LOVER

·CONTENTS·

·PREFACE·

THE WRITING OF THIS BOOK illustrated as well as any event can the "processes" of life on the farm. It was difficult and at times almost downright impossible to bring it to fruition. Many of the reasons should be apparent before looking further. Assume the role of "editor," request some steady and organized production from a dozen talented and temperamental prima donnas, and observe how effortlessly confusion and hesitance take the place of order and spontaneity.

Total Loss Farm, as its name implies, could never work that way, and it collectively and vociferously held to its principles of systemless accomplishment throughout the writing of this book. As that instinct had in the past proved to reap the most joyful benefits, we believe that once again the old and trusted rituals have borne us through. The material brought together here seeped into form slowly and often under great pressure. All of us had to take time to stand back from the center of our lives and our work as farmers of the soil and the mind and community, and look "objectively" at what we'd done, and how it mysteriously came to be that we were all gathered in this one place together, working for the farm and for each other and, up until the writing of this book, for some unspoken dream or purpose that kept us warm and moving. And although the introspection at times seemed valuable and educative for us as well as for the potential reader, the experience of that look into the power and ideas which remain beyond the appearance of our lives was often painful, and not a little disarming. Whether or not the reader will be offered a glimpse into that mystery, remains to be seen.

There is, however, an undeniable value to this book. For it succeeds in presenting one large and shared experience through the eyes and sensitivities of each of those who are a part of it. And therefore we, as well as you the reader, are given the opportunity to experience how the often obscured processes of "reality" are broken down into individual interpretations, and stamped with the particular watermark of the perceiver. In this aspect of the book, then, we have all been able to nudge the working minds' approximations of truth somewhat closer to the light.

Who knows how or why this place which I write from, just now caught in the statuesque freeze of December, sustains itself? And is it important to discover? Are the answers to follow, neatly presented and indexed? None of us can be sure. What we *are* certain of is that the scenes and stories that we've presented are a journey into the discovery of ourselves and our environment, which when gathered together, like the stitches of endless winter knitting, can reveal a shadow of the symmetry we call our love.

·THE OLD VALUES·

MUCH OF LIFE HERE is an attempt to recreate or rediscover the values and joie de vivre of Kajamunya, the land of our forefathers to which all of us are heir. All of that experience, now so vague, is scented with only the fondest recollections of a supremely tender and joyous history, almost as if life there were spun from some ecstatic dream or waking reverie which quickly fades when one remembers. Yet all of us know in a moment of quiet revelation, or in that mysterious acknowledgment that what is happening now has surely happened somewhere before in some other time, that Kajamunya did and continues to exist. And for us, all countrymen and lovers of that distant land which saw our exile, the moment is enough.

Although I, the son of the late, demented king of that land, now a marquis driven to exile in its image, am the only one who remembers clearly the language and history of the lost land, all of us at one time or another have found ourselves brimming forth with the foreign speech and manner of our heritage. And because Kajamunya is such a persistent memory and surprise in our lives, and because of my mutually tragic and happy memories of the place, I have been asked to relate what my heart can bear to recollect of our life there. Because it is easier for me to find my way through its language, I have first written this in the consonant sounds of Kajamunyan. What follows is the most proximate and lyrical translation I could transcribe.

Life there now seems as if it were a dream: centered somewhere in the heart of Eastern Europe (understandably I cannot be geographically precise), Kajamunya, an ancient and accomplished civilization, looms out of the foothills of a rocky yet fertile land as the largest mountain in all the neighboring country. It was settled, before time or history can recall, by a wandering band of scholars who had left their native land in search of a place which would be more suitable to their growing spiritual and intellectual awareness. Their leader, Bianafount, had been a temple priest and astrologer in the king's court who one day had awakened with the realization that his present life and occupation could no longer bring him the freedom of spirit and satisfaction for which he yearned. The ways of the court and country were in such a state of disharmony and anarchy of feeling that he felt it immediately necessary to create a new life for himself, and for those who would follow. In discussions with his family and a circle of intimate and abiding friends, he learned that others, too, had come to the same uncomfortable state of affairs. It was quickly decided that all former connections must be severed, and that a caravan would assemble when the moon would best be suitable for planting; then they would make their departure. Because the ruler of that land was himself a man given over to the mysteries and revelations of the spirit, he gave Bianafount his reverent and hopeful blessings. Bianafount assembled his family, among whom was his favorite grandson and pupil, and asked them to make ready for their exile. In the spring, on an evening when the moon was ripe in Gemini, the caravan of friends and family departed, never to return.

In his inspiration to move toward awakening, Bianafount led his people east, toward the lands of the rising sun. Their journey was a long and often difficult one, for everywhere the company traveled they found the same arid, flat spiritual and topographical geography from which they were in flight. It is recorded in the journals of that journey (rescued from the fire which destroyed the Kajamunyan National Library many years later) that the caravan experienced at least one attempted coup brought on by impatience and discontent, and that many of those whose intentions were at the beginning honorably set on seeing the journey through were forced for one reason or another to settle by the way. The spirits of most, however, were imperturbable.

After some time (the number of years or seasons or moons are the subject of another story), the wanderers found themselves face to face with the highest and narrowest mountain they had ever seen. Its peak loomed into the ether beyond mortal vision. Bianafount, amid murmurs of disbelief and discouragement, assured his followers that on this mountain they would learn to live and love one another as never before, and find the peace of soul and spirit which they had set off to attain. His wisdom and inspiration were quickly recognized and accepted, and the troupe began then the difficult years of settling into an unknown and precipitous environment.

Every man and woman and child eagerly began to climb the mountain seeking out a place to build a home and plant a garden. Those first few seasons, we are told, were a fury of construction and labor to make shelters. Some, exhausted by uprootedness, chose to settle near the base of the mountain, and others, committed to the idea that it was altitude which they were seeking, struggled into the higher air. But because those were the days of old, and men and women knew how to make what they needed, and because one among them had a brilliance for design (which is now unheard of or forgotten), each family quickly and with little effort created comfortable and hospitable shelter. In an unbelievably brief time all were ready to begin the project of building the temples and courts to house the ideals and codes of their new civilization, reserved for the summit of the mountain.

But first they sought a name with which to identify themselves. It was the favored grandson of Bianafount, a young man who had now grown precociously wise in the constant companionship of his grandfather and in the disadvantages and sufferings of growing up in exile, who suggested that not only a name be given to this mountain of their dreams, but that everything the whole company had been born into and lived through be renamed and rediscovered. He suggested that the place be called Kajamunya, which is translated "Dream," and that the language that they would all soon learn to speak be called Kajamunyan. The potency of the young man's mind, and the promises of leadership and awareness which he had revealed

in the long days past, impressed the elders as well as the younger journey-men, and the mountain was soon joyfully christened.

It was not long before, in the process of working together to build their new capital, that abundant joy and intensity evolved myriad new words for tools and objects, expressions and anatomies, fantasies and ideas and longings, all of which were carefully recorded in a series of dictionaries now lost in the damaging flames which struck the Kajamunyan National Library in a moment of passion, and blotted the history of those early and zealous years. But due to the skill and inspiration of the old scholars, who were willing at the crossroads of their lives to give up everything in pursuit of Kajamunya, the grammar and composition of a language conceived out of love and labor lives today.

It was apparent at their departure that Bianafount was the most willing and accomplished among them to put their dreams and desires into working order. He was unanimously chosen Neninka, or official leader, in a cere-mony which took place at the highest point in Kajamunya. (It became a tradition that every succedent regent of Kajamunya in its now long and arduous history was anointed there with prayer and celebration, to rule wisely and unselfishly over the lives of all Kajamunyans.) Some have said, and it is written in many delightful odes and tracts, that the choice of Bianafount as first overseer of well-being from the heights to the depths of Kajamunya was a sign and promise from the fates that Kajamunya was blessed by destiny, and that, in the person and governance of Bianafount, Kajamunya was thenceforward heir to the seemingly impossible good for-tune of an image and model of the best which life had to offer. And, lo, it is true that every ruler after the sublimely peaceful death of Bianafount had transmitted to him or her, by history or psychic connection, the love, wisdom, and profound governance which Bianafount bore for his people.

In his address to Kajamunya on the day of his election, Bianafount promised to begin to record and transmit the laws, codes, and ambitions of Kajamunya. He promised that none of those airy and adaptable obligations and contracts would ever be written, but rather passed on from father to daughter, mother to son, to be engraved in the memories and hearts of all of those who would hear them, and be willing to abide by them or alter them. He then appointed, as chief architect of the realm, Borimini, the dash-ing and brilliant student of design and imagination, whose purpose would be to design the Kajamunyan capital, which is called Kajamunya, and to introduce into the land a sense of design and taste which would represent

the spiritual harmony and transcendence that all Kajamunyans longed for and sought.

Borimini set to work, and under his sure hand and inspiration the town of Kajamunya came to life with fantastic and exquisitely habitable shapes. There has never been nor will there ever be a more joyously functional center of a nation's activity. He first set his mind to the palace, a structure of immense proportion and height in which there was one elegantly appointed room made to house all of Kajamunya on festive or solemn occasions. Next he put his lifelong dream into form and built the National Library, in which all of the history and learning and storytelling of Kajamunya was housed in the most ample and dreamy of circumstances until the great fire which Borimini watched toward the end of his life with tears and promises to begin rebuilding immediately. Death took him too soon.

The fire, as if lit under the soul of Kajamunya, destroyed much of the scholarly and practical learning which the Kajamunyans had collected and written down. But decidedly more tragic than that was the burning of Kajamunya's greatest source of pride, the parchment quartos which held the well-known stories and mysteries of Kajamunyan life. For, with their newly learned and growing language, rich and bursting with fantasy, the Kajamunyans had come to spend much time pleasurably spinning out the fabric of their daily lives and discoveries until the stories, (and every event, psychic or quotidian, remarkable or secret, was transformed into fable) became the most accurate and meaningful history of their sojourn on the mountain. There are tales filled with the reminiscences of friends, families, and neighbors sitting before their fires, perhaps under the unclouded sky of the mountaintop, creating in succession, one by one adding his or her particular commentary, the memories and circumstances, humor and sadness, of life in Kajamunya. Although the fire could not consume the spirit of those adventures, a Kajamunyan story, once so familiar, is rare.

Although our life here in some part is tuned to the rhythm and romance which those fables captured, we cannot summon them to come and be remembered. There are the flashes of revelation, as this has been, and if one is lucky he or she can write it down. But for the most part we must be satisfied that the story we are living here, in some deep and as yet untold of place, approximates and is infused with the spirit of that place so long ago and far away.

—RICHARD

·BEFORE·

FROM THE APPLE TREE you bear left and head toward the hill. At the end of the first field on a bank of wild grasses, mosses, and junipers was an old logging skidway and a decomposing barway across the logging road that wound its way through the sheep pasture. I often remember going up that road, sometimes to pick butternuts at the tree on the side hill, sometimes, my trusty .22 in hand, chasing a gray squirrel up a tree, then aiming carefully as he jumped from treetop to treetop, then marching proudly home with a couple of fellows which Ma would make into squirrel pie or put into the freezer for a winter meal. Of course, the tails were collectors' items, and it was no small thing if by the end of the season you happened to have more of them than your brothers or the kids down the road.

Up the main road from the barway, the grade grew steeper. Large pine and hemlock boughs hung over the road, blocking the sun, except for a few rays that snuck through, lighting a piece of white quartz here or a red partridge berry there. Under the cover of those boughs, snowbanks often sat around until mid-May. You soon came around the corner to the bridge. Its wooden planks would clop, clop, clop as if a team of Morgan workhorses had passed over, even if it were our Chevy hay truck. The iron rails often held me up as I leaned over watching the worm wiggle on the end of the fishline. I could see a native brook trout sunning himself near the edge of a large rock, but he didn't seem any more interested in my worm than he did in the swallow who had built her nest just above, on the bridge's stone foundation. Often I walked to this point in the road and fished downstream until the fields, barn, and home were again at hand. Dad used to tell how, when he was a kid living with his grandfather on the farm, that used to be the place he would fish the first morning of trout season each year. Then he'd proceed to tell the respective first-day fishing spots claimed by each of his brothers, cousins, aunts, uncles, and grandparents.

Up the road from the bridge was the Stanov stomping grounds. It seemed an odd place, usually empty. The outer buildings stood alone, one with a collection of books that in number at least equaled or surpassed the entire number of volumes at the free library in the center of town.

It was the cemetery that was my favorite spot. Up the two steep hills, down a slight dip, and onto the flat stretch ahead, there on the left was the opening. The wild grasses sprang up between my toes. (I never wore shoes in the summer, always cut-off dungarees.) I headed for the seemingly ancient, sturdy yet intricate, iron gate, which swung open with a creak of rust against rust, leaving an entrance into the past. History seemed to rush out, grab you, and pull you in. I moved slowly from gravestone to gravestone and by the end of my procession I seemed to know each of the bodies that lay there.

At the far end of the flat, the road dipped slightly again, then again, making a small twist each time. Again, the left draws your attention: under a stately pine grove a stone fireplace with its troops of picnic tables. It was here that the family made their annual pilgrimage for reunion. Outside of that, it seemed to stand there, just waiting.

Across another flat and up yet another hill, there, again on the left, were the remains of an old mill. I'm not sure what kind of mill, perhaps a sawmill or maybe even an old sugar house. I'm sure I've heard it told, but that bit of information must have slipped away some time ago.

Finally, up the last hill to the Corners. I remember arriving at the top and looking up the road in each of four directions, north, south, east, and west. Here, too, history seemed to spring alive. The old inn, lying dormant to the northwest, the schoolhouse to the northeast, the Franklin farm to the southeast, and Rosie's weedy garden to the southwest.

The old inn, like the Stanov place back down the hill, sat dormant most of the year, but even so it seemed to come to life if you looked at it hard enough. Sure . . . there comes the stage now! Maybe from Westminster or Windsor way, or perhaps over the mountain from Bennington or Albany. It doesn't really matter. The keg in the cellar flows freely, as the new arrivals fill their own private flasks and the "regulars" each grab their mug or flask from its peg on the wall. The old maid schoolteacher is having her problems in the schoolhouse across the road. She lost the attention of the children as the stage came over Belden Hill and is unable to regain it. Finally in desperation she screams, "School's out!" The mad dash out the door and across the road leaves the schoolhouse empty. Even the school-mistress is content with dashing across the road to hear the latest gossip and to meet the new arrivals.

Suddenly a monarch butterfly wings by and I'm brought back to the present as my eyes follow it across the road to Rosie's garden. The weeds are tall, and it doesn't really seem like much of a garden. But somehow, knowing Rosie, you know there's beans, tomatoes, carrots, and the such hiding among those weeds, just waiting to be plucked and preserved for those long winter months ahead. My eyes still follow the butterfly as it breezes by Forrest's dilapidated garage, standing there between those two huge sugar maples. I've heard it said that if those maples weren't there as guards, just inches from either end of the shed, it would've been down long ago. The winged monarch continues its journey across the yard to the chicken house. Several times I helped Rosie collect eggs, and I remember my amazement the first time I found a chicken had laid a glass egg! It took a moment's thought and an explanation from Rosie before I realized she had put it there just to persuade the old birds to do their duty in the nests and not on the floor.

Of course my favorite thing about the whole hill was Forrest's peach orchard. Forrest, the Yankee he was, never was one to do any more than he absolutely had to, but his peach orchard received all the care and atten-tion it needed. I remember marching up the hill to watch Forrest and Rosie pick and grade peaches. But they could tell by the grin on my face why I'd really walked all that way; and Forrest or Rosie would pass me a couple of big juicy golden-pink peaches. I'd sit there eating peaches and watching Forrest climb the ladder to pick basket after basket of peaches until the sun had gotten far enough down the sky so I knew I'd better head for home if I was going to be there in time to help fetch the cows, feed hay, and change straps for milking machines. So I headed back down the road past the Corners, the mill spot, the pine grove and picnic area, the Kroll Ceme-

tery, the Stanov house, the bridge and stream, the sheep pasture barway, the logging skidway, and, finally, The Apple Tree. I finished my afternoon's journey up the hill and back and there was still time to waste before milking. Perhaps I'd work in the garden for a while, go swimming in the brook, or maybe I'd play King-on-the-mountain in the hay mound with my brothers (that is, as long as Dad didn't catch us fooling in the hay).

At night I'd crawl into my top bunk (our bedroom looked like an army barracks: with five younger brothers and sisters, numerous visiting cousins, and a couple of other kids who lived with us, you had to pile 'em deep) assuring myself before I dropped off to sleep that I knew every inch of the road, between The Apple Tree and the Corners and most of the land on either side of the road.

In the summer of '68 I left for a job on the Maine coast. I was employed by some friends who owned some resort cabins and a gift shop at a place called Land's End on famed Bailey Island. Believe me, it seemed like the end of the world. It was probably the longest and loneliest summer of my entire life.

My only sanity came in thinking about home; the moody holsteins in the barn, my younger brothers and sisters, my parents, my friends, and just Vermont in general. More specifically The Apple Tree, the logging skidway, the sheep pasture barway, the bridge and stream, the Stanov house, the Kroll cemetery, the pine grove and picnic area, the mill spot, and the Corners. It wasn't that my bosses weren't nice. They couldn't have been nicer. I guess it came right down to being just plain *homesick*. That's why when I returned home at the end of the summer things seemed even more beautiful than before I left. Yes . . . *more* beautiful; even with the changes.

The sheep pasture barway and logging skidway had long since been bulldozed away and replaced with a modern turquoise suburban style home. It's not the house, but that color, it's so ugly. The house sits there on the knoll that once belonged to the skidway, not a tree or bush in the yard. Just green lawn that grows right up to the front door . . . except the door is four or five feet off the ground, and no steps! But there are good things about the house that greet you as you head up the hill. It's the home of a fine man and his family. It's their dream home, their pride, the first they've ever owned. Like with everything else the newness will wear off and age will mellow this modern home.

Up the road past the quartz and partridge berries, the bridge too is gone. I'll always remember it as if it were a living being protecting my favorite fishing hole underneath. I remember hearing the clop, clop, clop from a passing vehicle, even if I was at the foot of the hill by The Apple Tree or in my front yard. The iron rails . . . gone too, replaced by a few creosoted guard rails over the cold silver culvert which replaced the bridge's stone foundation . . . gone . . . not swept downstream by a natural disaster but, like the skidway, bulldozed away. Hopefully age too will mellow this once sacred bend in the road.

Up past the flowering tree hydrangea in the Stanov yard, up the two steep hills down the slight dip and onto the flat stretch ahead, there on the left is the opening. But something has changed here too. The creaking rusty gate . . . it's gone. Again, taken not by some mysterious force of nature, but by man. A super rip-off! It's still one of my favorite spots and always will be even without the gate.

Across the flat and down the two twisting dips the pine grove still stands guard over the picnic tables and the stone fireplace. But it has a new addition to its flock—a new cement block fireplace. Perhaps it's not as pleasing to the eye, but I bet its barbecued spareribs and hamburgers taste just as good as the ones its stone ancestor cooked.

As you head up the last hills to the Corners, you can tell that here the changes have been the most profound. The old mill spot has become a parking lot, its collection of dead or dying motor vehicles growing larger each year. As you arrive at the Corners you realize the inn no longer sits dormant. It's now the permanent home of an antique dealer, his wife, and their French poodle. The inn and the farmhouse across the road have been stained a deep brown. The inn, furnished only in original antiques, still smells of history. The schoolhouse across the road actually looks better now that those curtains Miss March used to have in the windows are down. The weedy garden still grows to the southwest, but it isn't Rosie's. Forrest has died, and Rosie has sold the farm and moved to the city. I first heard about the sale of the farm when I was in Maine. A letter from home said simply, "Rosie has sold the house and a bunch of hippies are moving in."

—RONNIE

·SKATING HOME FROM·
·THE APOCALYPSE·
·BROOKLINE: 1965·

IT ALL BEGAN WITH BUZZY, the wild man, jack-of-all-trades, first of the seven sons of George and Martha Dodge, our founders. Buzzy had come to live with us in Brookline from a mottled career, parachuting into Alaskan forest fires, salvaging scrap metal from bombers, long-distance hauling in Wyoming, a 1950 Mercury bullet factory on wheels, most recently mixing chemicals in a madhouse basement. He took the last empty room, filled it with old and soggy socks, and a dilapidated cat named Poo-Poo (RIP Mayday 1969, after a long and wearying illness, on the farm), in our flat: part-salon, part-flophouse, shelter to several Total Loss Farm constituents, and a kitchen which saw the rise and fall of many a soufflé.

One night over Chablis and Verandah's moussaka (cf. later), Buzzy leaned back with a smoke and said he was sick of rats in the basement and on the street. He knew where a man's soul belonged and it wasn't in Brookline. He conjured a vision of peace and adventure on the northwest coast of British Columbia—the Japan current, glacier valleys, undisturbed Indians, birchbark canoes, and we, like Noah's family, starting from scratch, to be saved from metropolis, the war, and our pasts. The house was in ferment. A map with pins marking the way to paradise accessible by sea appeared on the wall. It was our secret salvation. We plotted the schedule for our exodus, sans skills or dollars. We gathered together pilgrims, those of us who were able to see the dream waking, and waited for a sign. It never came. Most of us kept close, and waited. Buzzy left, sensing our distraction, to spin more private and viable fantasies. We were left with neither wings nor sails, yet the vision of a peaceable kingdom, and a compelling departure, endured.

·DIASPORA I·

Verandah left to join Ray and Marshall in Washington to chronicle the fall. Richard and Laurie and Connie and Hugh Beame and Elliot stayed home with the mimeograph machine on Laurie's piano, honking out Chopin and propaganda. They weren't bad times, filled with the fury of war, resistance, and other dreams.

·EASTER MORNING: CHRIST IS RISEN·

In a basement apartment in the nation's capital, in the throes of riot, how it goes on, V. watched Raymond sleeping. Keat's kittens in the closet had opened their eyes as Raymond snored. She noticed that his face was green. Gazing in the mirror, she noted that her own face bore the same pallor. She shook him awake. It wasn't easy. He dreamed a lot. "Raymond," she said, "I want to go home. I've had enough. The war is over."

"I know just the place," he said over his first glass of Washington water. "It's up the road from Don's. It's in Vermont. We'll be there by summer."

·SURPRISE·

Waking up hung over, Richard crawled to the phone in the bedroom —hall—closet, hardly responsive. It was long distance, Verandah from Washington.

Don't make a move, she said. We're going home.

Whaaa? I said.

We're going home.
Oh, that's nice.
Bring a toothbrush.
In a condition like mine, I need this kind of torture? I need competent medical attention.
That's what I'm talking about, she said.

·LANDING·

Verandah came to Boston with a map with pins and a date to meet the other half (Ray, Marty, Peter Simon) in downtown Brookstowne. Brookstowne? Laurie, Richard, and Verandah, three-man medicine show, high-spirited in the after dawn, with chart (you must find it with your heart) and lantern (in case it got dark), hours and many miles later, found ourselves in front of the Holiday Restaurant wondering, "Where's the other half?"

There we were shepherded by a young carpenter named Glen, God bless him, into the backroads for some local color. Stoned in Brooks. This must be the place. Good omens. Don't stop now. He dropped us off at the Paramount where we ran forthwith into our comrades who drove us down lovely country lanes that branched into lovelier country lanes, and many tributaries thereof, until we reached The Apple Tree.

The road to home. It was not warm. There were black flies. Richard had to piss. Peter snapped our photo in front of the farmhouse that was hardly the Ritz, or the one that you see in *The New Yorker,* or Marshall's find later in Gonamute. Forrest had died several years before, and Rosie, may her tribe increase, had moved to Greenfield, which was paradise to her after thorny years of struggling with the farm. All the doors and windows were locked. But we looked in and saw Home Comfort (the stove by which we are sitting and writing this now in the first November chill with coffee and nostalgia), and it was looking good. It was the orchard that arrested us. We were home.

Back in Greenfield, Marty and Ray stopped in at Rosie's to negotiate. Raymond could pull dollars from the air. The rest of us kicked around Greenfield, where Verandah was once arrested for hitchhiking, and ran into some longhairs (which was always an unexpected pleasure in those days), a meeting of our kind. We flashed the V and smiles. How long ago that seems. They said they lived in a tree house in Deyne. That made us neighbors. We talked about trading food and love. (Soon after, they were burned out of their tree house, a sign, they took it, from God to incorporate their empire and found the Spirit in the Flesh.) Marty and Ray came out beaming, with a date to sign the deed. Bring the money, Rosie said.

Money. Marty's life savings from a former life of editing encyclopedias and his Bar Mitzvah bonds, Peter's purse, and Raymond's indefatigable finagling, and change from the couch, made the down payment. We all split to tie up our loose ends.

·DIASPORA II·

Verandah followed her heart to California. Laurie followed V. with his toothbrush. Ray and Marty went back to move the News Service to New York, as a parting gesture (cf. *Famous Long Ago*). Peter returned to Cambridge. Richard went back to Brookline to sell Hoodsies from a truck with Elliot. Returning from a hard day on the wagon, I heard the phone ring. Laurie was psychically smoldering. Could I come out and save a friend? Yes. After contracting to drive Doctor Bernstein's beachwagon to San Francisco, Elliot and I turned in our leftover Hoodsies, disappointing an entire neighborhood, convinced Connie to resign her position as a hospital worker (more about that later), and set out.

Like an ambulance, we raced across Canada, and found our friends on the Solstice—a feast day in California. To celebrate the rite and return, Richard, Laurie, Veranda, and Elliot swallowed a little California sunshine, and set out to find the friend of a friend of a friend. Like a roller coaster, we raced up an down the pastel hills, stopping often to admire the sidewalks or the sky. San the Fran was the only city where one could lie on the sidewalks, stare into space, and grin while people nodded kindly as they stepped over. Of course we had a revelation.

The way would be easier if we divided the labor. While two of us hallucinated, the other two would guide them across the labyrinth of streets, night, and herds of cars like buffaloes. An enduring vision: all life could be divided in just this way. "To ped-x": to cross the street and look before you leap; perform the necessary tasks and functions which would leave one the greatest leisure "to hallucinate": i.e., to lie in a haystack, to dream, to make life play rather than work.

We finally arrived at Duncan Street to see the man who knew the man who knew. Julia came to the door, hardly pleased to see four drug-crazed strangers. She let us in. V. and Michael fell in love. We rode to the sea, where we cast a portentous hexagram: the Turning Point, Return, changing to the Creative. Michael gave Verandah a ring. It was time to go.

Who was Michael? Scorpio postman, rock and roller, a sharp dresser, a good dancer, a music master (music by Michael, lighting by God), a farm boy with an insatiable appetite for love and cars and dope. He drove us to Salem, Oregon, for his last farewell, and deposited us in the home of Loeta, his Scorpio-Indian mother, the Red Queen, who woke us each morning, hung over, with bloody marys, to play croquet with flamingos and rabbits. How do we get out of here? Michael suggested that we pick strawberries — after all, we were "farmers" — to make enough dough to get across the Great Divide. Three days with the braceros on the farm where Michael was raised, and where he returned every fall to drive the big machines he loves (where he is now), crawling through the mud of overripe berries, we gave up in despair.

Verandah called Raymond in New York: "Help." Raymond said, "You must come home, we need your help" (cf. *Famous Long Ago*); and Marshall, may his soul abide in paradise, sent us his last hundred dollars.

In an overcrowded car with Michael at the wheel, Verandah, Richard, Laurie, Jimmy, and Julia (Julia: Pisces, sister to Michael, who later came to stay, only to leave again; and Jimmy: Libra, with Scorpio rising, foster brother to Michael, and warlock of wit and circumstance, who came to stay, only to leave again, the Lord Buddha watches over them), we set out for the East and Vermont and an end to our wandering.

·BABYLON REVISITED·

Out for a beer on 125th Street, where angels fear to tread, overjoyed at our reunion with Ray and Marshall and Mad John (Australian Aubrey Beardsley witch doctor), we were followed by roving thugs who welcomed us with clubs. They knocked off Raymond's glasses, shades of Daedelus, and threw John to the ground. All fled but Richard and Verandah, who screamed in Spanish, "What do you want to do a thing like that for? They're pacifists. They won't hit back. And Michael in New York for almost the first time." They apologized. "If you get into trouble on 125th Street, ask for Paco." They let us know we had to get home.

·HOME·

Laurie, Richard, Verandah, and Michael head for the hills! At the edges of our auto seats, we passed for the second time The Apple Tree, and pulled into the driveway. We were greeted by the sight of "Gem Spa" in the pines. Our home was overrun with strangers from New York who had followed a mimeographed map to paradise.

On entering the house there was no place to sit down or sleep. People asked us who we were and how long we intended to stay. This is the most difficult to recount. What had happened in our absence? Ray and Marty left a couple to oversee the farm while they finished in New York. Peter and Linda made no distinctions between friends or strangers. They were under the impression that: property being theft, we had no right to pick and choose, to put down our own roots to the exclusion of others. How could we argue with that? But for us there was something more compelling and essential than opening the land to any and all who were willing to come to it. We wanted to sire a family. We were the parents and we were the children until such a time when we had enough faith to foster children of our own. It was not that our conception of the place made it an elite, secluded hideaway. It was, however, an inspiration to resurrect *this* farm, and to take our cues from where we were, without the hassle of immediate social problems.

Verandah threatened to leave. It was like New York City, she said. But Raymond, on arrival, pointed out that we were mortgaged to this land, mortgaged in Eden for ten years, in his name and Marty's, and therefore the fate, immediate and future, was in our hands.

Those of us who had shared the vision of this place from Brookline to British Columbia, and California and Oregon, came together to decide how we could live. We concluded that it was necessary to evict the others, and we felt guilty, and still do. Yet we knew we made the right decision, and naively began to prepare body and soul for the winter.

—VERANDAH AND RICHARD

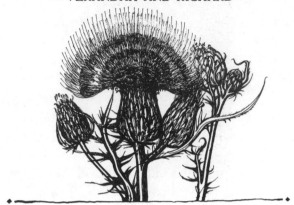

·WHAT THIS COMMUNITY· ·NEEDS·

·A SELF-INDULGENT ESSAY·

THE COMMUNITY NEEDS COMMON GOOD AND EVIL. These may be abstract and religious if you're Mike Metelica or Mel Lyman or Mao Tse-Tung; but they must be real to the people involved. They may be material and practical too—good in the leaves and trees and sun, bad in the inclement weather or threat of bankruptcy or the neighbors' absurd and wrong way of living. In the true sense we know that good and evil are but intellectual conceits, they don't exist, "nothing is better, nothing is best." Yet it is absolutely essential to the community to have a common enemy worthy of fear or contempt, we stand united against it; and a common joy incapable of tarnish, we stand together in loving it.

The community needs trust beyond reason. Trust with reason is good enough for neighbors but not for lovers. One must refuse to believe the worst of his brother in the face of conclusive damning evidence. Incidents or remarks which might be insulting or hurtful among ordinary citizens must be suffered and forgiven in the community. Every member of the community is responsible for all the others. If we believe we cannot be betrayed, we never shall be. If you go to Tibet for twenty-seven years, I must believe you are right to do so, and hold your place back home. I must trust you even when there is no reason to.

The community needs privacy and exposure. The members of the family need inviolable privacy from each other and inevitable exposure to each other. There is no blame in the lonesome heart. The community also needs a certain impenetrable privacy from the rest of the race, a privacy which nonetheless must prove itself against regular exposure to new people, groups, places. When a new person really joins the community, it is because she or he knows the secret. There is always a secret, and each keeps it in his way.

The community needs pleasant surprises and disastrous setbacks. A warm apple pie, a sudden batch of chickens, a baby; a storm, a great loss of resources, an illness.

The community needs freedom from tiresome ideological tracts that leave you right where you started, which is fantastic.

—RAY

·HOW I CAME HERE·

AND WHERE ELSE *could* I be living but on some down home Total Loss Farm where, as Uncle Luis says, the tree of goodloving grows? How'd I get here, this cold winter's morning, boots caked with manure, fingers stiff from morning chores; what route, what roots, what long lonesome highway directed me here to this chickenshack shanty tucked downwind in the hollow by the barn, where Verandah, Bessie and her day-old calf, and Highlee the goat are my nearest neighbors, and where twin centuries-old sugar maples peer through my window, framing the morning sun as it rises through the woods above the meadow announcing, along with the stirrings of the animals in the barn, a new adventure, a new day.

As one of the "elders" of the farm, I have become keeper of the historical consciousness. It's a self-assigned job, like walking the boundaries to see that the rock walls are in place; no one else seems to care. But I've always thought it good to keep in mind where we've come from the better to appreciate how far we've come. Like a skinny ninety-pound weakling in an old Charles Atlas comic book ad (remember *dynamic tension?*) I've experienced the before and after and know what it's like living on the other side of history. I've been a Bar Mitzvah *bruc'ha,* Democrat, college jock, advertising copywriter, encyclopedia editor, married and divorced. I saw Joe DiMaggio at Yankee Stadium and watched Willie Mays grace center field across the river at the Polo Grounds. I saw the first televised nuclear blast, Milton Berle, General Wainwright on his return from Japan, and once believed this country great. But, also, Charlie Parker bebop riffs careen through my head like the nation's madness. I can tell you the personnel of the Basie band during the mid-fifties and I remember the lindy hop, the cha-chacha, the twist, the fish, and the Miami Beach rumba. I've had sand kicked in my face by a bully carrying an American flag, gathered the grains, and created a castle. It's no accident I live on Total Loss Farm. I've been up and down the length of the track and this, friends, is the end of the line.

If there has been any logical pattern to my life I guess it has been a yearning for community. I don't know how or why it is but this feeling has always been there, like a vacuum sucking me out of the horse latitudes, those endless and deadly doldrums that describe so much of mid-century American life. My favorite memories are mostly of experiences with closely-knit groups of people, friends, whose own best resources were themselves. I have trucked those memories around with me for years, much the same way that Indians carry within them a collective vision of the future that is a continuation of their historical past.

There is no room for progress in this scheme of things. We are dealing here with emotions and feelings as old and as basic as time. One strives to experience in an infinite number of ways the most cherished moments of the past. These moments seem always to be found in the context of community or, if alone, with the community's blessing and support. On the best of days I think of us in Neolithic times, sitting peacefully around a fire, nodding silently to ourselves in complete and harmonious understanding. Left to our own devices we'd all probably choose community over anything else. It's always seemed to me that once we got the food, shelter, and other necessities in hand, community is the only objective worthy of our ambition.

My favorite recollections of growing up, for instance, are about what must have passed for community on the streets of New York. This happened before urban renewal, before the coming of the bulldozers, and before the city planners decided that neighborhoods had become obsolete. The best hours of my youth were spent loitering in front of Simon's Candy Store on Creston Avenue in the Bronx, doing nothing, just hanging out. Most of my contemporaries quickly abandoned this phase of life and went on to bigger if not better things. Some, I suppose, are even considered "successful" in their chosen fields. And I? I'm thirty-one and surely should have outgrown it all by now. But it struck me early in life that hanging out was one of the most sensible and civilized ways of spending one's life and that once I secured a minimum livelihood there was nothing as meaningful that I could possibly do. Of course, this view ran counter to the accepted values of society—the Puritan Ethic and all that jazz—and still does, though even this is changing. The trick I came to understand was to create a world—and if that proved too difficult for a start, then at least a small piece of turf as a beginning—where one could hang out with impunity. Total Loss Farm, I'm pleased to announce, is one such place and will suit me fine, thank you, until I reach that Great Street Corner in the Sky. In the meanwhile, friends and

neighbors, follow the words of the bouncing ball. "Don't drop out, hang out!"

The idea that we are a family is important to the people on the farm. This sense of family wouldn't be so much a part of our present awareness if we didn't each carry within us memories of what our family life was in the past; where it broke down and ceased being meaningful and how, now, it can be reconstructed to that end. We've all, symbolically or literally, left home and rejected our pasts. At first, this was merely rebellion, a necessary but negative act of breaking away. In retrospect, we seemed to be running not as much *from* our families, but in search of family, looking for the sense of community and family life we once knew but, in the end, found lacking at home. As we reclaim this sense of community life, we rediscover the tribal soul and within ourselves become family men and women once again.

Living on the farm has enabled me to look back at my family with a fondness that I once found impossible and to begin to reconcile my present with the past. Most of my relatives lived within a short bicycle ride from one another. We were a big family and very close. We used to go on big family picnics to Sherwood Island in Connecticut and play at each other's houses. One of my grandmothers lived with my Aunt Freda and Uncle Ruby and their children in a big, yellow brick house with garrets on the third floor and a backyard with a flower garden raised up from the concrete. It was the kind of old family home that brings to mind Silas Lapham, Booth Tarkington, and Orson Welles's *Magnificent Ambersons*, the kind of big private house you don't see much of anymore. Those that haven't been torn down to make way for high-rise apartments have been subdivided into lots of tiny living units, each with its own mailbox, entrance, kitchen area, sleeping corner, and toilet. That is what happened to my grandmother's house. Once it was teeming with family life, its walls bursting with talk and laughter. Now, I suppose, a lot of lonely people live there and everyone has a lock on their door.

Sometime during the nineteen fifties this kind of family life began to disintegrate. Remember the poor, pitiable mother-in-law who was the butt of what passed for humor in the early days of TV? She symbolized the de-sanctification of the family that was so much a part of that time. The family was under attack, forced into retreat, sent scattered into hundreds of split-level suburban Levittowns splattered willy-nilly across the landscape. We fled, too. Spades had moved in down the block, the spics were edging west-ward across Webster Avenue. We moved to improved digs in White Plains, Westchester County, New York, 1953. I was thirteen, creature of habit and citizen of the street, so spent the first year looking for a congenial street corner to hang out. But there are no street corners in suburbia, only meandering lanes and circular drives that never seemed to lead anywhere. Kids didn't hang out on the streets or in the schoolyards, anyway. Every-thing was organized for them and supervised by adults. The world I had grown accustomed to and actually liked had come to an end and I found my-self stranded in limbo, with no place exciting I could think of to go.

Disaffection with a way of life and a yearning to return to what was probably a romanticized version of a happier past are in themselves insuf-ficient to produce a direction for useful change. One has to glimpse a pos-sible avenue toward the future, a light that points to a possible way out of the past. My sister gave me such a direction. Ruth was three years older than me, a talented musician and a student at New York's special public High School of Music and Art. Her friends were writers, artists, musicians, and erstwhile bohemians in the days just prior to the beat generation. They used to hang out in our kitchen, devouring my mother's waffles and entertaining us with music and wit on into the night.

At first I didn't know what to make of them. I had the world neatly divided and they didn't fit either half. There were the street kids, like myself, who fancied themselves "rocks" and refused to acknowledge intelligent thought. Then there were the others, the sissies who liked school, brown-nosed their teachers, respected authority, wore clean clothes, and had no interest in the important things like gang wars and sports. My sister's friends were smart, all right; always talking about ideas and music and books, but they were also tough and cool. I decided finally that they were "with it" and followed after them seeing what I could learn. One of her boy-friends, an artist, even dressed like Marlon Brando in *The Wild One*. Motorcycle boots, black leather jacket and cap, greasy dungarees; my mother had fits. He became my idol. I guess I was about twelve years old at the time but Ruth and her friends made a lasting impression. I wanted to be like them, which meant—although I didn't know a word for it then—I wanted desperately to be hip.

Wanting to be hip put me in touch with the soft underbelly of American life. It was where my own experiences veered away from that of my friends, with me taking a series of hesitant steps left. I'm not sure of the exact route or of what led to what but certainly the path included Jean Shepherd, the *Village Voice*, beat poetry (though I hated poetry in school), existentialism (whatever *that* meant), Jack Kerouac and *On the Road* (Ruth gave me it for my sixteenth birthday). Neil Cassady/Dean Moriarity became my new hero (and remains so today), my snotty literary equivalent to the more popular James Dean. Through a set of fortunate circumstances, but mainly because The Birdland Show followed Alan Freed on WINS radio, I got into jazz, and from jazz there was no turning back.

For a long period during my high school years I led a solitary existence, went on no dates to no parties and had no good times. If I didn't think of myself as a terrible social flop I might have been very happy, but no one informed me of that possibility. Saturday night would find me locked in my room reading *Downbeat* and whatever literature I could get my hands on about jazz, listening to "Bird" and Mingus, and John Birks Gillespie and Thelonious Monk and Basie and Satchmo, Mulligan, early Miles, Lambert, Hendricks, and Ross, Art Blakey, the MJQ. What company! Charlie Parker telling me absolute truth right in the confines of my room. I was

alone, but never lonely, sad but satisfied, paying dues, digging blues. It was a period of self-discovery and an introduction to a world turned upside down. Jazz led me into black America and from there to the civil rights movement and into dope and nightpeople and into different levels of reality and awareness of which I never knew.

But I didn't drop out; not for a long time, anyway. Jazz, after all, with all its beauty, was a cry of rage, a pained but accurate vision of the coming apocalypse. But, like the beats, jazzmen were too far gone to have anything to offer to a future society. The only sign of its possible shape came in the small but beautiful communities one sensed wherever jazzmen gathered to jam. I was an outsider hovering along the fringe, nursing my two-drink minimums at the Five Spot, Birdland, Half Note, and Connally's Stardust Room in Boston. But I could see enough to know that I had come upon the right place. If only I had the courage to walk through that dark, inviting door.

It took me ages to finally do what I always knew I had to do, say "fuck it" to my accustomed world and go boppin' like whiteman saved into that other world. I finished college, dabbled in graduate school, embarked on a career, took care not to burn any bridges, and entered the bohemian world one small step at a time. In the winter of 1963, when I was but a thesis away from a master's degree (and still am), I got a phone call from two strangers. Dave Clark and Paul Johnson were doing research on a wildcat coal mining strike in the hills of eastern Kentucky, had heard, through a mutual friend, that I had a car and a sense of adventure, and asked if I'd like to drive them. Would I like to drive them? What a question. I was sick of academia, bored with my thesis, and apprehensive about going out into the straight world which at heart I didn't like. Theirs was the phone call I was waiting for all along. I packed my bags, vacated my apartment, left school, and headed South to Hazard, Kentucky.

Hazard was my Mississippi and, like many people my age who went South during the early days of the civil rights movement, it completely changed my life. In Hazard, the police chief interrogated us about our Communist affiliations and made veiled threats against our lives. In Hazard, an officer in a sheriff's uniform told us "the U.S. Constitution ain't worth a damn, you're in Perry County, now, boys." In Hazard, I met the good decent folks who had poison in their hearts and poor, illiterate miners who restored my faith that folks could be decent. And in Hazard, a carload of armed coal miners, their rifles pointing out the windows of an old station wagon, had to escort us to the county line to protect us from the police and the decent folks who tailed us down the road in unmarked cars. The experience was nothing when compared to what my brothers and sisters in SNCC and CORE were going through farther south, but the United States, once *my* country, could never be the same.

From Hazard, I settled in on the Lower East Side, East 11th between A and B (later I'd move eastward to between B and C), lived with and married David's sister, Nancy, and became one of the younger members of Paul Johnson's wide circle of friends. Paul, Becky, and their three kids, Chris, Torey, and Nels, lived first in a tenement in the farther reaches of Brooklyn and then in an old apartment building near the Staten Island waterfront which was gradually taken over by all our friends. Paul's circle consisted of writers and artists, some of whom by now have been "discovered." But at the time, none of them cared about public success or critical acclaim. They toiled away at their crafts with diligence and anonymity, working at whatever odd jobs were available to earn enough bread to buy food and pay rent. God knows why they put up with me. I worked in advertising by day and played hipster at night. But they were patient and eventually I saw their light.

I guess it was in 1965 that we all became aware that there was a war in Vietnam. A friend of ours, Maris Cakars, who was involved in the pacifist movement, was trying to organize a New York action group, a workshop in nonviolence, to provoke the public into an awareness of the war. I took part in the first large antiwar parade in New York City, a march down Fifth Avenue, and was delighted to be one of many in such a distinguished crowd. So I became active in The Workshop and discovered, quite pragmatically, that pacifism and nonviolent action made sense. But pacifist literature disgusted me. It was excessively self-righteous and lacked any spark of life. It turned Paul off as well and, with Maris' encouragement, Paul, Gwen Reyes, and I started *Win* Magazine, which gradually came to dedicate itself (much to the shock of many older pacifists) to psychedelic pacifism and the creation of gentle, joyous mayhem in the streets.

Working with *Win* was an experiment in a new kind of journalism. Not only did we have to report movement news, we had to create it as well. At times it seemed that the entire peace movement consisted of maybe ten people walking around in circles with signs reading "End the War in Vietnam." It was that lonely. Our primary goal, as an action group and magazine, was to reassure each other of our existence. We also sought to create

an illusion for the overground media that we were much stronger than we actually were. This meant that not only did we have to plan demonstrations, distribute leaflets, take part in them and write them up, but we also had to decide, beforehand, who would go to jail and who would try to stay out in order to get the next issue to the press.

It was a frustrating and unrewarding task. *Win* made incredible demands on our lives and for practical reasons forced us into communal situations which we otherwise might never have considered. First of all, it was a full-time commitment, seven days a week, with little time out for sleep. We were together constantly, meeting deadlines, planning demonstrations, arguing tactics and politics, dodging nightsticks, and attending farewell parties for friends being dragged off to jail. I spent one vacation from my straight job at a week-long vigil in front of the White House and most of my "sick" days sitting in jail. The passion of our cause forged us into a community. There developed an overwhelming love and trust among us. We operated strictly by consensus and everyone's opinion was respected and heard. It amazed me how we all learned to soften our positions so that the magazine reflected everyone's view and that we could frame our arguments and handle our disputes in ways that acknowledged the respect we had for our differences.

It wasn't easy. There were times when we got on each other's nerves, refused, on principle, to assign tasks and so contended with days of confusion during which nothing got done, and sat through tiresome all-day meetings that often had us all storming out of the room in tears. I must have resigned from the *Win* staff half a dozen times, letter of resignation and all. But I never left. At the worst of times my friends were with me, willing to spend hours talking my problems out, refusing to abandon me until whatever was bothering me was worked out.

We were also poor. Only a few people at a time could draw the subsistence salaries that the magazine could afford. In 1967, after quitting the last formal job I've ever had, I lived off unemployment insurance for six months. Our poverty led us to share our meager resources, something we had only dabbled in before. It strikes me now how weird we were about money. In college, I had a friend named Marty Mitchell, who I turned on to jazz and who then became my constant companion. Mitchell never had any money, so whenever I wanted to go somewhere with him, we'd have to go through a standard routine.

"Hey, Mitch, Ornette's at The Five Spot, want to go?"

(Fingering his empty billfold) "I can't afford it."

"How much do you need?"

"Oh, maybe a couple of bucks for the minimum and a bite to eat later."

"I'll lend you the money and you can pay me when you have it."

Of course, we both understood that he would never "have it." But Mitchell would open a little notebook, just the same, and record the loan in his list of debts. By graduation he owed me and his other friends hundreds of dollars. We never expected him to pay and he never intended to. Yet we kept the ritual going and he maintained an accurate list of his debts. In point of fact, we were functioning communally, but none of us were aware of the concept. Instead, we continued to phrase our system of sharing in terms that budding capitalists, always conscious of creditor-debtor relationships and the importance of defining private property, could understand.

This finally broke down at *Win*. It became too much of a hassle to keep track of who owed what to whom. Whoever had money footed the bill. If we went out to a movie or to dinner, everyone was invited and whoever could afford it paid. It worked smoothly and without plan. No one in the movement figured ever to get rich.

Private property also lost its value. We took to opening our houses to the many movement people who always seemed to be passing through New York. Some stayed and so shared whatever apartment, food, bed, clothes that were available. We stopped being guests at each other's houses and no longer felt the need to entertain or be entertaining. Kitchens became liberated territory. Women still did most of the cleaning and the cooking (that would become an issue later), but we stopped thinking of our little apartments as *ours*. All kinds of people, some whom I didn't know, lived in my apartment. I spent most of my time at Paul's. What a pleasure it was to live in New York those days. There were four or five apartments scattered throughout the city where I could spend time, eat, sleep, and feel at home.

Slowly, we were becoming a family. We weren't aware of the process, one step suggested a next step and circumstances dictated the direction. In the spring of 1967 the Beatles' *Sergeant Pepper* album came out. I remember doing little else during the evenings of that best of all summers but visiting with friends and listening to Sergeant Pepper, stoned and silent. Sergeant Pepper was our catechism. The Beatles gave us the words to describe our feelings. "It's getting better all the time" and "I get by with a little help from my friends." The world seemed to be coming apart all around us; yet in the growing hippie subculture we were experiencing an unprecedented ecstatic high. Our world, at least, was getting better all the time, and, if nothing else, we had our friends, which seemed more than enough. "With our love, we could save the world," we felt, "if they only knew" and, by God, we were more than ready to share in the good news. The *Win* staff became the *Win* family, and with thousands of other small families scattered across the nation, one big spaced-out tribe.

After that summer of love, the bubble that the Beatles had created burst. The pieces fell all around us but the vision that was at its heart remained as ever, dazzling and clear. The problem, we thought, was that we had created our beloved community in the eye of a hurricane and that the hurricane, which was the movement, was spiraling out of control toward a head-on confrontation with the government. The tension, obviously, helped bring us together. But the pressure was too great and the speed with which events were unfolding worked to drive us apart.

Between the Pentagon demonstration in October '67 and the Battle of Chicago in August '68 we were in continuous confrontation with the police. Every weekend saw a different street action. Throwing money away at the stock exchange. Running through the street to declare "The War Is Over" as if the power of our self-prophecy could make a reality out of an illusion. The Resistance was at its peak with morning induction refusals, picket lines and rallies, and Yippie was chipping away at the sanctity of the state through satire and obscenity. Demonstrations became social events, what one did every weekend. We lived from action to action, the weekly encounters with authority defined our lives. By the time Chicago came up, we were all tough battle-hardened veterans of a score and more

skirmishes with the police. It dawned on some of us, too late I suppose, that we had entered into a cycle of escalation similar to the pattern of the war. The more disruptive we became, the more force the government would muster to keep us down. Our desperation seemed justified at the time, and I suppose, if it's any consolation, history will be kind. Our radical views about Vietnam and about our government, as events have proven, were in every respect right. Yet neither the press, the public, nor the government took us seriously. It seemed that trying to disrupt the orderly workings of sociey was the only thing left we could do.

The desperation of the movement caused problems for those of us committed to nonviolence. We were advocates of disruption, of course; in fact, pioneers of the more gentle aspects of the art. But the threshold of anger had become so high that nonviolent action was no longer possible. As more and more movement people started to bait and then fight the police, the pacifists found themselves in the compromising position of trying to cool both sides out. Chicago was the last demonstration I've ever attended. I went, planning to write about it for *Liberation* Magazine. But I never wrote the article. I saw things happen in Chicago about which I didn't want to write. The police riot didn't bother me. Mayor Daley's police were only a little bit more violent than were the U.S. marshals at the Pentagon or Mayor Lindsay's Tactical Police Force at various demonstrations in New York. If the Chicago police hadn't beaten up newsmen they would have gotten away with their violence as other police had before. But they attacked the press, it was shown on TV, and the whole world was watching. Big deal. The press and the public finally learned something about the system that we had learned over and over again long before. But the system grinds on.

What frightened me at Chicago—and I wish I had had the courage to say it in 1968 (though no one would have been in a frame of mind to listen) —was the violence of our own people and the way it raged out of control. The few movement veterans who came to fight police and did so didn't bother me. They knew what they were doing and did as expected. It was the hippie kids who answered the call to a festival of life and the McCarthy followers who came to Chicago still believing in the system. Overnight they were transformed into an angry and hateful mob without any political understanding of their violence except sweet and righteous revenge. You cannot build a movement for social change on the emotions of revenge. The turning point was 1968. Some of my friends became Weatherpeople. Others disappeared into the woods. The peace movement had reached a dead end. There seemed to be no middle ground.

Chicago confirmed an earlier instinct that it was time to drop out. Earlier in the year, I went to Washington, D.C., to help Ray Mungo on Liberation News Service. I first heard of Ray when he was editing the B.U. *News* and raising the same kind of hell in Boston that we were stirring up in New York. Since I had dropped out of B.U. grad school I wrote Ray a fan letter urging him to keep up the good fight. Ray, it turned out, was a fan of *Win,* so we continued our correspondence, which led, right in the middle of the riots after the death of Martin Luther King, Jr., to me going to Washington to lend a hand at LNS.

Two busts during the rioting—one for curfew, the other for dope—

turned us instantly into old and trusting friends. I met Verandah when she sat next to me during a double feature of the Marx Brothers' *Duck Soup* and a Mae West feature, title long forgotten. Now, nothing, absolutely nothing, can distract me from the brothers Marx, but with Verandah sitting next to me with this big floppy hat on and eyes which I couldn't see (she, at least, was watching the movie) yet knew were glowing fire, Miss West was all but forgotten. I moved into the LNS communal pad on Church Street and staked my future on Ray and Verandah's gift for fantasy. It wasn't long before we were headed up to Vermont (after a brief detour to California) to buy a farm, of all things; but perhaps I should explain myself further.

By 1968 the *Win* family had pretty much burned itself out. Gwen had taken her family to New Mexico, the Johnsons planned to follow soon. Politically, we had staked our pacifism on the success of The Resistance. We believed (and I still do) that if all the people who opposed the war had actively supported The Resistance (by turning in their draft cards and refusing induction if they were young males of draft age) we could have ended it. (As it was, if the Pentagon Papers are correct, The Resistance probably forced a limit to American aggression, some solace, but we didn't know it at the time.) But though many people gave lip-service support, relatively few people put their bodies on the line. A lot of our friends went to jail. I was lucky and never got indicted. But it didn't seem at the time that pacifism had anywhere to go, or at least I no longer felt I had anything original to contribute. So I needed to phase myself out of *Win*.

Yet, the experience at *Win* propelled me further in the direction I always seemed to be going. I didn't want to be just a writer, or just a person who functioned in some capacity in the movement. I wanted to build on the idea of community that had started to take shape at *Win*. That is, I wanted to start all over from scratch, reshape my own life and see how far a small group of people could take the idea of community together, hoping that out of the experience I'd have something later to write or offer the movement. Remember, we were all heavily into politics and committed to "making a revolution." I was very self-conscious about these motives. When Ray and Verandah had their fantasy about Vermont (and I never considered it more than fantasy at the beginning), I immediately agreed to go along. Though we only knew each other about a month, there was a lot of love, trust, and respect between us all. Those were fast-moving days and we all formed allegiances, made friendships, and fell in love on the basis of vibrations and elemental instincts. The fact that we got along and were headed in a common and communal direction was sufficient for each of us to commit whatever it was that shone dimly as our future to each other.

Well, one step led to another and much to my astonishment we were soon headed to Vermont to buy this farm which, somehow, Ray and Verandah knew about from this friend they had . . . I never quite understood the details. We looked at the farm, satisfied that it had a house on it, grass and trees (noting little else), and I met some of the other people who were going to live on the farm. Everyone seemed weird, but so was I and it seemed that if the farm was really going to happen I should go with the flow.

In June, 1968, we bought the farm. I assembled my life savings of $2,500, half of the necessary down payment, and threw it into a common pot. We signed the papers and I still had a hundred dollars left. Ray decided we needed to buy a car or maybe I heard wrong and he needed to buy a car. At any rate, I said "Far out," and with my last hundred dollars Ray bought an old Rambler sedan, which he named Nelly Belle, registered it to himself, and drove off to Washington, D.C., to close out his affairs. For a very brief instant I was stricken with an explosive flash of paranoia, a blast, I suppose, from my not quite forgotten straighter past. What in God's name had I gotten into? Here I'd invested every cent I had in a farm which we knew nothing about, with some crazy people who I hardly knew, and then Ray had taken my very last penny and absconded with what I believed was to be *our* car. But that feeling didn't last for long. Our lives, by then, had become structured on faith. If I couldn't trust my brother, who could I trust? The farm had to work out because I couldn't think of what I'd do next if it didn't. It was, as I said in the beginning, the end of the line. There was and is no place else to go.

As you can guess, everything did work out. Not without a few hairpin turns and a trip to California thrown in. But, read on, dear friend, read on. The adventure has just begun.

—MARTY

·THE GANDER·

VERANDAH AWOKE in the middle of a dream. She has not told us the dream. Or we no longer remember whether she first told us the dream, and neglected to tell the rest.

Something had seemed to awaken her. She awoke knowing that something had spoken, but the sound, if sound it was, passed in the instant that sleep did; and she awoke as if in an unfamiliar room and threw dew-sparkled nets of waking senses round, as when a wind gust through a storm-opened window blows a drowsing spider from her nest, and her eight feet spread to balance her on the trembling threads—so her mind moved, though she lay not stirring in the bed, lest a movement frighten whatever it was away; perfectly still she lay like soil, and one by one, like seeds, images of what was told her by cells warming up to language broke through her deeper surface in words—so we have heard: as the wind blows, everything grows.

What was it? We no longer remember the order of the possibilities she thought of in those seconds—surely it didn't seem to be a sudden drop in temperature (it sometimes was, so late at night, so nearly morning); no, a damped sibilant told her ear that a slow fire lingered in the stove below; she had *her* way of stacking wood, Verandah did: first the dry scraps of someone's carpentry: two hundred-year-old splits and chiselings of spruce, and then on top of them the narrow quarter-rounds of yellow birch, for the way that the feathers of the bark flared, and kindled in a moment the very flesh it had shielded from all weather for twenty years. Then the solid fuel itself, oak or beech or ash or maple, round, thick, or thicker than the arm that sawed it, or something special, according to fancy, or her sacred calendar: apple, cherry, a knot of hickory; and above these, if there was room, and there always was, after she'd pounded the splintery butt of the ax down on the topmost wood and packed them into the fire, she'd wedge a half-section of unseasoned black birch or cherry with clots of ice in the bark, so that by the time the rest of the wood had burned down, the last, on top, had baked dry enough to burn till she got up. No, she was warm; it wasn't a chill that locked her chin as deep as it could burrow in the warmth of her own shoulder—

In time, not much, her eyes opened: you and I are travelers now, pilgrims to a place that's still a mystery, and the third concentric space we have to pass through is visual space, a field not infinite as mind, nor spherical as hearing, but ovoid, forward, and deep enough—her eyes opened; she saw that first light was growing through the window on the east; it raised a glimmer not yet pink on the east faces of the rafters just above her; the dark shapes took on their familiar edge: roof-boards, joists, tears and creases in the vapor barrier—can you see her, as we who know her can, winning her night's rest in the cramped loft of Farmer Franklin's chicken slaughter house, her ladder a straight (or not so) birch sapling split right down the middle for six feet or so, joined by rung-shaped branches as thick as, no thicker than, a Coney Island Red Hot, leaning on a concrete floor with a

drain in the middle (for the blood), reaching up to a pile of blankets, quilts, and sleeping bags that looked, we imagined, like a dark mass of bread dough she'd just twirled a spoon through: twisted, no mattress below, and the roof so near above that she could sleep on her back or her front, but not very well on her side, her feet dangling or just saved from dangling over the side in the heat rising from the stove, and her head by the window, three of whose panes let a passable amount of moonlight through the dust sometimes; the fourth frame had given up its glass, and the same old towel was wadded there in winter. It was winter seven months of the year.

If it wasn't the dawn, or a sudden, distant light, already faded, or a strange shape among the shapes she knew, her eyes couldn't say what had broken her sleep.

She reached her right hand over her head, slowly and curiously as if through seaweed, turning all the while till she leaned on the other elbow; she pulled the towel from the hole and stuck her face through like a bird being born—there must be smells! and there were: wood smoke from her very fire, borne downwind and around on the draft from the top of the knoll, then caught on the level space, suspended in what would have been mist if it were August. The smell of the barn, the steaming mound of hay and horseshit by the door, the presence of the animals inside; and sources of coolness: the water forever flowing from the tap that drained the new well, the nearest apple tree, that somehow still had leaves that rustled, and a dozen sodden apples still on the limb; and snow, a fresh inch of powder over the tracks and stains it was time to erase—she knew these with her nostrils, and the skin of her face.

For just a few seconds, perhaps—she couldn't say, for sure, how long —she let herself go, let her face through the broken window be the surface where "this side" and "beyond" came together, and wave upon wave washed over her being: swells of sense breaking into words, or wordless pictures instantly etched, as if in frost; *we* have no words, either, for what we cease to wish to know.

She took in with no question, no power to question—the very outlines, very names of things, seemed to withdraw like snakes from the strength of her sensation—she absorbed, she became, as all of us have, time and rare time again, the farm, the rolling, rocky pasture pitched to the north, the forest advancing again across stone walls, the buildings that never blow over for the wind wails through not against them, and the hill itself holding all, and turning its own face to the certain waves of the seasons: to take in this without question is to approach what one was born to know, and what one came here to caress.

This moment passed: what else is annihilated in the instant that it's accepted? Was this why she had awakened: To awaken again, and again?

—PETE

·HOW I CAME TO THIS PLACE·

HERE IT IS, December; it's almost the last week of the year, and I could swear I haven't a thought in my head. I'm bound to write a story for this book of ours, but instead I've been biding my old time in the bottom of the barn, building a stall for the calf to be born this New Year's Eve —our very first calf, Bessie's first here on the hill, though Lord knows she had a couple before she came here. I'm glad to have wood to work with: we took down a two hundred-year-old barn in West B———, and all the old beams and boards and planks are stacked here neatly under the fresh snow. So I've been working very slowly, as I like to do, down where it's sheltered from the west wind, and where the only sounds are Bessie's patient chewing of hay, and the trickle of the gravity-fed water system, and each hen's shattering cluck of triumph as another egg is laid. (We get twenty a day from twenty-four chickens.)

Sometimes as I work, my spirit takes a little leap, and I realize that somewhere inside me a young boy is busy throwing a straw up into the wind: I mean to say, my mind's thrown free, it's glancing about to see which way the vision's going to come from, then just floats back down where I'm working. One of the things I love best in this world is doing some careful job, in wood or ink or flour or words; it's my way of moving meditation, "arranging space," slower by far than muscles themselves can move—a whole day can pass by and I'm happy; the space around me has changed, but somehow feels as if it's always been this way; my mind's been here but been wonderfully quiet, like a newly obedient dog who's staying around, hasn't shit on the rug, and hasn't strayed far-off to find something to chew.

But now I'm through for the day, see stars in the east; I finished the new grain storage bin, and I walked over to where the calf is curled up, still inside the cow, and pressed my hands as close against him as I could, and pressed my head against his mother's soft black winter coat. "I think I'll go up to the house and write," I told the calf; "can you wait a little longer?" He kicked and rolled around as if to say it was okay. He'd stay in there a few days more.

I come up to sit at our sunset window. There's a big chunk of beech burning in the old Woodmere No. 20 stove. The wind's roar seems both near and far away. I am searching for a word that means "pertaining to the eyes of him who has just seen the sun go down again."

We're approaching the fullness of the Moon of the Howling Wolf. I can see its first silver light—a light that chills—come on the crust of the snow; I'm looking down through the toast-shaped window: how easily the vision shifts, from one side of the glass to the other, the while dumb fingers move over the objects on the desk, hesitating one last time to tell this story, now at the year's end, at sunset, in my third winter (and winter is the best time) on the farm—

When I first visited this place, I remember, a few years ago, I was alone, in a way at last blind to humor; I was preoccupied with a longing for something: to fill up this life gently with more people, to know them; to put on faces I knew I had in me, to work hard but not for money or reward, to know the world and the seasons I worked in, to live as slowly and reverently and lovingly as I could, and to halt, just *halt*, the headlong, totally unwilling, seemingly ordained drive I was on, toward a life of further separation: into secrets, into the spoken desires in my heart, into couples, into a job, personal cash income, small house, little incomplete family, private car, visits with friends I grew estranged from and tried to outperform, all with one jealous woman I lived silent seething life with and dreamed myself away from, and against whose fragrant, mysterious body I hatched (bless her) visions of violence.

Well, toward the end of this time I was a graduate student at Harvard, in Sanskrit and Indian Studies, in the little room in the big old library, where all love I ever felt for ancient texts was wrung out of me, though I knew that somewhere behind those words lay the Dharma itself—I sat and sweated with the same old fear of the same old recitation; the seats in that steam-heated room had built-in hemorrhoids: Generations of key-carrying scholars had come into that room and passed on. I, too, passed on; I leaned out of the wired window once, chanting a chant of what was locked in there with me: Krishna and Radha, bellies and stones, stars and sighing ganders, cymbals, digits of the moon: I left that place, though school was all I knew. I talked with a dean. "Pick peas," he said.

I drifted. One night in Boston, a beautiful thing happened to me. It was 1968. I smoked a little piece of black Lebanese hash. It was perfect. It bore the seal of the grand vizier himself. I laid the pipe down and walked out into late August night (Alone! Girlfriend off in Canada! Me, and the summer night in the city, and happiness of not knowing what might happen): the good, good feeling is what I'm trying to share; of more than this feeling, which was so new to me, I won't write; it would take too many words and introduce faces that don't really appear again, would lead elsewhere, but where I can't say, for to have followed the events of that first night would have led somewhere other than the farm. So we all must have nights like this in our memories; just as some of the objects on my desk are memory-symbols of whole universes I've traveled in and loved in at one time, so other objects or images seem to open into futures that never existed except in potential, and have passed away.

And that's the difference between the first and the second night. The same quiet room, perhaps a record playing: Laura Nyro, or *Lilacs Out of the Dead Land,* or Mick Jagger singing "Back Street Girl" with the concertina lilting in the background; some good food, the ceremony of the black-and-silver pipe, and the blue flame on the tiny perfumed flake. I descend the stairs, and soon I find myself in my car, driving ever so slowly out of Boston very late at night, my mind peacefully empty (in the state I have described to you), looking out the windshield that's bordered by artificial flowers and

Greek saints and an incense holder, and a bejeweled card that says "Trust in the Lord."

I decided I would. On the seat beside me lay a map my sister had drawn: "How to Get to the Farm." I'd never been there; it was in its second month. I knew Richard and Verandah, but not well. (My sister was married to Richard's brother. She still is. You can read her writing later in this book.) How could I know it was nearly impossible to find the farm on a dark night? I expected, perhaps, paper lanterns strung around "the lake," and a streetlight beside "The Old Apple Tree where you turn up the hill."

I didn't know how dark the night was, but my head felt good, and the first well-accompanied fifty miles gave way to a long stretch of empty road: no other cars and seldom a sign, bumpy old Route 2, and quiet throb of the engine, so that my memory wandered for a second: in how many other states and countries, from how many situations, had I hurtled downroad late at night, with destination and feeling of belonging where I was about to go, and sense of a perfect life-space pattern I could see if I were a hundred miles above: that old Ozark highway that hundreds of turtles were crossing, separated by swaths of mist; or the cross-isthmus truck road in Oaxaca, where I stood the night through (eighty passengers, no seats, my toe broken) pressed against the huge bus windshield where the mountain rain lashed, and the Indians in work-clothes talked to each other about how much my armpits stank—or the stretch west of Billings, Montana, where I was driving in just such a mood, and a jackrabbit darted in front of the car, turned and blinked at the lights for a second, then vanished in the talons of a great snowy owl that swooped down: I'd been lots of places. I didn't know what this night would yield.

Many turns; I sensed, but couldn't really see, the long pond and then The Apple Tree. I felt I was led to the dooryard of the farm. I turned off the engine, stepped out to incredible quiet, to August night air so fresh and cool, borne in on a slight breeze from the mowing, and sweetened by the damp of the lower well's hollow: what a deep breath I took!

I can still see it: a narrow beam of house light falls on the weeds and stones, and I guess that's Dale standing in the doorway, wondering who's there. She's wearing black pants and a faded green T-shirt; there's a cigarette dangling from her fingers; her thin lips purse thinner; she doesn't know me. Behind her I can see Verandah, and she calls out my name: I know I can stay and visit, so my shoulders relax from driving, tired, as a strong smell of dust and cat-piss pours out of the house, and I meet Ellen and John and

Michael and Connie; I settle back, too, on the ratty couch in the Green Room; before long I'll sleep in the hay in the barn, on my first night on the farm.

My visit lasted two days and two nights. The farm by day was beautiful. I remember rolling down the great hill in a white shirt, the dry scratch of hay gone to seed. The people weren't doing much, so there was no one I could help. I was introduced to Raymond. He talked a lot. We took a mild psilocybin, and the afternoon came bright as goldenrod in flower; at night I cooked French-fried onion rings and Dale made two peach pies; we ate in what seemed to be a garage. Walking down to the graveyard in dark as dark as any, I held Ellen's hand. We read the inscriptions by matchlight. Walking back, we held hands, too. Nearly two miles of holding hands. (Aren't we there yet? *Another* rise in the road?) It felt good but uncomfortable, as those things do. She seemed to be Raymond's girl. That night in the barn the chicken came to sleep with me. She clucked along the beam and settled beside my head. I lay low. I thought she was a rooster.

Before I left I said how nice it had been. I said I thought I'd like to live there. Nobody made any offers. I said I'd come back soon, and they said I should, but in fact the wind blew me many places before it took me there again. I started to tell myself what I tell myself now: that I knew I'd live on the farm or someplace like it some day, but I had to go through some other things first; it was my task, and not the farm's, to bring myself to it. Clearly, I wasn't ready, or someone would have asked me to stay, it seemed to me.

Now, unlike my other friends here on the farm, at this time I was not involved in the movement, except as a fool or a jester—I was one of the first freaks at Brandeis, as I remember. Revolutions need mummers, and I was growing in that direction, although at the time, had I been admonished to "involve myself in a cause greater than my own destiny," I might have taken that to mean "pursue broad knowledge," or "experience Love of and with a woman," both of which I did to the extreme, more or less, with fitful excitement and adequate discipline. My parents were very proud, and so was I.

You know what happened at that point. I choked myself with knowledge for its own sake and grew to hate the woman I lived with. What's worse, those two binds had twisted about me so tight that my tongue was as lame as ever, and I had to admit that, in living as I was then living, I was knowingly prolonging the very cause of the crippling sorrow that had first hit me years before. The block between me and just being with people was still my center. I didn't know where it came from; I feared and bewailed it.

Yet live inside it I did. It was my house.

At this time also, the world really seemed to be falling apart; its state overwhelmed my private grief; its disintegration overshadowed the breaking up of our long-ago-lost love. In the middle of this period, I visited the farm. It felt good there, and I sort of wished I could stay. It reminded me of the farm in Pennsylvania I'd played on as a child. I thought I knew a lot about plants, had grown and grafted hundreds of them in my apartment. And one of my secrets was, for a couple of years I had dreamed of living on a communal farm; I'd read all I could about tribes and primitive families. But I wasn't free, and, as I've said, the question didn't really come up.

I wasn't surprised at the lack of warm welcome; I didn't know the people well, and I hadn't presented a very convincing case for myself; I was uptight, though I made a good show of looseness. (It wasn't easy to visit the farm then; so many had come that summer, and it was automatic that after one day there, you wanted to stay. And it's just not possible. In the past two and a half years only two new persons have been allowed to stay on. And they didn't ask.)

But I felt lucky. I had a pretty good sense of the change I wanted to see happen in myself, even though I couldn't name it, and had no vision of the steps that would help me on the way. My friends and I and the media all rehearsed alternative ways of living, and how to understand, believe in, and survive the crumbling of the American Empire. But more important, I (surely all of us) had a dawning, growing faith in another reality, a separate reality—everywhere around us; it had always been there and would always be: perfect, beyond time, unborn, unchanging, undying; it had only to be perceived, and then you'd know and love it, and seek a place, a life, where knowing it could be your power, your own version of it, renewable each time you breathed deep, or heard the low, motive hum behind the seasons— Reader, if you've heard this song a hundred times before, and still don't believe it, then listen once again, and believe *this*, if you can: it just doesn't matter if the vision is objectively true or not. If you have faith in its existence, then it exists. If there were "give" and "take" to it, I could say, it gives you power, and it also *gains* power from your acceptance of it— time and again on the farm we are surpised by the gaiety, fullness, and power unleashed when a group of people lets itself go, just a little, and slowly such rituals grow beyond their origins, till they repeat almost on their own, till they become our worshipful way of saying, Blow, wind, and splash, rain, and Earth, heave if you will; we know what's behind you and we're going to keep it all humming—we are hanged men; we've traded our own power for a Greater. "One must die to the social order to continue on one's path of growth."

Unless you've been born into a family of such mind, you have to seek it, and feel where and how. It helps to have a teacher, and I had two of them before I came to the farm.

Luis was the first. You'll see him described elsewhere in this book, because he, too, lives on the farm. He came shortly after I did. Eight, nine years ago I met him; a large, bawdy Cuban he seemed, his face as big as the full moon. Meeting him turned me around; quickly I learnd that he had accumulated about as much knowledge as it seemed to me a man could gather, but all of it somehow transmuted in his brain, stripped of its weight, and piled haphazardly at the precipice over which truth topples into absurdity. I'd come to him with some new delicate insight and he'd say, Well yes, man, that's very good but on the other hand—and stick out his tongue, accompanied by an apelike sound. Other teachers took pains to put on knowledge like suits of clothes; for him it was food, and the sooner it got to be shit, the better. For the first time I had to consider that at the end of my road lay nothing. And then I had to take that image down to its extreme, where it dissolves in irrational laughter. We studied voodoo, and Pablo Neruda, Cesar Vallejo, and Miguel Unamuno, in all to uncover the instant in which this world melts away— I am thinking of all this now, for the first time since I moved to the farm, but I know now how important this time was. I ignored the lessons and forgot their source. We moved apart. Some of his feelings, some words, and a cackle or two stuck with me, like rats that had boarded a ship in port.

In time I came to know an old, old man named Leo. Luis grew aware of him too. He was as ghostly a man as ever walked on the ground. He was teaching a course in Indian Art. He stood in the darkened room before a slide of a massive North Indian stone carving, elephants bathing each other and trees turning into snake-bodied women; you could just make out his frail body dancing outside the arc-light; he couldn't see the slides; he was losing his sight, so he *became* each image he told of: "Ah," he would whisper, "the unseizable totality of that moment! Its formlessnessness! The deerness of the deer! The mobile rigidity! Forgive me; I know nothing! Change the slide." He couldn't see the people taking in each word and sight of his dancing body, to a place inside them that had rarely been touched in their lives. When you told him so he blushed and said, You cannot mean that. You are trying to make me feel good. When he said he knew nothing he was telling his truth: he didn't know if he was Russian, French, Catalan, or American; they all kept coming and going inside him; he didn't know if he was young or ancient, flesh or spirit, blind or seeing, male or female, loved or despised. Each moment of his life came as a surprise to him. His senses stirred on his surface like hair that grows on a dead man. Yet to every person who reached out to grope for where he was, he sent out an almost indiscernible beam of pure love, undemanding and unattached. How could a man want nothing from his friends, yet love them more and more? It was his last year of teaching—he had appeared as a parentless child somewhere in Eastern Europe just before the First World War, and he was going back there. His "foster father" awaited him. I haven't seen him in two years and I'm afraid he may have died.

I said good-bye to these people. I went to California to live for a while. Sold *Berkeley Barbs* in the winter rain, visited David in the redwoods, slept on a lot of old friends' floors, saw my old friend Kathy, moved among strangers, walked all night long in the hills above the bay, got tear-gassed on Telegraph Avenue, and took some LSD in Organ Pipe Cactus National Park. Now you may say: so, here's another one who went to California and dropped some acid; they're all alike. Well, if so, you've been misinformed; anyone who has ever gone on a massive and solitary trip will tell you that once you are flying, and breathing in the unending, silent Law, that kind of talk is nonsense; it no longer matters how many thousand others have gone before. They don't exist anymore. It's just you and the bull. The crowd has vanished. And then the bull vanishes, and then you do, too.

I wandered from dawn till sunset in a land of twenty-foot-tall cacti; the colorless February desert sun melted me and I left my clothes on a rock, climbed a mountain as a winter wind came up, making the spines of the great saguaros hum on the canyon floor. I took shelter in a mountain lion's cave, lay on its wild-smelling bed, scratch-marks and bits of fur on the walls around it, bones and a half-eaten mushroom near the entrance of the lair; soon I climbed higher and hunkered on the top, and an eagle flew down from an advancing thunderhead, and spied and circled me, flew lower and lower and swooped down—would he pluck out my heart?—screaming my new name as it dived right by me, warning me to get off the mountain before the storm and sunset hit; so I did.

A few friends and I had decided to form a mime troupe and commune. We went back East to bring more of our friends into it. I visited the farm again. Verandah said, Why don't you stay for a while? I said I wanted to do this other thing, to be in it from the start. I left after two days again.

For weeks we held long, intense, and ultimately pointless meetings of the commune-to-be. But we came to know each other a little, ate well, and finally wrenched ourselves away from drugs, more or less. We did hours of mime exercises every day; our teacher, David, moved so well and taught us how. In two months we put on a show that was as beautiful and silent as snow in the night pine forest—I got to be what I had always wanted to be: a masked but bright-eyed gesturer in silence, speaking by just being, and getting through; each muscle speaking for itself yet not alone; my friends told me: Go out there and at last declare what you were born to be. Don't avoid it or deny it anymore; your silence is not your enemy; it is a part of you, a gift, your power; let it be.

I guess I mean this image to be instructive: if you're not feeling as loose, as freely and beautifully embodied as you'd like to feel, mime or dance may help you—like a piece of clay or a pen or a violin, your body's just waiting for you to use it, play on it, push it around, even to the point of transfiguration; you forget who you were, and know yourself to be creation itself at its moment, moving through births unceasing—it feels good.

The events of that year began to move so rapidly then, that at times I couldn't keep up with the sense of it, but moved like a startled bird far from its home; I'd certainly left just about everything I'd thought of as central to my routine: my plants were given away to friends; my books lay somewhere packed in boxes, and everyone "owned" the blue car; we shared clothes and food and the floor we slept on; the deliberate, demanding encounter-group techniques we used in our meetings soon had me talking as easily as ever I had: my mind was up front with my tongue; it had to be, that was the rule.

One afternoon I woke up in the hospital emergency ward. I had been mugged in downtown Boston. I asked where my girlfriend was. My friends looked at each other. "It's all right, Pete," one of them said. "She's not here. You broke up five months ago." I caught sight of my ruined (so it seemed) face in a mirror, and went into shock, and woke again, thinking how far in a strange space I'd traveled, how disintegrated my life seemed to have become, if it could scatter so easily. What was my presence? The kind nurse, who thought I'd taken LSD and fallen off my motorcycle, rammed my face against the X-ray plate, to demonstrate that my nose wasn't broken. They say salvation, or certain kinds of happiness at least, lie at the far side of experiences like these.

We packed up our cars and went West, nearly thirty of us; summer was just beginning as we straggled into Berkeley, the day after the Guard erected the tall fence round People's Park; they sure looked silly standing there among the flower beds and children's toys. We settled into the life there, attending meetings of the outraged populace, practicing mime and working on a new and perhaps more political play; we met every night for dinner and the talking, and sent expeditions north to search for land. Weekends we met with other freaks for softball on the campus. Nothing was more important for me than this. So this is the first pulse of climax to my Horatio Alger tale; my ego can have no greater flowering in this world: mind and body and mouth, all loose, dreams of sad childhood come to this: bounding like a deer at shortstop, fielding those grounders (almost all of them), chattering "No batter!" and "Life is a Dream!" and the entire team running, chanting, laughing for the fun of it.

I remember the rest of the summer as a bright and emotional dance— liberating, yet pointing homeward, too. We never found the piece of land we wanted, and just as we thought of a name for ourselves—the Big Rock Candy Mountain—we grew irrevocably apart; having talked ourselves into two more or less opposite corners: those who were content to flow with time, and with the gradual, casual brotherhood that might come; and those who wanted to structure and anticipate, leaving nothing to luck or the cosmic play; the second group felt that the first had let them down by not being honest enough. My own spirit alternately soared, then dived a little, in love, in growing close with a few friends, in a kind of mystic apprehension of the week that men first landed on the moon, in a few weeks spent deep in the

Marble Mountain Wilderness, bathing in glacial cataracts and eating trout and berries and wild salads.

Toward the end of the summer a sad foreboding had crept upon me, and there wasn't much my friends in the West could do. Some were starting to work with the Portola Institute, and some stayed on in Berkeley. My thoughts turned to the farm—I was happy to see our own group break apart, for that's what it was meant to do, but I felt winter coming soon, and longed for my journey to end in country land among good people. You might say I felt this as a passion and a need, made manifest in a strange uneasiness I couldn't explain or shake; I drove across the country about as fast as one person can, stopping only to walk where Custer Last Stood, and to sleep a few hours each night.

The next thirty days or so are crystals I have sifted in my fingers so many times since: pulling into a Sunoco station just off the thruway in Allentown, to scrub the country's dust from my face, then going home; a few days spent in the old house, the best ever, my mother and father and I very close and quiet: I baked bread and our eyes met many times: what can I say? Soon it was time to leave there, too; I can still see my father waving under the sycamore as I drive away, so anxious to travel the last few hundred miles I have to go.

I arrived at the farm in time for breakfast; the October sun was warming the mist away. The people seemed happy to see me, Connie and Michael especially. I remember, now, a slowness and quietness in me, and evenings when I walked some new way from the Corners, I wondered a lot to myself: the farm was beautiful but could I stand to live with the people—such an improbable group, and such a dialect of English, and did they really know and love each other? It didn't seem so, and that was something I needed to feel. Was I doomed to move on from here, too?

Marty was leaving; he didn't say why. Raymond and Verandah were canoeing on the Concord River. Ellen came and went in a day; we hugged once; she was going to California. There were no spare rooms, so I slept on the dog couch in the big room, right under where the rotten tomatoes were hanging. They fell on me during the night. But there was plenty of work, and I started building a room over the shed, and the wind whipped over the moine; the leaves turned and the insects sang the loud death-song, and I tasted the apples of every tree. Sometimes I breathed like a reed in the wind, and sometimes the air was so heavy you had to swim to move it. Raymond returned and announced that death was stalking us; he felt it. Kerouac died in Miami and Marshall Bloom was about to die. And that same week, just as the sun entered Scorpio, my father died dancing in Allentown—the smile I'm now known for is just a shadow of his.

I pass over the two weeks spent at home again; I moved restlessly in the house and the familiar streets. I knew his death as if I'd been there, but the greatest sadness of all was that I couldn't tear or scratch away the film of ego over my eyes, and just *see* him; every image I saw was cloudy: what a loss! And my own heart felt as if it, too, would stop. The prayers I prayed were like this: God help me to let people deep into me, unclothed, unchanged by my eye, by my "I"— before it's too late. I left as soon as I could. "I must go be with my family now," I said.

As the car came over the last rise in the road, I saw Michael. He was trying to disk the hard sod of the lower pasture. He ran my way, leaping over the low wall. He put his head through the car window and started to cry on my chest, and I did, too.

I finish writing; my mind flies over the years that have passed since. I wrap a great blanket around me and go out to piss in the snow. It's very late; the snowcrust on the hill is heaving and cracking in the cold. There's no wind, no other sound. The animals and humans are asleep.

Up in our room again: I drape the blanket over the chair, throw a round of black birch in the fire; then I lie down beside Ellen, who rolls over toward me, aware but not waking— I lie still and listen to the wood take fire; first the stray sawdust combusts minutely and whispers up the pipe, and soon the log itself's aflame; the stove makes a sound like a great moth beating its wings inside a jar.

But sleep doesn't come to me that way tonight; my mind's too full and wild, my mind and the world are two new lovers who want to embrace again before sleep stills them. But I would believe you if you said this seems like a dream. It doesn't matter. We know, because we trust each other, that whenever one of us is awake in the night, then we are all awake, "clothed with the heavens and crowned with stars," and we also know, with the stubborn certainty of ten old men and women trudging somewhere in the universe carrying nothing, that when the last board and shingle of these houses have rotted away, and beings unthought-of rub their backs on the piles of broken bricks and roll their red eyes, we will all be together somewhere in the dream, for our dreams are slowly becoming one, like puddles coming together in the rain.

So I move off into a dream—as close as I can to be waking, it may be—I dream that the big, slow, happy dog I loved, who was shot this fall by hunters, has come back to stand once more on hind legs, his huge black head leaning level with our heads, in our bed that's four feet off the ground, his tongue out and his brown eyes like deep empty caves a soul might sleep in: it seems he has come to ask me to go with him, and as it is nearly morning now, I do, after first waking Ellen a little, to ask her to follow if I don't come back soon. She murmurs a word formed of sleep-sounds and then sleeps on, and the baby inside her kicks, and is quiet.

I get up and pull on soft wool clothes and hat and boots and go outside; the good air rushes into the lungs; the barest wind above sighs like a gander in the twigs of the two great maples, and the chickadees' song weaves the first translucent threads of the veil that day drops over men's eyes; dawn can't be far away.

There's a slighter, more mysterious sound among these; I hear it come down from the hill, where the jewel is in the lotus, where the dog has already gone: it may be a laugh, or the tinkling of glass. Walking uphill, walking uphill. The crust is solid, and here and there suggestions of objects protrude from the snow: the weeds above the wild strawberries, the old harrow, the cut-off sunflowers, a mound I don't remember—there's a lantern burning in the pub; someone else must be awake; the light comes through the thick glass of the window and slides a little way over the snow. And a little bit of it drifts up and dusts the bristles of the overhanging thatch.

I push open the big door with a creak—it has always creaked—and glance around the room: nobody. But again, the room bespeaks a presence; the brown tiles of the floor are warm and traveled-on; a great log's burning in the fireplace; the flagons remain on the board. The cellar door is slightly open, and a glow and a woman's laugh float up from below, and then a belch that seems to rumble out of the earth's core itself: surely Hugh is down there, and not alone, by the sound of it. What a night this has been!

Soon I'm a part of the candlelit group in the vault. The dim light reveals our faces: Hugh, the Marquis, the stranger, and I. The stranger is a woman in wanderer's dress. She's smoking a pipeful of leaves gathered "somewhere out West," and we're all drinking cider, golden and tiny-bubbled, pressed a year ago of Macs and Baldwins and Macouns. How long the other three have been here, I can't say, but their eyes sparkle—the first long swallows

give me a scent of the road they've taken, and I'm off, too. Behind our heads the stacks of barrels stand and bide the years.

The traveler is speaking of things she "has seen" in the world. Some of what she tells us she has surely seen, and some just heard of, perhaps in a tavern like this. And some must have welled up from her own imagination, as is only right. Tomorrow must come from somewhere.

Anything we hear on nights like this is news: most people have ceased to travel, except within the communes; as time goes by, very few people still choose to gain knowledge by moving about on the face of things. At last the long moment had to come when the peaceful minds, the abundant farms, the increasing tribe stood still, and breathed deep where it stood, of the power entrusted to it, while the planet itself gathered its own voice—you've heard all this many times.

I won't—I can't—repeat the things she said, although I meant to when I started out; it may even be that her voice which was low and beautiful had just grown weary by the time we came, and now she just sat and cradled her drink in her hands and slowly looked around at us, eyes wide. In her eyes we see all the time she's traveled, and the past places where she's found hospitality, and the tenderness and ease we share with no effort nor motive, and the silence and calm that listens and hears, that loves, and is free, and makes empires fall—

The particulars, her words—our plans, our visions—I leave unspoken here; you have your own. For me, the quiet and knowing glance represents what's happening in this instant, and what must happen times without number, in place after place after place, till the planet is ours, till it's saved; it's come down to that! I look at you, you look at me; our eyes hold each other for the time it takes; the past woes, the learned defenses, the civilized fears, all fall away from our faces, and we know each other, we trust what's inside, we share each other's rhythm, it's the same; most of all, more than ever, we finally know what we have to do, and time, Time, will grind down and stop for us while we do it: it sometimes has, in history.

We will help each other; it's not hard; we will not murder, harm, spite, or judge each other; we will not take profit from, scorn, or exploit another person's work; we will repeal the never-wished-for orders to consume, consume, spend, waste, and exhaust; we will dismantle the war machines and choking industries that feed them; we will ignore the ill advice that separates us into silent children at our desks, into locked apartments, into nations—we want to be joined, and responsible; we want to spend the rest of our days taking care of the planet, as we are learning to take care of the farm; we will be gentle with it; it will be our center; we will be responsible and grateful, we will know and love our own nature, far beyond words or political thoughts, know what we are a part of, just a part; we will eat good food and not spread blindly, unfairly over the earth; we will be together with each other, and with the animals and plants who will love us, in the ritual, seasonal dances that call up, name, and exorcise the violence, darkness, and ignorance in us: we will master them, and not need masters. We will have, and be, light and dark, spiritual, sexual, the same, city, farm, and wilderness; we will have no enemy; we will look into each other's eyes and no longer see the division that's made men blind to the one vast being that mystics and physicists stake their daily lives on—

I don't know if I'm awake or dreaming, don't know if it's night or morning; we seem to be sitting in a quiet room deep in the earth; our gazes meet as if we know each other very well, though we may very well have been strangers a moment ago. We all have stories to tell, and we'll tell them. Though we may feel we have been here all our lives, though we may never leave, we're still travelers, in paths whose direction and rhythm you have to look deep into nature to see—like the swallow flying back to the barn, like Sirius, the Dog Star, over the peach orchard hill, we are all travelers.

What do you seek here, since this world is not your resting place?

—PETE

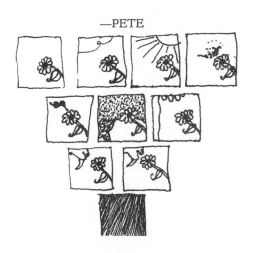

·PEPPER'S VISION·

Five o'clock in the morning.
No one awake.
Downstairs, Pippy greets me with wiggles and piles of
    caca.
That first trip to the outhouse is chilly and cold.
Freezes my fanny but not my soul.
Last night's stars are still in the sky.
This is morning?
My dreams are still so close.
By six o'clock M. has left.
He has an early date with fifty girls of Gordon's.
Pippy and I are alone again.
But something's happening in the sky.
It's pale gray where just a short time ago it was so
    black.
The stars have gone and outside the big window it's
    pink, and purple, and twelve other colors I can't
    describe with words.
Sun's coming up!
Got a lot to do today.
Can't remember what just now, so I'll sit and watch the
    sun while Pippy, who only has to be a pup today,
    begins by attacking a pillow.
She's got it made!
Right now, I think I do, too.

—PEPPER

·WHO'S IN CHARGE·
·for L.N.D., wherever·

I REMEMBER HITCHHIKING TO THE FARM on a number of occasions and drivers asking me what did we *do* up there. And who does the dishes on which nights. And where does the money come from, and how is it controlled, and who makes decisions, and who leads the workers, and who . . . blah . . . blah . . . blah? I was always tongue-tied for an answer. What decisions? What organization? There were none. Yet every night the dishes were done. And every few days someone would venture off the safety of the hill, go to town, shop, write checks, spend money, bring home food to fill the refrigerator and pantry, and most likely be applauded for the good deed of the day. Cue: smiles and reinforcement. And obviously, I knew, there was no omnipotent paternal or spiritual leader who by sheer wit and psychic force or chicanery had subtly organized or scheduled the quotidian destiny of life on the farm; obviously no one had tricked us into believing we were finally free of obligation and routine while hiding behind the arras pulling strings with joy at our delusions.

If none of that, then how (as the ride continued with growing curiosity) did it all get done?

Well, I suppose, in a way, there is a schedule of sorts. But let me tell you how and why it worked.

When we first arrived here with an enthusiasm which was rabid and full of doubts we did "organize" ourselves. Most of us knew nothing, and all of us had that starry-eyed zeal of coming from the city to this place to make a farm or found a new life or make a last political stand or learn or whatnot—the kind of awkward if not embarrassing eagerness to plunge without the slightest idea of how or really why. Our quaint farmhouse with the blue shingled roof was enchanting and rustic but terribly small for a population which had suddenly bounded from the farmer and his wife to ten noisy and teeming neophytes. Laurie was a carpenter, and because he knew something, a craft and art, he earned the immediate respect and willingness of all of us. The garage attached to the house, under his hand and

tutelage, was transformed into a spacious living room filled with lofts and platforms, and paneled with old barn boards. He told us how to bang nails, staple up insulation, distinguish 2 x 4's from 2 x 8's, the uses of tar paper and shingles, etc. Winter came. And because he knew that we'd need wood to keep warm in the new room, it evolved that Laurie once again became "the man who knew" and led our first search parties and chain gangs, with saws and axes, into the woods behind the orchard, to gather fuel. He was the foreman and we the willing students and workers. Laurie freaked out. He became itchy in the role of boss and Mr. Know-it-all, began to feel guilty about being pushy and arrogant. And the ranks too were beginning to feel the incipient and creeping feeling that we all as well as Laurie were at a disadvantage—that our education lacked spontaneity or initiative or error. Not long after that, for a number of intrapsychic as well as external reasons, Laurie left.

Then began a short history which found many of us feeling that it was he or she who had to willingly or unwillingly assume the role of organizer or teacher. Marty bloomed to the fore as a woodsman, and took charge of wintry forages into the woods. The idea of bossman freaked him as it had Laurie, and he eased off, only to become manifestly discouraged at the lack of accomplishment. Threats of departure, wringing of hands. Could it be true that we'd get nothing done unless there was some one person to cast a cold eye on all our strivings, and that it was therefore necessary for all of us to wink back the signal of submission, and punch the clock?

That role passed onto the shoulders of a number of us, and each one in turn shrugged off the responsibility and pain of "seeing to it" that things got done.

But in the kitchen something else was happening. Every evening, come frying July day or 30° below and snow in January, a sumptuous feast was laid (at first perhaps less than festive cookery—we called it "something for nothing" or "cheap but good") which was invariably cooked and served by a different, tired farmer. And every night (almost) the dishes were done by some new face at the sink. No kitchen manager. No list tacked onto the fridge or over the sink specifying menu, cook, dishwasher, bottle cleaner, sweeper, etc. And it was there, in the kitchen, at the evening dance of a crowd stepping out of one another's way with arms and hands flailing spoons and wire whisks, one baking bread, one throwing vegetables together in some as yet untasted and innovative way, and the coffee-hounds jostling the tea-totalers for the hottest spot on the old Home Comfort, amid laughter and intermittent "ouches" of burned hands, and the final rush to the table to be seated before a splendid and orderly meal, that I first observed how things got done, and what made them happen. By this time the whole rhythm of the farm began to look and feel like what I saw in the kitchen, and of course it would be food, which this whole crazy place worships in a way, that pointed, for me, to the symbols and their meanings.

A bit of trouble arises here. Because although I want to tell you what I think I learned in the kitchen and henceforward found all around me about the process of the place, there's a gnawing hesitation to put the unspoken into words, to pretend to make the subtle manifest and cogent. Yet it's all really quite simple, and what the hell.

What I think is this: that you come to the country a bumpkin in the face of the elements, and you try to make some impression of yourself on what's around you. You struggle, in a way, to make the environment a counterpoint to your own action in the same way that you learned to control your urban destiny. After all, you *are* the source of cerebration, of power, of will, and if your education has taught you anything it's taught you how to use all of that to make life work for you, and those who are best at it have the benefits of immediate gratification. But if you're willing to doubt all of that even for a moment, and you find yourself courting all the frustrations which that knowhow and attitude will inevitably bring in the face of a northeaster, or, say, facing wet kindling on a December morning, and you find yourself slightly eager to take all of that, something begins to happen, and your first introduction to it is of some unidentified flying object circling in your solar plexus. And perhaps you're moved to take a long hike in the snow, alone, and there is nothing under your feet but absolute untainted whiteness, and the birds are singing some spicy winter ditty, and the wind moves through the trees like February into March, and there's nothing above you but up; it's there and then that you fall down, not to pray necessarily, but to die in order to give it all away, and become what you thought you were not. The ax falls, the bough bends, you are, at last, *no longer in control*. Blown away. All gone. Ha ha ha boo hoo hoo.

If there is a secret, and it's oh so ancient and so recognized, that experience points the direction to its unraveling. In some quiet or not so quiet way you've learned that the controls, the bossman, the superintendent of rhythms and schedules and motion and rest, is out there somewhere beyond the medulla, and it only takes the slightest bit of recognition and submission to make friends, and take cues.

That's what I think happened here. That the wind and the snow, the explosions of green and summertime blew us all down, taught us lessons about time and the sequence of events, and especially about where direction comes from.

Now the rhythm of our work is that rhythm. And the farm as a whole, its plantings, plowings, harvests, business transactions, decision makings, etc. can be seen as a mirror image in the larger picture of what each one of us learned in his relationship with . . . whatever it is that's out there. As it was, in the kitchen, the power of food, the need to appease some insistent hunger, grew larger than particular issues: the image of smoke curling around the nose, beckoning, and pointing out direction. In the image, the farm becomes a power or an idea or a movement greater than each individual or even the group as a whole, which like a simile for what's out there, has a rhythm, a process which gives the cues, and which one, not necessarily submitting to, becomes a part of. And stretching the image further, each one of us, having learned the rhythm and power of the others, learns the individual cues which each one of us puts out and which each must either submit to, become resigned to, or flow with.

So the dishes get done because they have to be put out of the way, and the person who does them, occasionally suspiciously silent, does them because he or she feels that it's necessary to make some space, move some air, unstop the flow, clear the room for dancing.

It wasn't so unique or terrible at all—simply a matter of learning who the real manager is and learning the rules which are set down all over the face of the earth, in the ground which has to be tilled for food when the winter thaws, in the orchard which has to be pruned to bear the sweet peach, in the wood which has to be cut and sawed and dried before winter to keep the body warm, in the teats of Bessie the cow which have to be, just plain have to be, milked at morning and when the sun goes down. Some of us hear the call of some of these things more clearly than others, and so have an interest and excel. But Bessie, like the farm growing and calling all over, won't take no for an answer. And she'd stamp her foot, and you'd know it's as simple as that.

—RICHARD

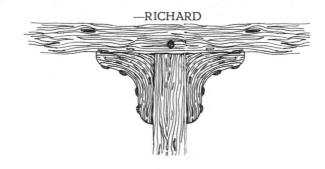

·THE MAKING· ·OF A· ·CULTURE COUNTER·

·THE MILKMAID'S LAMENT·

I wonder who's milking her now.
I wonder who's milking my cow.
I wonder who's looking into her sty.
Shoveling pies, telling lies.
I wonder who's drinking the wine
Of udders I used to call mine.
I wonder if she likes them better than me.
The goat has run off with the sow.

SIX O'CLOCK P.M. in the winter of 1968, saw Perry Mason closing his briefcase to the crackling tang of potatoes frying in the kitchen. Perry Mason held court in the Green Room with static and station breaks on the TV set Don had carted to the farm to help us idle away the cold. It hardly seemed peculiar then. We were so recently unplugged. The telephone John Kaplan needed for the school to call him had been shut off around Thanksgiving. John's teaching career followed suit by Christmas.

Still, the days of the news service (cf. *Famous Long Ago*) and the taste of what followed were fresh for many of us. So when the telltale tele-type began to clatter, we gathered on cushions and sofas near the heat vent in the floor, to greet the avuncular Walter Cronkite. Never Huntley or Brinkley. Some thought him a subliminal peacenik, but most maintained a tepid indifference. He sat among maps that lit up trouble spots, and news-reels of the holocaust. All sighed as he finished his litany, and repaired to the living room to digest it with our tuna and potatoes.

Some returned for the late show where Raymond featured coffee and popcorn during the commercials. One night there was a thriller called *The Man with the X-ray Eyes,* starring Ray Milland as a scientist who took a drug and saw the world as skeletons. That was the last movie I saw on TV. The set itself was returned to Don that spring, because a young child who stayed a while with us would watch it all day, his head a foot from the screen, like a tiny android.

The spring of 1970 found me homesick at a cottage on a loch inlet of the Atlantic in Scotland. Our host would don his Wellingtons each day, and standing majestically on a rock, he would cast his line over and over into the water until teatime. He never caught a fish. He never wished to. But often a neighbor who lived in a castle would bring us kippers or fresh mackerel, which we dined on, to their consternation, in the manner of the French.

Night time passed with a blink of the eye, and the moon above the water seemed the eyelid. At dawn a herd of milk cows would wake me with their faces at the window. I would don my red robe and chase them with a bucket, eager after butter and cream scones. But they sidled off at the sight of me. I swam across the loch in my nightdress, only to be jeered at by some insolent swans.

The moorlands were soft and moist underfoot, and speckled with pink fragrant flowers. Seabirds with their prehistoric cries swarmed above me. A short walk from our cottage loomed ambrosial jungles of wild rhododen-dron. A tiny red rowboat bore us out to adventures on the high seas and back to the sitting room in time for high tea by the coal fire, with curried haggis, barley bread, sweet cakes.

The postman brought Raymond his galley proofs and tales of home-folks on the farm. Pepper sent a picture which I carried with me like a holy card. It showed Bessie the cow, black and shiny as anthracite, with her bull calf Leroy, who was mottled brown and two days old.

The final weeks of June saw us walking and hitching where the wind tilted through Ireland. A kind farmer outside of Yeats's Sligo let us sleep in his barn when he heard that we knew enough not to smoke in the hay. His mother mentioned that the barn was built on the foundation of a Celtic castle, and that we could tell our friends that we bedded down with kings.

Next morning his children followed us a mile down the road hanging on our sleeves and tales. We swam to the Lake Isle of Innisfree and slaked our road-parched throats on water from the Holy Well.

Then the powers that were, brought me by jet to Montreal and home to the hill where the bugs were vampires, and home again to the barn where Bessie welcomed my weary head on her ample flank and my faltering hands to her full udders.

From the couch where I write I can hear the bull calf lowing his week-old cry.

How can I describe our Bess? She's a holstein-jersey cross, first lady of the farm, as long as I am tall, and unfathomably black but for a white spot on her left hip. Pepper says her body recalls the arched suspension of the Brooklyn Bridge. Looking from the bump and tuft of hair atop her head, her body flares at the shoulders and hips which are joined by knobby vertebrae. She's seven, spry, and light on her feet, wily, hungry, and foolish. It is as slanderous to call a cow bovine with all that it connotes, as it is to call a pig and a policeman by the same name. Bessie is no more docile than the hogs are self-righteous.

One summer Bessie wandered a mile up the Bloom Highway to see how the other cows lived. A neighbor found her making conversation with some of his ladies. She was marked as a hippie cow by the bell around her neck. Which reminds me of a riddle. How did Bessie get a swollen knee? That was what we wanted to know when the middle of her leg swelled up to the size of a cantaloupe. Finally Ralph Rhodes came to have a look at her. He squeezed her knee, which didn't seem to give her much pain, and he chuckled.

"It must be that bell," he said. Indeed, it was a big bell. "When she's walking uphill and she throws back her head to swat the flies, the bell knocks against her knee." Now there's wisdom and kindness living right over the hill from us, so nothing can ever go that wrong. You can learn more in an afternoon in the Rhodes's kitchen with Mother, Sister, Ralph, and Sherm, than you could plodding through this book from start to finish. In fact, if there were more people like the Rhodeses living close by, then there would be no need to compile books of near-forgotten ways.

In spite of our best efforts to fence Bessie that summer, she managed to get to where the grass was sweetest and the apples were ripening. At dawn, with stars just beginning to give way to daylight, I would be off down the road following hoof marks and turds to where she was grazing. Bessie would notice me and chew with mock scorn, until I waved my willow switch, and she skipped back to barn and stanchion. There were mornings when she was nowhere to be found. I would grit my teeth and perch myself at the window, lying in wait. Sometime around seven-thirty, when her bags started to ache, she would stroll back through the woods and look at me as if to say, What are you waiting for?

She ate the neighbor's corn but never our corn. It was less than a disaster. We grew enough for several households. This past summer we put up electric fencing for Bessie and Windy. By midsummer they had out-witted us. Weeds knocked out the current. We escalated with a stronger charge, though it was clearly a Pyrrhic victory. Someday we'll put up a split-rail fence which will hold them and all their progeny by virtue of its honest and sturdy construction.

One day we went down the hill to ask Maynard to come and see if Bessie was in heat. With one lone cow it's sometimes hard to tell. By the time the characteristic discharge appears, the time may have passed. Sometimes they moo when they're in heat, but sometimes they moo for reasons of their own.

"Will you come and have a look at our cow?"

"Maybe we'll bring Freddie to have a peek."

"Who's Freddie?"

"The bull."

There was a thick mist in the hollow. Maynard set to calling the bull. The echo seemed trapped in the air. "Come, boy," he cried. And "Boy, boy, come, boy, come, boy." Across the pasture cows parted as Freddie came trotting, followed close behind by blond boys with sticks.

Maynard passed a rope through the ring in Freddie's nose. He stomped and snorted, pulled, and Maynard yanked on his end until Freddie's nose bled. With much fuss and bother, the bull was loaded onto the cattle truck and all headed up the hill. I was in terror for Bess, and I knew in my bones that she wasn't in heat. The ends met in the dooryard and nothing happened. All shuffled and cleared their throats. I hid in my house. Maynard offered to leave Freddie in our keeping until Bess was more ready.

By the next evening Freddie, being homesick, had walked through our fence and was headed home. On the way he got lost in Linton, but eventually he was rounded up and brought home, where the next year (I am told) he "got ugly" and was sent to auction to become roast beef.

After one more try: Bessie meets Smitty; we had her bred by manhandling to a Scottish Highland bull. "You guys ought to have a long-haired cow."

Bessie has taught me many lessons: care of the cow brings good fortune. First off, don't milk barefooted. I was doing just that one evening while bales of hay were being tossed into the loft. One bale bounced above our heads. It shook the ceiling. Bessie balked and shifted, cracking two of my toes. Now I can tell when the weather is changing by a stiffness in the pinky and next toe.

She taught me that dawn and dusk are the most ineffably beautiful times of day, and that repetition is often prayer instead of drudgery. I know no greater happiness than waking to face the animals, except, perhaps lying by my window with my dreams and knowing that Marty, Pete, or Ellen will do it with pleasure.

In winter, I wake the night fire in my house, traipse up the hill to the kitchen. There I skim the evening cream and funnel the milk into jugs washed in iodine. This morning I heated some whey from the cottage cheese that's hanging up, for the calf to drink with his milk replacer (which smells like vanilla pudding). Next the pig pail is prepared with extra buttermilk, old apples, rancid cereal from the health food store (for the world's original health food pigs). With this burden I head to the barn, pausing perhaps to warm my hands by my stove.

The bottom of the barn greets me with the cacophony of beast and bird about their business. I edge past Windy with my spoils. First stop is the pigpen. There's big pink Dolores hurling her bulk (which is considerable) against the door. She's six months old, in heat, and, alas, not long for this world. Yesterday Pete patched up the hole that Wilbur (RIP June '71) made and Dolores reopened in the chicken wire, which enabled the hens to hoard and hide their eggs. Little Long John, who hails from our sister farm in Gonamute, is squealing by her side. I lean over the barricade which prevents them from running rampant (hog wild) in the chicken house (as Wilbur did for kicks), and set down the pail so they can drink. Then I upend the pail and spill the swill on the corncob floor in two piles. Dolores and Long John are living high off the hog, as the saying goes. Though Dolores will be in cold storage in a month, I feel no remorse. I know she will be tasty. Soon Long John will be teasing our next piglet and warming his bristles in the spring sun.

It's hard not to step on the hens as they swarm in for their grain. These twenty-four Rhode Island Reds are the best chickens we've had. Twenty-two eggs a day and they just began to lay this autumn. I don't know if God made these birds, or whether they were developed in test tubes. Surely we could not be more proud and grateful had we done anything to inspire them.

Many hippie farms have poor luck with chickens. We've had several batches of bargain basement birds given to us as part of a package deal with a baying dog and a library of dusty volumes in German. Iago at Wellden says that chickens need stern discipline. He built several sliding mobile homes for his so that they could peck insects from the garden. Nina at Gonamute claims that they need special attention and compassion. She has sixty-five birds under her wing, of varying age and gender, sorted and housed in four different quarters of the palatial barn on their farm. At Tree Frog, where most are vegetarians, an ax displayed at the door was said to stimulate egg production. Pete played the mouth harp to one group of hens he was trying to whip into shape, but then he went off to Persia for a time, and no one carried on his program. Stinging nettle grew high in the chicken yard. (This year I cut it down, let it putrify in a crock until it smelled like pig-shit, and watered my eggplants with it. They grew like beanstalks.)

Ronnie, a dear friend from over the hill, bought these girls for us. Pete, Ellen, and Bob spent the night before their debut whitewashing the chicken room and building roosts like motel boudoirs.

After a chorus of "Lay, Lady, Lay," I repair to the yard where the Chinese gander and his dragon bride bite at my knees. The geese, named Chang and Madame, foment rebellion and internecine warfare in the fowl world. Last summer, Taj, the rooster, was unceremoniously pecked to death, an event which followed on the heels of the hatching and mysterious demise of the tiny green gosling. The geese have no use for us. The handful of feed we dole out twice a day is hardly wages enough to buy their loyalty. They

are regal and indifferent, exiled, and existing in a Formosa of their own apart from the mainland of the barn. Four ducks, two brown and two white, form their meager entourage and live as their serfs. In warm weather they snarf around the nettle copse. We turn flat stones to let them graze on bugs. They lay enormous eggs.

Back in the barn, I carry water and feed to the larger beasts—Windy, Mama the goat, and Bess—and serve breakfast to the calf, which he swallows in a slurp. What shall we call him? Porgy, Mr. Boogie, MacDonald? Soon he'll have a curly mop, horns, and a mane. But now he's brownish black like mink, with eyes full of idiot wonder. He's a miracle.

The week before Christmas, Bessie, who was enormous and barrel-bellied, tiptoed around the barn to where the grain was kept. She was surprised by Joan, who came on a whim. Bessie had downed forty pounds of dairy ration. She was so fat we could hardly squeeze her through the door to her stall. The days which followed were an agony of force feedings, pumpings, injections, visits from the vet, who said, to be honest, that we might lose mother and unborn child, or that Bessie might not milk again.

Now, our vet is a wonderful person, Doctor Bob La Due, and so is his wife, Judy. Last year Pete made a cradle for their baby, and we've been friends ever since. He saved our Bessie (and words cannot tell how grateful we are), aided by medications and her unswerving will to keep on being normal. Yesterday I was telling Bess how much I love her son, and she said, "Lookit what I had inside me, boss. I was kinda hungry. Gotta feed four stomachs and that too." She's glad to have her maidenly figure back. Her step is dainty. She holds still as I milk her. Bessie peers over her stall at the nursery. Mr. Baby curls up in the hay. She croons a lullaby.

·THE CULTURE·

The great cheeses of the world can be made in the home kitchen.

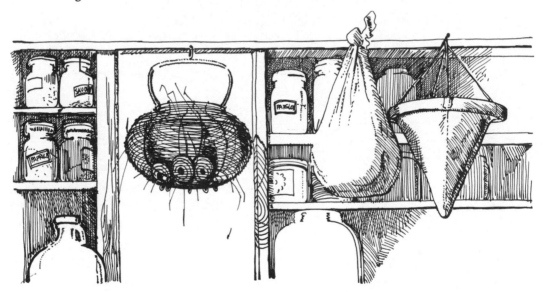

COTTAGE CHEESE:
The Short Method

Simmer on the stove raw skimmed milk, a gallon or more.

Disolve 1/2 tablet of Junket rennet in warm water.

Set in a warm place to curdle. It should take less than an hour.

When the milk has separated into curds and whey, pour into a cheese bag and let it hang overnight.

In the morning, if the whey is drained out, turn the curds into a bowl and crumble it with a knife or fork.

Add soy sauce, or salt, pepper, chives, thyme, or sweeten with honey, and serve with fruit.

The whey can be used as a nutritious drink or as the basis for a hearty bread. If no one cares for it, dogs, cats, or pigs will thrive on it.

The Long Method

Add a drop or spill of vinegar, lemon juice, buttermilk, etc., into a gallon or two of raw milk.

When milk is good and sour it will curdle. Hang it up and proceed as in short method.

SOUR CREAM:

Set out cream to sour in a warm place. You can add a souring agent if you wish to. The milk solids will separate out and rise. Scoop out the thick cream and serve. Use the whey for something else.

CREAM CHEESE:

Proceed as above. When sour cream is thick, hang it up to finish draining the liquid.

For a description of the hard cheeses, see Pete's treatise on cheese-making on the small farm.

From here the reader is on his own. He will notice that each batch of a dairy product has a different taste. Through trial and error, one learns to cultivate the taste he prefers. At the farm we have a counter with hooks and nails above it where we hang our various cultures to dry. There is no complicated equipment required. Anyone who is lucky enough to be on milking terms with a cow can make delicious concoctions in the home.

—VERANDAH

·CHEESE-MAKING ON THE· ·SMALL FARM·

THAT'S THE TITLE OF A MOVIE we're going to make someday on the farm. It'll start with some tinny music in the background, and then Arthur Godfrey's voice (we haven't asked him yet) intoning, "How to make cheeeese on the small farm," and Bessie the Cow will come on the screen, cropping the pale green shoots of mid-June clover, dew-dappled, as the sun comes up red down the road, and by the barn Ellen, in some summer frock, bangs the bucket and calls her name—Ah, it'll be a film like those twenty-minute ones they used to show you in school, when suddenly some gray morning the teacher would say, "We're going to have a film now," and you just didn't care what it was (*Rommel Invades Israel* or *Heredity and You*); all that mattered was that for a few moments those big manila shades came down and the room was almost dark, and you could laugh at the teacher fucking up the projector, or the drunk violinist on the sound track. You could even lie back and shut your eyes; no one was going to call on you; you weren't even in school. Such simple happiness when that mind-embalming routine was broken up.

That's what kind of film it would be, but full of truthful imperfections: Bessie taking one of her long pisses in the rotting hay, the hairs and dirt on the milk-straining cloth, the pots piled in the sink, the dogs licking whey off the press; then bringing up the moldy cheese from the cellar and blowing the dust at the camera, and the ravenous freaks crowding around the table laid with eclectic and preposterous elegance—the ooze of the cheese on the fresh brown bread, the smell you can almost see, the slosh of hard cider deep in the cheek. If only, ever, once, I had seen a film like that in school—

Legend has it (I wrote it myself) that I don't talk much, but in fact I do have plenty raps, some of them shorter than others. One of them is my cheese rap. Here it is.

We cannot overestimate the importance of cheese: since humans first began to deal with animals, men and women have set fresh milk aside to sour in dark places, till time and some little-understood divinity in the air or earth transforms it to a substance that's good to eat, and keeps a long, long time. The Himalayan yak-herder boring holes in chunks of dark gray, rock-hard cheese to string around his neck; the Macedonian truck farmer fishing a white goat cheese from a barrel of salt brine; the Andean workers dipping flat corn bread in curds: they all know that today no less than ten thousand years ago the care of the cow (mare, llama, reindeer, goat, buffalo, sheep) brings good fortune, and much more—something I've thought about in images that rattle around in my head, and I have yet to pursue to the extreme.

In land upon land all over the earth, except perhaps tropical jungles or other places where dairying is not practiced, cheese-making is one of the principal ways of preserving needed food, and cheese is one of the major available, natural, beloved, and cheap sources of nutrition. It's peasant food, or poor people's food. It's always amazed me that in the vast U.S. of A., where geographic, ethnic, and bovine diversity could make for such a rich variety of local cheeses, encouraged by government and all lovers of food, cheese has become for the most part pasteurized, processed, sealed in plastic by the slice, and/or priced so high that it's a luxury poor people can't afford, except *as* a luxury. We've asked all the dairy farmers around here (and all the farmers around here are *dairy* farmers) about cheese, and they all say, "Ah, yes, used to make some when I was a boy," and you can see, in their eyes, the memory of the wooden hoops and the press, the damp cellars where what dust there was helped in the ripening. Most dairy farmers no longer make cheese, and the small nonspecialized farmers who would are being forced to grow, specialize, or sell out. In some states cheese-making in the home is illegal; elsewhere, advice, materials, and cultures are rare or obscure; everywhere, one is encouraged to buy the antiseptic, standardized, expensive product stacked on the bright shelves of the Super-*Duper*: no pun intended.

Why? Don't people want to experience the entire range and variety of tastes? How many generations does it take before one's human desire is limited by the narrow field of what is offered for him to buy? There must be a problem here, and it must have to do with the decline of the old values, a movement that's continued too long.

Now I just happen to take this matter personally. Here's why: All my life I've had two unfortunate problems centered in my mouth: more specifically, in my lips and tongue. The first is that my lips just don't form words the way my brain would like them to; the process is painstaking and subject to fits. Well, for a while now I've understood that my mouth just goes on strike when my brain instructs it to produce words that my heart isn't into saying, and the situations of everyday conversation, and my involvement in often unwished-for worldly activity (like recitation in school, for example) make that happen, more or less, all the time. But it's getting better.

The other problem is this: for as long as I can remember, I have been a very slow eater. When I was six, I would sit at the old table in the half-darkened dining room after my father, mother, sister, had gone their ways, nursing a mealy cheekful of potatoes or lima beans. I just couldn't swallow it; I didn't have enough saliva; I guess I hated most foods, mostly vegetables, 'cause they gave me such trouble. I stayed skinny and small. My mother, who was concerned, advised me, "You'd better learn to eat those beans, and quick, because you have to eat everything on your plate when you go into the army, and they don't give you much time." So I had a vision in my head of myself at seven, in a baggy uniform, with all the other soldiers gone out of the mess hall, and me left crying over a tin plate heaped with chalky late peas, and the sergeant snorting over my shaved head.

Luckily for me, and for the military, my mother's prophecy of woe never came true. The army turned me down, although I somehow grew into a man, strong for my size and healthy, and in time I learned to love fresh vegetables, potatoes, and grain so much that I spent a recent year or two eating, more or less, no meat. But I remained a slow eater, although, again luckily for me, fate had landed me among a group of people who took deliberate chewing to be a sign of spiritual development, real or feigned. It all worked out pretty well.

But I had never ceased to wonder at my deficient spit. In summer camp when we'd line up and see who could hit a spot on the cabin wall, I was lucky if I doused my toes. When I was eighteen and had my life in my own hands I took leave, more or less, of our family doctor, who had always struck me as a conservative man. (Today, I'm sure he would tell me there is "no medical evidence" for the health I know I have from the foods we eat here.) Very seriously I described the dryness of my mouth to him. He suggested I should, quote, "suck a lemon."

Fortune called me to France, a Catholic country where, I'll admit, they do strange things to food, but, God be praised, I'll never forget what happened the first time I sat down with my friend on the bank of the Seine, and broke the long loaf of bread in two, and unwrapped the soft lump of cheese we'd just bought and held it up to my nose: my very hair stood on end, odoriferous flowers blossomed on the boulevards of my memory, great tears rolled from my eyes; but, most important, saliva flowed in the canyons of my gums as never it had before.

Now I'm not saying that the only good cheese is a soft and subtly pungent one; I'm not even saying that when a big healthy American peasant family sits down to spread a farm-cured cheese on bread hot out of the oven, it's got to stir up the old sensual nostalgia-for-mud in their brains, or it's not good cheese, and I wouldn't eat it. No, all I'm saying is that there, with that morsel of aged milk in my mouth, I had a religious, or insightful experience, which has gained definition over the years, as much as it has recurred.

Cheese-making on the farm, I saw, is a form of art, one of a special number of transcendentally earthbound handicrafts that once flourished in the world, and, in America at least, have died or are dying out. The government and its public relations men, the supermarket owners, the souvenir-makers, they'll all try to tell us that such local crafts are flourishing in an atmosphere of encouragement and good old American liberty, but who believes them? Certainly not the old craftsman, long since forced to work in a factory to earn money for taxes, rent, and food. And certainly not the poor consumer, disappointed again in his search for a product to eat, wear, admire, or whatever, that's made with half as much care as those things used to be made.

So I decided that the good French man or woman who had made that cheese was an artist. The memory of spring and summer grass was in that food; for me the cow's milk had been transfigured into a substance that had a mysterious physical presence, soft as a breast. It smelled like the place where "Love has pitched its mansion." (Reader, if you're laughing, I am, too.)

I decided I would learn how cheese is made. Perhaps someday I'd understand why I'd never found that sort in America. Although, to be truthful, I couldn't call up, to the mind's eye, a credible vision of a gray-suited executive driving home in his just-washed Mustang Cougar Sting-Ray to his air-filtered house, crossing the spick-and-span floor of the stainless steel kitchen, and taking out a cheese alive with microbes—soft, changing, unprocessed food—I just couldn't see it. But I hoped that somehow the kind of cheese I loved would be eaten, if somehow it could be made.

What follows is a fairly technical discussion on how to make cheese at home. (It assumes that you know the easier, more accidental ways of just letting cheese happen.) As far as we have discovered, the process works well. The results vary, and you'll see why. (Get to *know* and master the variables.) I have further observations on American life, in the same spirit as the above, but I guess I'll save it for another time.

THE PROCESS:

Here's what you need:

Fresh milk, all the better if you've milked it yourself from your favorite cow. Two gallons is a good amount, half from last night and half from this morning. Milk from high butterfat cows makes the best cheese, I guess. (Our own cow is a holstein-jersey cross. Holsteins give a huge amount of low-fat milk, and jerseys a smaller amount of high-fat milk.) Best to make cheese in spring and early summer, when the cows are grazing on fresh light-green grass, full of nutrients (i.e., not yet gone to seed). Pepper has reminded me to write that care should be taken in spring, lest the animals freed from their winter confinement gorge themselves too quickly on the rich grass. All of us who eat sprouts know how concentrated a food they are. Much of this food value will end up in preserved form in the cheese.

You'll need a huge pot—tinned copper or enamel is best, and if it's big enough to work five gallons of milk, no reason not to try.

You'll also need a dairy thermometer, the kind that floats upright, and rennet—either unflavored Junket Rennet tablets, or Hansen's Cheese Rennet tablets. Or you might like to learn how to gather it from the stomach of slaughtered calves. The function of rennet is to cause part of the milk to coagulate; the fat, casein, calcium, and some sugar, salt, and vitamin A are caught in the curd as quickly as can be, before the milk has soured. What is left over is whey.

First, clean the dust out of your pot with scalding water.

Next, pour in the milk. I've heard that if you want a softer cheese you should make it as soon as possible after milking. Perhaps, toward making a particular ideal cheese you may have in mind, you may want to skim the milk a little first. I've never tried it.

Very slowly heat the milk, with the thermometer floating in it. When it reaches 85° it begins to ripen. If half your amount is from last night, it'll ripen faster.

Let the milk sit for at least an hour, at no less than 86° and no more than 120°, a temperature too hot for proper curdling. To hasten the ripening process, you may, if you want, experiment with adding a little sour milk or buttermilk to put extra microbes in the stew. It's up to you how far you want to delve into the area of sour-milk cheeses, which are usually strong and delicious. (Indeed, you needn't use rennet at all.)

The next step is the adding of "cheese color." We always skip that step.

Add rennet, enough to curdle milk in half an hour or so. The usual amount is 1/4 tablet to two gallons of milk. Here's how to do it. Take the milk off the heat, but leave it where it'll stay about 90°—either in a large pail of warm water, or on a warm part of your stove. (Wood-burning stoves have such places, use the space over the pilot light on gas stoves.) Dissolve the rennet in a few tablespoons of cool water, set aside; crush and disperse it well. Start stirring the milk and then add the rennet. Keep stirring for a minute more. A wooden spoon is best.

Now let the milk just sit in that warm place for a good while. They say a firm curd should form in thirty to forty-five minutes, but most of the cheeses we've made have needed at least an hour at this stage. But this is dangerous: the stillness and warmth allow certain acids to increase, which in time may affect the flavor of your finished cheese. Yet if you hurry to cut the curd while it's still too soft (which we did a couple of times), then you will lose some butterfat solids in the whey.

To test the firmness of the curd, stick your finger in at an angle and lift straight up. If the curd splits smoothly, it's ready to cut.

The process of cutting the curd is to allow the whey (mostly water) to escape from the curd. No hurry—it doesn't all escape at once like blood from a wound. It's a process of cutting passage for it, and then heating the curd so the pressure forces the liquid out the passage, like sap out of sugar maple trees.

Cut the curd into "cubes," about one or one and a half inches on a side, with a knife long enough to reach the bottom of the pot. (Experiment at this point, too, with the size of the cubes you cut; reason and experience should show you that the larger the cubes, the more moisture is retained in the cheese; the more moisture retained, the softer (and probably less acidic) the final cheese.

We call the forms "cubes," though really they are shaped like squarish fingers; you've cut down through the curd, two ways across the top of the pot. Some people recommend further cutting, till the fingers are actually cut into cubes. However you end up doing it, this part of the process is delicate and fun. The curd is solid yet spongy; its surface is smooth.

Now the cut curd is to be heated. It is probably satisfactory just to put the thermometer back in and heat it slowly; you'll get a softer cheese if you don't heat it very high. But you may want to try the long method; you'll learn how the good harder cheeses are made, and learn some things about heat and pressure, too. (But if you want, you can skip the whole next section, in your recipe.)

Put the thermometer back in, near the side of the pot. Don't put the pot back on the heat. Tip it a little, to spoon out a small amount of whey. (Some will have already collected.) Be gentle, so as not to break the curds. Heat this whey separately in a small pot to about 135°. Then pour some of it back into the big pot and stir it around a bit. Several ways of stirring are recommended: gently with your hand or with a wooden spoon, or gently tipping and rocking the pot itself in a slow circle. You're trying to distribute the heated whey. Why? Because you'll find that the added heat stimulates the curd to release more whey, and the stirring also helps to keep the newly cut curd from matting back together, which is not desirable.

You'll repeat this process many times in the next half hour or more:

spooning out whey, heating it, putting some back, taking out more, stirring now and again, so that three important things happen: (1) the temperature of the curd keeps increasing two or three degrees at a time; (2) the curds are growing more and more firm and compressed; and (3) you've taken out a lot of whey, much more than you can use in the heating process.

(Most American cheeses are made this way, drained of all whey. "Americans don't like soft cheeses," the factory owners think as they dump the "useless" liquid in the nearby river and the fish downstream die. We could eat it. Fish can't swim in it.)

Whichever way you've heated the curd, you're here now. It's about 100°; you may have taken out some whey, but most of it's still sitting in the pot. The next stage is a variable one, in which you just let it all alone for a while. (An hour is recommended.) The curds sit in the warmed whey; they compress even more, and you stir them a bit to keep them from matting. Here's the variation: somehow leaving the curds to soak in the heated whey increases the acidity of the cheese, and in general acid cheeses are dry— a little bit helps the flavor develop while the cheese is aging, but you'd best not let too much be formed.

So, in a short or shorter while pour off all the whey. You can do this by straining the whole contents of the pot through a cheesecloth, or just by pouring out the juice. You'll probably wonder what to do with the whey. Drink it; it's good. It's also a good liquid for use in bread-making. A small amount of it is good for your organic garden, although I couldn't say exactly what minerals it contains (perhaps some calcium more than anything else, and many soils are calcium-deficient). Most important, dogs, cats, calves, and pigs love whey; they'll never turn it down.

Now you have a potful or a cheeseclothful of fingers or cubes of new cheese, plump and pliant to the touch, but solid and shiny, off-white in color, that don't stick together when pressed lightly in your hand. It's time to add salt, about a tablespoon for each gallon of milk, a little less if it's sea salt you're using. This is more than just for flavor; it helps in the curing, slowing down the ripening process so the finished cheese is more mellow. Too little salt, and the process may be hasty; too much, and the cheese may dry out and not cure at all. I have a hunch that the soft French cheese I love gets little salt, and is allowed to ripen quickly—too long an aging would permit the encroaching molds to devour the cheese.

At this time also, you might add an herb from your garden: sage, thyme, caraway, dill, or some other. Mix it and the salt quite well among the curds. Then hang up the cheese, wrapped in cheesecloth, to drip for a half hour or so. While it's dripping you can prepare for the next step, in which the cheese is pressed.

We pressed our first cheeses too hard. We used an old cider press, as a dairy book recommended, but didn't really need to; a small, hard cheese was not what we were after. Cheddar cheeses are pressed at a final pressure of five hundred to eight hundred pounds, but for a soft cheese the weight of a couple of bricks ought to do. (Kneeling on a cheese is what some Frenchmen do.) All that's needed is to squeeze out as much whey as you mean to, and to start the process of amalgamating the curds into one solid mass. (Understand, also, that it's difficult for novices to know how hard the finished cheese will be inside. We've found that things like the amount of salt, acid, captured air, the temperature, the mold, the ripening, all affect and alter the texture inside the cheese while it ages.)

· a cheese press ·

First dress the cheese, in a more or less cylindrical shape, as best you can, with clean white cloth. Wrap the sides first, tightly, so the cylinder stands about three inches high. Pin the cloth, or put a cheese-hoop or some other container around it, so that it won't all fall apart when pressure's applied. We pressed our first ones inside a Number 10 can with holes punched in the bottom (punched from the *inside* so as not to rip the cloth); you only need support like that if you're applying a lot of force.

With cheesecloth on the top and bottom, press the cheese, between boards that can't tip, with the weight of a brick or two above, or in a press of great force; it's up to you. Turn the cheese over once or twice in the next twelve hours or more. If you happen to suspect that the curds are not congealing, a little warm water might help. Cold curd won't unite.

When you've taken the cheese from the press, unwrap it completely and let it stand for half a day, till the rind has dried.

Some sort of sealing should follow. Paraffin is most commonly used, though I've found it difficult to get the cheese totally sealed this way. Some people rub a vegetable or mineral oil all over the surface, instead. I've eaten cheeses that were dipped in wood ashes or crushed grape seeds, or just left to float in a salt brine. It's good to experiment. The best cheese we ever made was sealed like this: it was June, and the wild grape leaves were growing big and yellow-green all over the farm. I picked about ten of them and boiled them for half a minute, then wrapped a spherical cheese, unpressed, in them, binding the bundle in a clean rag tied with twine—it stayed perfectly white all the while it ripened. I wonder whether burdock or maple leaves would work well, too.

(Before wrapping the cheese, you may want to inoculate it with a culture from some favorite moldy or smelly cheese. This could be accomplished almost any way. Spreading a little of the old on the new works well. The difficulty would be to maintain some control over the process. Someday when we have a curing cave we'll do it right—get the right spores in the air. We'll travel overseas and tour the famous caves in the Auvergne; we'll bring home their mold in our dirty socks. The customs inspectors will never know.)

Find a clean, cool cellar to age the cheese in. I leave it to you to live through the horror of exploring your own basement: the dank dirt and dripping pipes overhead, the old junk and the dust and cat-shit, the rotting vegetables of last year's root cellar, the broken canning jars and moldy shoes— Clean it all out, throw everything out; you'll feel like a new person when your cellar's been flushed, and then you won't mind going down there, and finding a place for the cheese. But build a rack that's mouse-proof, or hang the cheese, and keep an eye out for flies.

Let it cure for a month or two or three; more, if it's a hard cheese and you feel reasonably sure it's doing okay. If you notice a mold that you don't like, sponge it away with salt brine. You'd better eat that cheese soon. Fifty degrees is a good temperature for the curing room.

That's more or less how we go about making cheese. I guess I needn't go on about how good it feels to do it, and how you come to understand how important it is that farmers continue to make cheese in this country. I can almost guarantee the wonder you'll feel as these few, specific, repeating words take on physical form and color and what you have created will taste good.

—PETE

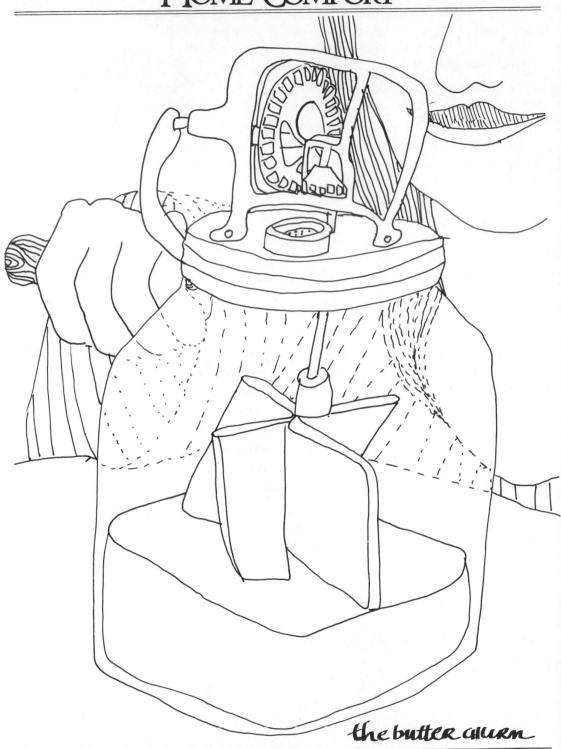

the butter churn

You may have trouble locating a butter churn, but making one is very easy.
OUR FIRST CHURN looked like this:

Fill not more than ½ of JUG WITH HEAVY CREAM. IT WILL WORK BEST IF cream is about 50° OR 60°.

BEAT THE STICK UP + DOWN UP + DOWN ETC.

DOWL

HOLE IN LID

GALLON JUG

a PIECE OF WOOD CUT INTO a CROSS

WHEN THE BUTTER HAS FORMED, IT WILL BE YELLOW (BRIGHT IN SUMMER, PALE IN WINTER) AND STUCK TO THE STICK OR FLOATING ON THE TOP OF THE BUTTERMILK.

POUR THROUGH CHEESECLOTH. WASH BUTTER WITH COLD WATER AND SQUEEZE OUT MILK.

SOMETIMES WE PRESS OUR BUTTER WITH THE STAMP BELOW.

·BREAD·

EVERY OTHER DAY OR THREE, someone walks into the kitchen, opens and shuts in succession the cabinet door, the warming ovens, and the refrigerator, and mutters, "No bread, huh?" Depending on the weather, the available ingredients, the state of the oven and wood supply, appetite and mood, someone is bound to make some bread. If they don't, someone else will.

If there are rye berries and/or rye flour, Peter will begin to assemble his Real Rye. First he puts on a "soup" of water, caraway seeds, cider vinegar, a little blackstrap molasses, and a big handful of salt. The soup may also include soy sauce, malt syrup, barley or kasha, potatoes, onions or garlic. He roasts some of the rye berries before grinding them, and looks about the kitchen for anything sour, salty, or fermenting. Beer, because it is the same composition as bread—being grain, yeast, and water—is one of his favorite ingredients. Once Hugh made beer from bread (according to some information in the 1935 *Britannica*), and Peter made bread with some of the yeasty, doughy dregs. Stinky whey or other milk products, mustard, dill, leftover beans, basil, corn meal, and buckwheat flour—all these I've seen him slip into the batter, but there are many more still secret. On the West Coast, he was known as Sourdough Pete. After the dough has risen slowly and repeatedly (after being punched down) a few times, then comes the shaping. Braids and long fat loaves are common, as are bread sticks (salted), pan loaves, and round ones. For Richard's birthday breakfast this year, Pete even made rye dough croissants, rolling the dough out with cream over and over again. They were fit for a king, or the son of one at least. Whatever its shape, Pete's rye bread is salty, tangy, rich, and Old World.

On another day, when form is more interesting than content, perhaps Peter will make pretzels, the favorite of his childhood and youth in Allentown, Pennsylvania. Pretzels are a simple dough, mostly white flour, water, salt, and yeast, shaped after one rising into thin praying pretzel figures. After a bath in a pan of boiling water with eggshells, where they must puff up and float to the surface on each side, the pretzels are placed on a cookie sheet sprinkled with kosher salt, and popped into a very hot oven, emerging shiny and brown. We have yet to duplicate the crisp thick pretzels that Pete brings back from the factory in Allentown—Miller's Pretzels, A Perfect Health Food. Still, the attempts toward the ideal are delicious.

Verandah's bread has the same Jewish roots and delight in salt as Peter's. Her basic ingredients are rye and barley, sometimes corn, ground coarse or fine depending on her strength and perseverance level for the day. I mention these factors only to point out some of the conditions under which bread is made at our house. The flour mill (one of those Corona mills made by slave labor in South America for sale here) is not merely hard to turn, it is on a counter that's too high, and behind the stove, which can get very hot. The two trash cans, the organic garbage pail and the pig pail, are also clustered beside and in back of the stove, where you must stand to grind. If you approach the job as a yoga or a muscle-building sweat treatment, or if you really want to make bread, it is no great trouble, the pace and the grindstone being infinitely adjustable. We repeat the mantra "fresh stone-ground flour is good for you."

Back to Verandah's bread: V. likes to mix up most of the ingredients—being the flours and meals, sour milk or cream or whey, pickle juice, leftover lentils, potatoes, soup stock, or whatever's at hand—all to sit overnight before adding the yeast in the morning. The finished loaves are triumphs: dark and solid, high-topped and shiny, being greased with oil or butter while hot. The taste is richer, more varied, and less caraway than in the other rye.

Bagels are Verandah's alternate specialty, made about as rarely as Pete's pretzels. Her bagel dough is lighter than the rye, having more white flour and an assortment of other flours and spices. If she gets an assembly line going, Verandah can turn out bagels all afternoon. She cuts or hand-twists the rings, drops them into the boiling salted and egg-shelled water, while a partner flips them, takes them out, and puts them in the oven, ex-changing trays of baked bagels for the boiled. We are always careful to have cream cheese and fresh-churned butter from Bessie when Verandah starts mentioning bagels.

Hugh Beame is usually moved to bake bread after a period of the heavy ryes. He uses only oatmeal, molasses, oil and salt, whole wheat and more than half unbleached white flour. His secret is the sponge: letting the oatmeal mixture rise with just enough flour to absorb all the water (about four cups) in the recipe, before adding the rest of the flour to make a stiff dough. This last step he does in a large pot on the floor, where he can stir and knead at the most efficient angle. One of the pleasantest highs a person can get is seeing Hugh kneading bread on the floor while his famous baked beans bubble in the oven, and bottles of his homemade honey-malt beer stand cooling in the old refrigerator in the cellar. Hugh's bread rises from the loaf pans in a classic bread shape. Sometimes it has raisins and once it had ground peanuts. During the summer, the big slices were a favorite vehicle for tomatoes, chard, and mayonnaise (next year, we will have let-tuce and tomatoes at the same time).

Hugh says he learned this bread from his mother, and he has always made it the same way. I remember the first summer he was the only person who could make a real loaf of bread that you'd want to eat. Verandah and I were beginning to learn, but she liked to experiment with the stash of health food flours left by Linda LeClair, and we discovered by trial about the properties and tastes of cottonseed, soy, and barley flours. It took me quite a number of flat wet breads to infer that nutritional yeast is not the same as baking yeast.

It was Hugh who taught me then the basics of mixing ingredients, dissolving yeast, and kneading. To this day I almost always start with a cereal, as he does. My favorite bread, on the sweet side, starts with cooked familia—oats, wheat germ, dried fruits, nuts, sesame seeds, to which I add salt, honey, oil. If the mixture is sweet enough to cover the taste, I'll add some brewer's yeast, too. Powdered milk or whey, scalded, is the liquid, and the flour is as much whole wheat as is needed to make the dough easy to handle, with white flour added as I knead. I like rolling out a cinnamon (or nutmeg) dough and making braids, rolls or sticks with the remaining dough. Plain loaves, though, are quickest and best for toast in the morning.

Moving up on the sweetness scale, there's Marty's corn bread and Pepper's banana bread.

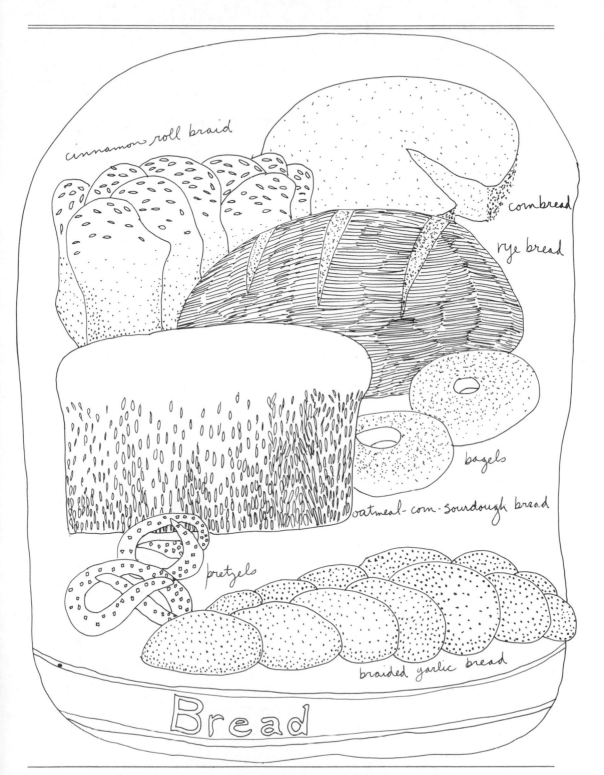

cinnamon roll braid

cornbread

rye bread

bagels

oatmeal- corn- sourdough bread

pretzels

braided garlic bread

Bread

Marty makes his corn bread fast, usually because he's hungry or it's just before dinner. His secret is a tiny bit of molasses, a slightly high proportion (more than 2 cups), of cornmeal, a sprinkling of cinnamon, and cream as well as milk or buttermilk. He claims that he forgets the amounts, not only from bread to bread, but while he's mixing, as well. This year we have both eggs aplenty and dried sweet corn from our summer crop that we grind into meal. Whether it comes out round, square or oblong, dry and crumbly, or rich and moist, Marty's corn bread is always a favorite.

Pepper makes banana bread whenever we get a load of old bananas, either from an eclectic shop in Brookstowne that we call the Used Food Store, or from a market in Leanfield, on the way to the bus stop, or Gonamute, known to all as the Cheap Banana Place. Pepper uses wheat germ, honey, milk, eggs, and whole wheat flour in a modified Adelle Davis recipe. It always rises and splits on the top and fills the kitchen with a spicy banana smell. Pepper also has a way with dates and nuts, and once she made a shortbread (butter, cream, eggs, flour, honey), served with peaches and whipped cream, that sent a visiting T'ai Ch'i student into ecstacies. The only trouble with her breads is they disappear even faster than Marty's corn bread.

I should also mention Hugh's buckwheat cakes, served at least once a day in maple sugaring season, and Bob Payne's chocolate pancakes (what can I say?). We also make New England tortillas with our ground corn and white flour, salt, and water, rolling or patting them out by hand. The uncooked tortillas, filled with day-old black beans and fried, make empanadas, which Pete introduced to the farm, which even Bob enjoys, though he professes to hate beans.

Some final observations: With everyone, the bread he or she makes proceeds from an idea in the soul. Experience has taught the properties of the ingredients we use, including watching and loading the stove and placing the goods so that they will bake slowly and evenly, or quickly, or fast at first, then slower, etc. A yearning or a whim leads the baker on to discover what mixtures produce salty-sour, spicy sweetness, moist darkness, golden wheat lightness. Shaping and kneading, the plastic arts, are also areas of innovation and expression. Our goal is Art You Can Eat.

—ELLEN

When I left the farm after my first visit, I took with me a sandwich of Bessie-milk cream cheese on dark homemade bread. I presented it to Raymond, who was still hiding out in Manhattan. He refused it.

"Eat the food of the earth and you'll be One with it," he said. "I am living on the moon."

I ate it and remain earthbound as ever. I'm an addict.

—ALICIA

·BANANA BREAD·

Sift together:
2 cups unbleached white flour
1 cup whole wheat flour
4 tsp. baking powder
2 tsp. salt
Add to it:
2½ cups mashed bananas (the rottener the better)
 ⅔ cup of honey
1 cup wheat germ
6 tbsp. oil
grated lemon rind
Mix gently, then pour into bread tins. The batter will be thick. Bake at 350° for 45 minutes or until a fork can be stuck in the center and come out clean.

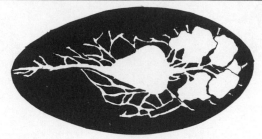

After the softball game at Gonamute, between our boys and Rau's Sunoco Sunday professionals, Janice brought out some loaves of deep golden-brown moist sweet-spicy warm bread. Said it was CARROT BREAD, and as it disappeared to a universal murmur of *oh wow*, Janice showed me the book she found the recipe in and how she had changed it (using some molasses instead of sugar, egg yolk instead of some of the eggs, whole wheat and graham flours for white). I wrote it all down, and carried the little piece of paper with me through a few days of brick loading and blueberry picking. On the first real Day At Home, I thinned the carrots to get enough for four cups of grated vegetable, but it was too hot that night to make a fire in the stove; I was too tired to begin the flour-grinding, egg-beating process. And, besides, the chickens, all fourteen of them, couldn't come up with more than four eggs.

Such a richness of taste is impossible to forget and love must find a way. So always retaining the image of The Original in my mind, I grated the tiny carrots to two cups worth, sending the rest off to market with Pepper and Joan and Luis. Then as the heat of the day started to gather and the breakfast log waned, I stuck the carrots in some water in a pot on the stove (Oh sweet magic roots, simmer) and went out to pick New Zealand spinach leaves. The sun got more shimmery and daylight expanded and in the middle of it all came friends and homegrown. In each lazy adventure, the carrot bread had some part. I made a mush and froze the spinach, mixed the flour and spoke to some people who came to give us a health manual for communes, kneaded the bread and watered the animals and on and on. This particular batch of bread (yes, it tastes pretty good) would not have been possible without the August light of a cloudless day, with a change of weather (hurricane) just beyond the western horizon.

The season for eating this bread might really be winter or late fall. Then it might be a pumpkin bread or acorn squash loaf, or carrots-from-the-root-cellar bread. In whatever season you bake it or eat it, it brings the sun into your kitchen.

·CARROT BREAD·

2   cups grated carrots
1   cup corn meal
      scant cup porridge (if it's left over)
1½ cup molasses and honey mixture (at most)
1   cup oil/margarine
      salt and cinnamon to taste
3   cups liquid, including carrot broth
1   cup buttermilk, if available
1½ oz. yeast (I used ¾ of a 2 oz. cake)
      in ½ cup warm water
5   cups whole wheat flour (a variety of whole grains
      is good. I used ½ cup rice flour, ½ cup soy flour,
      and the rest wheat)
3   cups white flour (be prepared to use more)

    This is not a quick bread. Let the carrots cook in water, then add rest of ingredients except yeast and flour. This is the point you make sure you have the taste you want. Let sit as long as possible on a warm stove ("so the flavors will marry" as Peter's mother says). When lukewarm, add yeast and flour, stirring until you have a cohesive soft dough. Let sit. Add more white flour (it may be another 3 or 4 cups, don't be alarmed) to knead. When kneaded, let rise and punch down at least once (the more it's punched down, the finer the texture). Shape into 4 or 5 big loaves and bake in a slow oven for another hour. Don't worry if the tops burn a little, it must be thoroughly baked. Like all bread, this tastes better the second and third days.

—ELLEN

·THE STRUDEL·

RICHARD HAS HIS "FAMOUS," Marty his pumpkin pie. I make strudel, pronounced "shtroodle." It doesn't manifest itself often: as with anything else, the time's gotta be right. You can't rush through making it; try it when you have lots of time. The second time we ate this strudel —the time we added a layer of mushrooms—Michael took a bite and cried out, a long wail of ecstasy; I'll never forget that sound.

Before I came here I used to travel a lot, getting round on little money in Latin America and southern Europe. When I reflect on what my senses took in there, I find that the sights and sounds have mostly mellowed or dispersed; there were few touches: a little love and sickness, not much more. But the smells and tastes remain inside me, close to the springs of my memory, and when I cook the dishes I love best, and when I'm cooking well, it's just because creation and quest are active in me. I'm trying to rematerialize a memory. My brain and my hands set to work. Smell and taste stand off, waiting to judge. It takes a while; there's no recipe. Now and then we take a taste.

At last something happens; the elements are all there on the tongue, and suddenly the old dormant circuit in the brain sputters to life again, and I see, for the first time clearly, the village in the Balkans, the old bald-headed bearded men drinking coffee under the plane trees, the premier's picture on the wall, the woman in the hot kitchen putting her hands beneath her apron, and rolling her belly in two strokes of a dance; the demijohn of resined wine. I'm not traveling; we rarely leave the hill, so these faces come to me here when I sit and eat.

There's a standard way of making strudel dough; I imagine it varies little from household to household:

3   cups unbleached white flour (I add wheat germ,
      and sometimes ground sesame to this.)
½   tsp. salt, or a little more
⅔   cup warm water
2   eggs, beaten with a drop of milk or cream
      Later, 1 cup of butter.

Mix the flour and salt, and then mix the egg in. Then add the water, and stir it all around with a knife. Knead on a floured board, keeping in mind that the finished product is one you'll have to stretch. So knead by pulling and stretching, not just by folding and pressing. Now leave the dough in a warm place, on a well-floured board, and covered. It has to rest for half an hour at least, so that it will stretch better. You can forget about it while you compose the filling.

The filling I'm writing about is spinach and cheese, though you may prefer to do sweet autumnal ones, full of apples or peaches, raisins, nuts, sunflower seeds, molasses, and honey: a dessert strudle.

The last time we made it, I had the three separate components of the filling a-growing and cooking at the same time; that can be confusing, if this is your first or second try. So remember that, if you want to, you may prepare the cheese, and even the spinach, well ahead of time.

(1) I dug around in the freezer for a couple of quarts of the spinach we froze last summer. It's not easy to know exactly what you're getting, if your freezer's as big and as stuffed as ours. I managed to find two frosty, vaguely green bags; I couldn't tell if they were spinach, New Zealand spinach, or Swiss chard. It didn't matter. I knew they weren't brussels sprouts or corn, though I wouldn't say out of hand that corn in some kind of strudel wouldn't go down real well.

I defrosted them a while, then cooked them in a little boiling water. To approximate the taste of Greek or Yugoslav spinach, I added a little salt, pepper, lemon, and perhaps a trace of basil, rosemary, a dash of vinegar and oil. Keep tasting; you know how you like it best, but keep in mind that a well-defined tang or sourness will marry well with the cheese, whose flavor is ripe and full. Now drain and put aside, but drink the juice, or save it.

(2) The traditional cheese is goat cheese, feta cheese. When I first started to cook this food, we couldn't find any goat cheese. (Things have improved since then: they have it at the new health food store, and we now have a mature goat, due to freshen this spring, if that billy served her well. It only took him a second, and, if you ask me, he missed.) So lacking that, I set out to reproduce the remembered flavor: salty, fresh, sour, soft but not creamy, a little gamier than grass-fed cheese. This part was pure fun, and I still think the spinach-cheese strudel is so good because I don't stop blending bought, found, discarded, and hoarded cultures of milk till it tastes as dank and musky as I can stand it, like a block of feta that's floated in brine for months. The first time, I used farmer's cheese as a base, and threw in

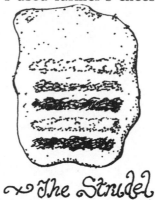

The Strudel

some mozzarella for stringiness, and a bit of homemade Romano for its moldy age. Then I stuck in a cup of sour cream culture Verandah had been saving for we didn't know how long. And there may have been more things: fresh cream, sharp cheddar, salt, an unresolved curd or a spoonful of yogurt that hadn't yogued: use what you have, and keep tasting; you'll hit upon something good.

(3) The third part of the filling was really not there, in the strudel I remembered. But it seemed as if the tart green spinach and the odorous white cheese needed a third coordinate to complete them: something sweeter and darker, but not foreign to the cuisine. Recently we found what that implied: fresh mushrooms, cut up very small, sautéed in butter, and then mixed in a bowl with a cup of lightly roasted pine nuts. It tastes just right.

Now the fillings are ready, and we return to the dough.

You should work in a draft-free room, if you can, because the dough needs a warm atmosphere in which to stretch easily without tearing. Lay a sheet on a big table. Cover it liberally with flour. If you don't, some juice may work through the thin dough and the whole thing will stick to the sheet. Place the dough in the center. It should feel soft, fluid, and warm. Dust with flour and, with a rolling pin, roll it out evenly till you have a rough rectangle about one foot by one and a half. Now brush with melted butter, ¼ cup of it or more. This ensures that the dough will not rip as you pull it thin.

You need assistance from here on: one or two more people to pull the dough across from you. You all put your hands under the dough, *palms down,* well in toward the center so as not to leave a very thick part there. The next part you will soon learn by feel: lifting, relaxing, rocking your knuckles, pulling, gradually stretch the dough toward you, each toward himself, away from the center, till the strange golden thing is nearly as thin as paper—but not so thin that it won't hold a good lot of filling, and watch out for holes; they don't have to happen. What a wonderful thing to make with a friend!

At last, a few minutes later, you have a surface maybe 24″ by 36″ or much more; the extra dough will serve to fold over and keep the stuff in at the ends. While your friend sprinkles another ¼ cup or so of butter over it, bring the fillings within reach, and lay them out in thin alternating rows perpendicular to the longest side. (See illustration.) Fold the extra dough over toward the center to envelop the filling. Now pick up one end of the sheet in both hands: the strudel will roll itself up. Be careful of leaks, and be careful when you transfer it to the baking pan.

Brush the top of the strudel with melted butter, and bake in a hot oven (about 400°); let the heat drop down to 350° or 325° while it bakes; forty-five minutes should be enough; perhaps a little longer.

Sometimes you may find you have filled it so full that while it bakes it flattens, and spreads alarmingly over the pan: but that's OK; the shape and composition of a strudel is nothing if not organic, and it tastes so surprisingly new and delicious that its appearance, fresh out of the oven, just adds to the pleasure of taking it inside you.

—PETE

EVERY YEAR ON VINTAGE DAY THE MARQUEE HIMSELF
PRESSES THE FIRST BUSHEL OF GRAPES WITH
HIS GOOD FOOT. THE YOUNG *CHATEAU*
WIZANSKY IS BORNE TO THE CELLARS
OF THE 'BARFING DOG'

·THE MARQUIS' GOOD FOOT·

EVERY AUTUMN NOW I collect both the wild and trained grapes around the farm to make the year's supply of our domestic wine, Chateau Wizansky. The first year's produce, which earned the wine's name and reputation, was the most fun and rewarding to make. It was then that we had the concord grape arbor by the stone wall in front of the house, where lush and purple grapes grew like a jungle across the trellis, and had climbed through the years up and around the apple and maple trees guarding our yard and giving us shade. But, alas, in the following spring, one of those furious wind and lightning storms which the hill is known for ripped the maple from the ground, which felled the apple tree, which felled the arbor and mutilated the grapes forever. Now I must search for the essence of Chateau Wizansky in less likely and less nearby places. Ah, but that first autumn my dreams of becoming an Italian peasant boy who crushed the grapes with his feet in the bacchanalian festival of wine-making all came true.

Gathering my cohorts, I climbed the trees like an acrobat and tossed the purple clusters to the baskets and friends below as we sang the Kajamunyan grape song, doting on the heady wine our labors would bring to fruition. After bringing the grapes into the house, the moment I had waited for since early adolescence was about to come. I threw all the grapes into a twenty-gallon crock (an earthenware crock, the best kind for making wine in because of the unlikelihood of its interfering with the taste). With nervous ecstasy, I pulled off my shoes and stockings, and was about to press my foot onto that purple magic when one of my brothers exclaimed: "What about the bad foot? Keep it away from the wine!"

But the bad foot, a psoriatic right ankle, had been uppermost in my mind, and to prove the point I brought the left foot, twitching with passionate eagerness, down upon the grapes. Ah, the thrill of that first step. Shivers careened up and down my spine as all of my fantasies were finalized in the oozing of the grapes below. Someone added their right foot to mine and the precious fluid bathed our feet in evanescence. Soon everyone was eager to join in, and as one would withdraw a purple foot to rest from the tiring motion, a new foot would be added to the fray. I've never forgotten the ecstasy of grapes bathing my foot and dyeing it the color of royal robes.

I soon discovered, however, that the process of wine-making is hardly play. For it takes much time and effort to remove all excesses from the precious liquid, to clear it, and rack it, strain it and fine it and bottle it, and wait at least a year until the labors reap rewards. As the years have passed, and the six or so bottles of Chateau Wizansky which were the result of all those grapes and labors have long ago disappeared into our spirited history, I've developed my wine-making into a tiring and organized art. In the midst of the process, I must confess, I'm always tempted to give up under the strain of knowing how little wine one gets from the bushels of fruit necessary, and how quickly a bottle of wine will disappear at a family dinner. But I persevere, and the benefits of falling into the dreamy stupor which comes about by drinking your own produce are enough to keep me making more and more wine. The recipes and methods for making wine are many, and you can find them in a number of places. I suggest Moritz Jagendorf's *Folk Wines, Cordials and Brandies* as the most beautifully written and informative book on wine and wine folklore I've ever come across.

—RICHARD

·How I Came to the Farm·

BY THE TIME I FINISHED STUDYING Chinese history at Radcliffe, all I wanted to do was make a children's book out of my thesis and marry an old boyfriend from Harvard. The excitement and curiosity of my junior year were too weak to withstand the distractions and cynicism in the university my senior year. It was 1968, the year of teach-ins, sit-ins, and so-ons against the Vietnam war. Especially for students in East Asian Studies, there was a fever pitch of intellectual righteousness, impotence, and paranoia. I couldn't take it.

I got a night-shift job in a hospital the spring before graduation. The job eased me out of the university, a longing for sunshine brought me out of the hospital, and a trip to see that old boyfriend in California sent me back to the East Coast in tears. I dropped out with a Harvard degree.

In a moment of anguish I wrote to Ray Mungo, whose letters had been a source of comfort and delight since we first met over draft resistance the summer before. Sure enough, Ray's letters, some of them LNS mailings and his mimeographed Occasional Drop, came from a world vastly more optimistic and grandiose than my own. There was news of long cross-country car trips, and an idyllic farm in Vermont, where he envisioned Merrie Frolicks, nymphs, and shepherds.

I happened to be visiting Ray in Washington, D.C. (there was a demonstration going on), and traveled with him to New York and back to Boston the week that he and Marty closed the deal on the farm. There was a lot of big talk—secession from the union by the newly liberated territory, and alliance with Free Quebec, printing currency of the Democratic Republic of Vermont, swimming in beaver ponds naked, and eating peaches from trees. I watched incredulously as Ray drew a map to the farm, with apple trees and cows as landmarks, on an Eddie Leonard's napkin.

Two months later I was in Wayne Hansen's black VW following those very directions out of Brookstowne. Not comfortable with the prospect of pure hedonism in Vermont, I had been reading Utopian tracts from Thomas More to B. F. Skinner, and had quite a muddled but idealistic picture of what this new commune should be. We would work together as equals on different tasks, all of which would surely be self-evident. Our lives would be cheerful, cooperative and, above all, orderly. It never occurred to me, despite these visions, that I was actually planning to move in, or that I would love and become part of the people who came with Ray.

Verandah, of whom I had heard great praise, was the first person I met. She looked at me as if I must be another in the long line of Ray Mungo groupies (which, in a way, I was) but she didn't hold it against me and we got along fine. Richard put me even more at my ease with his jokes and candor. Gradually I met Michael, John, Marty, Connie, Laurie, Elliot, and Dale, but I think I kept pretty close to a sink full of dishes most of the time.

I was so eager to find a helpful niche, to be doing a job, that I wasn't surprised or offended to find mainly women doing cooking and cleaning. It seemed quite avant-garde that we split wood for the stove by ourselves. Men took up their familiar occupations—driving cars, carpentry, playing music, and telling stories. Everyone considered themselves artists, writers, or intellectuals of one sort or another.

Now years later it's funny to look back on our daily lives those first fall and winter days, for our routines were not far from the lives we had so dramatically left behind. We bought all our food at the First National in Brookstowne: hot dogs, tuna fish, canned cream soups, cartons of Winstons and Camels. Ray slept till midafternoon, lived on coffee and cigarettes, and wrote things all night. Verandah finally broke up with Michael and ran away with Harry and wrote proud, exquisite poems about the states of love. Richard went to graduate school and Laurie built a small room with windows in a corner of the living room, which he imagined to be a soundproof isolation booth. Marty went to the Chicago Democratic Convention, wrote articles for pacifist magazines about acid consciousness, and set up housekeeping with Connie in a room where the twelve cats were welcome. Dale painted a huge warm brown canvas suggesting entwined arms and legs, which she argued was *NOT* sensual and represented only pure form. John taught science at the local elementary school, but left in the spring "for reasons of health" because he was losing his mind. Elliot made tuna fish sandwiches for the late shift, smoked a lot of dope, and finally joined a newspaper in Boston. Michael worked on cars, including a 1934 Packard and a 1949 tractor, and went back to Oregon for the first time. I got a job at the hospital, three to eleven shift.

These sketches tell only a small part of the story, for in spite of our old selves, we reached moments of ecstasy and wonder. More than a few times each month the peach orchard hill gave us a view onto a world we yearned to grow into. We climbed the hill through tall weeds and bright leaves in September to discover red juicy peaches for the plucking. Now we've learned to prune, replant, and fertilize the trees, and to can and freeze the fruit. Nevertheless, each summer's peaches are no less than miraculous, and we still have a rule that in climbing to the orchard, you can't look back until you reach the top, so that the view will hit you all at once.

The Aurora Borealis swept across the sky one night the first March. Richard had stepped outside after supper to take a piss, when he came back in, shaking his head. "Am I hallucinating or is there something out there?" Everyone got up to see and soon we had crunched up the hill on the snow to gape. Later we learned what the lights were, and now we watch for them on the days in the Farmer's Almanac. The sky, especially the morning and evening skies, and the new and full moons, is now an integral part of our emotional daily lives. As we grow more familiar, more intimate with our surroundings, we recognize our dependence on the elements: earth, air, fire, water, wood.

That winter was our first experience with wood heat. We stayed warm, grouped around the tin stove in the big room, the kitchen stove, or the furnace vent in the Green Room, largely thanks to the stock of dry wood Forrest Franklin had got into the cellar before he died. With Laurie or Marty at the chain saw, we too had helped provide heat from the woods nearest the house. It felt like the beginning of a new life, our need for heat leading us out of doors to watch the woods for dead trees and areas to be thinned, to scavenge power lines and other construction sites. No more turning up a knob on the wall and paying tribute to a big corporation for each day's warmth. As the winter night air would hit me in the split second between undressing and jumping into a sleeping bag in the attic, I'd laugh: Oh, we'll outlast you, winter, and meet you every time you come again!

I laughed, but I dreamed of California, curled on the floor. Many's the night I'd see sunshine on golden hills leading down to a bright blue Pacific. Sometimes I'd dream of that same young man who lived there and the tenderness we'd shared years before. Rubbing naked backs at the hospital and dancing with the gang gave me ideas, and I yearned to be held very close.

Things might have been different (that is, I might not have fallen in touch with the man in California nor left the farm in the spring) if I had not been working in the hospital. If I had been at home, sharing in more adventures, troubles, and earnest conversations, I might have been able to let go of my private fantasies and frustrations, might have found and returned closeness, warmth, and support.

But I was a Hospital Worker, and anyone who's ever been anywhere in a hospital knows what perversity that is. I performed the most menial and unsavory tasks because, personally, I got off on pain. Besides, at the end of the day I could fly away home healthy while the people in the beds (many of whom I came to admire) would be there saddled with suffering. I imagined that I had a power over them in my servile position: I knew more about them than they of me. As for the nurses and staff, I thought they could only know what I showed them of me, thought that my uniform made me invisible.

In point of fact, my uniform was so tattered and sometimes splashed with mud from riding to work in the back of Laurie's truck, that the Nursing Supervisor had to tell me there had been Complaints. That's when it dawned on me that in spite of my education I was the lowest on the pole. I looked, smelled, and lived like a dirty hippie. I decided to be a doctor.

In school I had studied history, looking for causes and effects, tracing major changes in consciousness as if they were inevitable. Finding the farm disturbingly day-to-day the first winter, I looked for some pattern in my past or in the times to show me A Future. I tried to have reasons instead of regrets, goals instead of inclinations, a role instead of a life. The doctor idea healed all my pains: I would rise to the top of the hospital hierarchy, go back to academia's familiar routines, make my parents happy, radicalize the profession, and save humanity as well. Besides, I could go to school in California.

I waited until spring to leave. I had to see the trees turn green again, and it was not all that easy to separate myself from the farm. By the end of April I had put together quite a theory for myself about how the place "worked," giving myself lots of points for self-sacrifice, responsibility and Hard Work, giving Ray many demerits for lies, exaggerations, and leading people on, Verandah for never combing her hair and still being compelling. I remembered that Ray and Verandah always used to say that "the drones carry on," and I thought that Connie and I, Marty, Mark, and Dale must be the drones who kept up the place while the more verbal and literary types thought, wrote, dreamed, and fed us myths. It's needless and impossible to go into more detail—the point is simply that I had to work up a lot of self-righteousness (it came easily, I admit) in order to leave. I reverted

to a world view in which people had positions, not feelings, in which money was essential to life and you had to know where your money was coming from, in which living in a group was basically distracting and frustrating, even if it was fun sometimes.

If my leavetaking had anything in common with other departures from here, perhaps it was in its uneasy silence. I couldn't discuss with anybody my feelings about the farm, and they became ossified. Although Richard, earnest and caring seeker of truth, talked to me at length about my unhappiness and my hospital career, I wasn't listening or explaining much. I needed to change, to be able to relax and see and be. I needed to let go of an old pain before I could accept and grow in this new setting of undefined relations, unfamiliar skills and demands. Everyone has one of those private hurts, I guess, that gets associated with the ego so tightly you think it's yourself and you'd die without it. Unready to change myself, I only considered changing things, that is, changing places.

What I mean to suggest is that everyone who leaves, goes for good reason, is right in feeling that his or her "condition" is not being helped by the farm or the relationships on it at the time. If they've been as confused and uncommunicative as Marty and I each were, they're also right in feeling that no one really understands or knows them. (Without seeing what Marty is writing about his "break" with the farm, I suspect we may be repeating each other.) Everybody gets to feeling cramped, restless, and even haunted sometimes. What distinguishes those who go from those who stay (and the returns are not all in, by any means) is if you think there is somewhere else you *can* go, you go. In the other case, you take a vacation.

I should say at the outset that I spent a total of eighteen months in San Francisco, and only eight on the farm before that. Draw your own conclusions, make your own observations about time. What follows are some stories of my life in San Francisco, which I include because they may be amusing, and it's possible they might have something to do with how I came back here. At least they're about how I lived, and others like me, in groups mostly, in a mild and beautiful city where everybody's secret dream was to move to The Country someday. It happened very gradually and unconsciously, the realization that I could live on the farm in Vermont, changed as we all were, unchanged as we all were. It wasn't a conviction, just a hope, a trust that the "myth" of our relatedness still held on both sides.

Once in California, I discovered that I had already dropped out too far to get back. A temporary job with the phone company rapidly became, I knew, the last straight job I would ever hold. More alarming, though I went through the motions of battling bureaucracy and applying to every college in the Bay Area, I knew I couldn't go to school again, that I wanted to live in the present instead of finding myself years hence with only the choice of where to practice. Besides, suffering had lost its old glamour for me. In a new social setting, I found that my attachments on the farm were intimate and binding still. I met a number of friendly people, associated ironically enough with the West Coast branch of LNS, but it wasn't until John and I started living alone together that I found I was quite unfit for the life we had planned. I panicked: this stranger doesn't know me, nor I him. We only remember what we thought of each other. The folks on the farm know me, will they remember?

Fortunately, before we lived there too long, John went East on a business trip, leaving me alone with the house, the dog, the eucalyptus trees, and a bottle of cheap California wine. I had quit my job and wasn't looking for another, though when I saw a young woman driving a mail truck, and our mailman came with hair past his shoulders, I signed up for the Post Office test. I began to just take what came, enjoying the sun, space, and silence. There was time to consider the farm and the year past in a relaxed and charitable light.

Into my dreamy solitude came a special friend, a man renamed Rex Leghorn as a baby when his mother married an American in Japan. We met as freshmen when we both considered majoring in Asian Languages and both decided not to (he chose sociology, I history). Whenever we saw each other after that we had serious and searching conversations (as undergraduates will do) about East and West, ideas of time and history, and how each society makes a person think of him or herself. In San Francisco, our conversations were a lot less academic (though Rex was only on vacation from a thesis in Ann Arbor). We talked about our lovers, families, doubts and hopes, my farm, his school, and the eternal quest. Once when we were pleasantly stoned he observed, "You know, happiness is everywhere, it really is, but fulfillment is only here," touching his heart.

As it happened, that same week came Steve Diamond from Gonamute, and as soon as I remembered who he was, we indulged in a feast of memory and hallucination about the farms. We gossiped about everybody and I had to admit I loved everyone.

I woke up one morning in bed with Steve from a dream in which I had been walking on a straight, paved road, striding forward, aware of the progress and effort my feet were making. Then I had turned, in the dream, to look on my right, into a grassy field full of flowers, and saw myself step, almost float, off the road into the fragrant, soft place. I seemed to lie down but I couldn't tell where anything ended or began, there were no edges or directions at all.

I would like to say that back in Vermont I am in that meadow, in an ancient Chinese scroll painting called "The Peach Blossom Spring," where all elements of the universe are in harmony, as the corresponding elements of our souls, where we respect and care for each other as brothers and sisters, where our work with the soil and animals and trees goes on as in the earliest dynasty. I won't say it. But in my mind, and maybe in practice, the farm is a place where there's work toward progress, if you look for it, where beauty surrounds you, and there's really no direction at all.

Sometime that fall, after a summer in the underground press, I was on my way back to the farm. I actually drove across the country, but I was going too fast to stop when I hit the East Coast and my old homes: Cambridge, family, and the farm. Before I came to rest I was back in San Francisco, where a notice awaited me that I had a job with the Post Office. Soon began the longest and most enjoyable procrastination of my return to the farm: eight months in the San Francisco Post Office.

Being a postal worker let me live in San Francisco as I had always wanted to live there, as one of the people instead of as an East Coast radical. I became a self-supporting freak on the street, who rode on buses, read the *Chronicle,* listened to FM radio, got high, went to the Farmers' Market, to the Park, to cheap old movies and Chinese restaurants, to the laundromat and the corner store. By the time I left the P.O. and was collecting unemployment, I was sharing a little house in the Mission district with three other women from our newspaper days, a boyfriend from the Post Office, and his three-year-old daughter. We had a backyard garden, homemade bread, and a number of hobbies. It wasn't a bad life at all.

My place of employment was an old condemned building called the Ferry Annex, being across the street from the old Ferry Building, the new World Trade Center, the docks, and the dockside bars. It was full of junk mail, magazines, and fourth-class parcel post to and from the Pacific, all low-priority items, so they put low security people there to work. On the fourth floor there were newly hired hippies and young blacks sorting and

throwing around bundles of junk mail for distribution all over the country. The supervisor had a glass eye. On the third floor again were young freaks of two or three races, handling the free samples being sent out by drug companies in the chemical-industrial suburbs south of the city to doctors in the area. The parcel post subculture also lived on the third floor, near the men's room, where it was said that lipstick was applied, wigs tried on, and behinds patted. The supervisor there took a lot of dexedrine.

The second floor was all magazines and newspapers going to every island in the Pacific, including Australia. That's where they had most of the Philippino ladies and the old-timers, who ranged from functional paranoids to totally disoriented schizophrenics. It was bedlam there, constant movement and chatter. There was one man who liked to repeat the sound of air-brakes on a bus, and another who received messages from his hearing aid. There were no windows, the Muzak was always too loud, and I don't even remember a foreman.

The first floor was the loading pier, where sacks came down from the other floors through a chute, greeted by shouts and curses from burly black men who drove the forklifts and had their own way there. People from other floors were called almost every day, men to load the trucks with the teamsters (a small, steady, hard-drinking group) and women to check off the bags as they went onto the trucks. When the weather was good, as it almost always was, and especially after the lunch break, a mood of raucous hilarity prevailed on the piers. In the basement, old men folded dusty sacks in neat piles on the floor.

The Ferry Annex was small enough so that everyone saw the same faces every day (and grew to count on it), decrepit enough so that no one took its postal operations very seriously, accepting it as meeting place, marketplace, tavern, street corner. There were some who could not exist without the place to come to every day and the paycheck to keep them independent. For others it was a friendly, stimulating interlude in an otherwise lonely city life. There were also brawls and bad feelings, compulsory overtime and lay-offs, a strike that split the hippies from the blacks and from the union, and one death. But when the place finally closed down in the late spring, we all knew it was the end of an era. We'd have to go back to Normal, work for the real Post Office, or find something else to do. (The Personnel Office made pretty sure that most hippies who'd been on strike would find something else to do by assigning us to a shift from 4:30 A.M. to one o'clock in the afternoon.) After the wrecking crew had come, I found other former inmates of the building rooting about in the rubble for souvenirs (a brick, a blackboard, a light fixture). Most, of course, had taken what movables there were before the end.

The best thing I carried away from Ferry was a friendship. On my first day at work I met Theresa, a round, beautiful woman my age. I could see from the way she moved and tossed her head, laughing, that she didn't take shit from anybody. She told me she was a Scorpio, had grown up and gone to university in Oklahoma, had been working in the Post Office with those same crazy people for over two years. We began to tell each other our life stories while magazines rolled off the conveyor belt; in passing she insisted that I shouldn't consider my scars from college deeper or more distinctive than most just because the school had a fancy name. She forced me to wonder whether valuing the name of a hurt, be it ethnic, racial, local, medical, familial, made it impossible to overcome the hurt itself. There's probably a name for that, too. In any case there began with our friendship a mutual process of exploring and lightening the memories that made us unhappy, delighting in the things that made us glad. We talked and talked, gossiped and joked, all around life's riddle that you can be whatever you want to be, and you must be what you are. We were part of Ferry Annex for six months; its personalities and customs, its schedules and routines were integral to our days. But even after it closed we kept in touch and eventually Theresa and her man Big Rich moved to a neighborhood near ours, right across Mission Street.

Late in my second summer in San Francisco, two jolts from the farm turned my wandering mind back toward Vermont. When I finally decided to leave, after a heartwarming visit from Pepper and Michael on their way to Oregon and back, it was difficult and sudden and we all cried a lot. In some ways my leavetaking was no better than it had been from Vermont, except that I felt more connected with the people on the farm, even after years, than with the people in my house. I got Ray's book in the mail, and though I knew it must be full of exuberant lies, the part about the road from The Apple Tree to the Corners grabbed onto my heart and would not let go. From a pleasant, floating life in San Francisco, I saw the farm as a way of life that endured. I felt I could not afford to stay away any longer, for the greatest changes, the drawing togethers would be taking place this very year. Lured again by magic and by myths of our oneness, I knew at last that the hopes our myths represent take work, participation day in and day out, or they are empty indeed. As Theresa and the Ferry Annex had taught me to enjoy the entire dance, its pathos and awkward steps, so I was eager to join again with the folks on the farm, amid woodsmoke and dog-shit, quarrels and confusion, work and celebration. I took the chance they'd take me back and tried not to count on anything.

There is usually someone leaving for the East from San Francisco, and in my case the ride was my good friend and housemate Kathy Bailey (who knew my brother when they both went to a college in New Hampshire, and who had visited the farm in the late spring). Our trip through Arizona, New Mexico, Texas, and the Louisiana coast to New Orleans was full of wonders, of fears confirmed and dispelled, of highway patrolmen, state parks and rest areas, hitchhikers and old friends, wild birds, and the spell of backroads. Something very attractive in New Orleans made us hurry north to Chicago lest we stay too long in the South. After a few days, we drove right back again, charting our confusion and our freedom on the continental map. Kathy stayed in New Orleans, with its mystery and watery sunsets. I took a Greyhound bus to New York and got to Vermont the night before Christmas Eve. Peter was standing outside in the dark when I arrived, asking who was there. Tomorrow night is Christmas Eve again, and Peter's baby is moving inside me. But all that is another long story. . . .

—ELLEN

THE GARLIC WREATH

·Summer·

·WOOD·

I AM CRADLING A SHORT LENGTH OF SEASONED GRAPE WOOD in my hand. I cut it out of its parent vine last spring. Twenty years ago, I guess, the brambles first overtook the vine, and it sent out canes along the shaded ground on the hill, till buds at the ends of the cane found sunlight and pushed out leaves. And so on every year: the brambles spreading uphill from the party tree, and the grapevine stretching with it, trying to keep its fingers in the sun. By the time Marty and I came to cut it back to the roots, to revitalize it and to make room for the next tier of asparagus, it had serpentined a good forty feet along the ground.

Its wood bent in my hand; it was early May, and the vine was full of juice—a little late for pruning, but this wasn't pruning, it was clearing land, and the light crimson, vaguely woolly buds clustered on the stub we left behind foretold a second, more mellow youth for the vine. We seasoned the earth around it with a bit of phosphate rock, and lay a protective mulch above, made of its own broken canes and tendrils—someday we'll have a few sweet fox grapes to eat when we walk up there to stand among the dry asparagus, golden and gone to seed.

The green wood bent in my hand, stripped of the brittle threads of its bark. I put it on a shelf in the Green Room, right beside the old Horse Clock that always reads six after four. It gathered dust for nearly a year, and the hot afternoon sun in summer and the stove's heat in winter dried out the room and drew out the sap through the twisted canals; it gathered at the two ends and then it, too, vaporized in time leaving only its smell, like its unborn child, wine, left in the bottom of a glass.

The wood no longer bends in the hand—I found it today and wiped off the dust, and rubbed its smooth length with a drop of safflower oil—but the play that's gone out of its fibers lingers in the undulating, sinuous grain of its dark brown surface. The next time I happen to be pruning old wild grapevines, I'll cut them in three foot lengths or so, and weave them while they're green, and make a crib for our baby—the posts of carved apple wood I've got drying in the shed, and the sides of woven grapevine, the bottom of hand-riven cherry boards, and a pine-needle mattress, and a small quilt of duck down or milkweed fluff: what a nice place to sleep that would be!

—PETE

·I HAD A DREAM·

LET ME TELL YOU ABOUT IT. It's simple.
In my dream, I was snug and cozy in front of a warm fire.

It was winter.

There were no strangers in the house and anybody who came into the room was a lover and a friend.

There was no talk of articles, books, or movies, at least not by us.

There was talk of building, cooking, baking, driving, animals, weather, and love.

In short I dreamed that everything was normal.

It was a vision worthy of higher poetry than mine, but requiring no word to be said.

—RAY

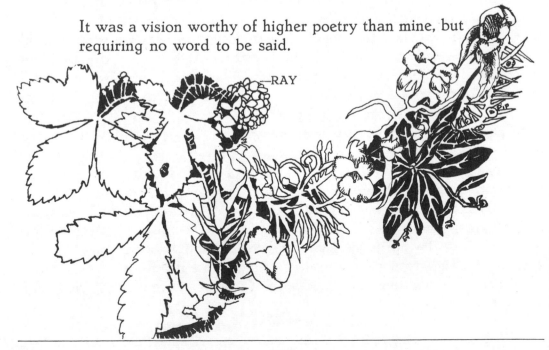

·Psychic Farming:
·The Organic Method·

I WANT TO TRY to say some things about process, about how work gets done here and about how we have managed to live together (no easy feat) and change and grow, so that when the farm is really together (or "honking" as Luis would say, no doubt thinking of Lester Young leaping above the superbly disciplined mayhem that is the roar of the old Basie band), the collective energies of the dozen or so prima donnas (as Richard describes us) who make up the whole is far greater, as the equation goes, than the sum of all its parts. Process is a subject we've never much talked about on the farm, preferring to let the natural flow of events determine the structure around which we want to live. We've rarely held formal meetings and I cannot remember any time meeting to assign chores, choose tasks, make lists, or in any way try to impede this natural flow. Even writing about process presumes some small risk. To describe our way of doing things on paper at once freezes the action—gives a definition that is essentially stagnant to a phenomenon that is always fluid. But I think we're strong enough to take that risk. Tomorrow everything will be different, I don't know who will do the chores, cook dinner, and wash the dishes. But everything will get done in its fashion.

I think of our structure (even a lack of structure implies structure) as being much like a free-form jazz band—the music of Ornette Coleman most easily comes to mind (it was he who first introduced me to the idea). All the soloists are improvising their own personal melodies, some in anticipation, others lagging behind or coming down hard at the center of a beat which, itself, is fluid and changing, continuously recharging the rhythm and the energy of the band's polyphonic wail. And that is how our music goes when we are all honking. Everyone has a song to sing and is bound to be heard. The music defines itself as it is played. The rhythm of our life is responsive to the different songs that we sing. It takes its cue from the melodies, lends shape to the contours that determine its harmony, giving it direction, and provides the energy to keep it flowing. Freedom gives us form. Our carefully nurtured chaos suggests order. And the blending of our music defines our structure which, at its best, neither represses nor stifles the most barbaric a-communal yawp.

I think it's fitting that those of us who talk about process (and nearly everyone has a say; it's become, without planning, a major theme in the book) do so through our own particular subjective filters. Contradictions abound through this book and in our lives, but nothing is false. Each of us contributes to the farm his or her own precious reality and we accept them as true, equal with our own. Learning to live and accept all the different realities was probably our first and most difficult lesson. Though we've learned this lesson, each of us a dozen and more times, forgetting it is still our major hangup and I can think of no worse feeling than believing that you are frozen out, that your reality, what you see and perceive and want out of life, has no place on the farm. Let's start now from the beginning.

It's been said before that we came to the farm without any concrete idea of why or what we were about. Some of the people wanted a place to be with their friends in a more decent locale than Boston or Washington. Some of us had political fantasies. Some of us had the idea of an anarchist haven, a liberated zone, with land open to all. Peter and Linda were fresh from the Columbia uprising and an open commune was their idea. Had the rest of us any notion of our idea we might easily have made it clear at the very beginning that open land wasn't what we wanted. But none of us even had an idea of what constituted a commune and, even, whether we wanted to give ourselves that name (it took us a long time to become comfortable with that word). What was a commune? We had read about them in the underground press and seen a story about them in *Time*. Verandah recognized an old chum in a picture from Morningstar Ranch in California. Is that what we were hoping to become?

At summer's end, the immediate family and its special friends purged the summer guests and claimed the farm. It was an awful time and an inauspicious start. Was our dream (again, unstated, but it was there) of creating a new society already compromised? Ray and I had title to the land. Did that give us right to choose who could stay? I was given the task of telling

Dale to leave. Or I volunteered, because I was the only one who knew her from New York. I felt like Ko Ko of the *Mikado*, "a dignified and potent officer," which is not what I wanted to be. Dale left, visited friends in the north of the state, returned, and was welcomed home. She became part of the family. Others didn't. Somehow we all sorted ourselves out.

Yet, we were still lacking a reason for being. Friendships and family worked in the city, because everyone had outside interests. But all we had were ourselves and the farm and nobody knew anything or had any intention of becoming farmers. We were miserable the first year. The first months of autumn bliss, of tripping together, falling in love, exploring the woods, swimming in the beaver pond, were soon blanketed by the stark, harsh reality of winter, a winter of discontent that lasted, for some of us, through the following summer and fall. The forest was stripped bare of its foliage and we of our illusions. The wind blew through the cracks in the house and we shivered in our nakedness.

If anything sustained us during this long drawn out winter, of days sitting idly around a wood stove, set high on a platform so that most of the heat escaped through the chimney, it was Ray's ability to create meaning out of nothing, excitement about what I remember as mostly long, interminable periods of boredom and frustration. Ray gave us our first reality, a mythic one woven from mixed strands of fantasy, hyperbole, a vision of the apocalypse, a sense of the absurd, and a generous portion of bullshit. Ray could really rap; everything we did, in his retelling (in a sense we did everything twice—did it and then heard about it), was a magnificent achievement of cosmic significance. A walk to the mailbox was a journey through time. A day in town was an encounter in Dante's hell. That the engine of one of our ancient automotive junks (a 1940's Dodge truck, a 1939 Packard, a vintage Rambler, circa mid-fifties, a '61 VW and later a '59, etc.) that cluttered up the front yard actually turned over and ran was a triumph for Michael's automotive sensibility and a tribute to the genius that was built into all old cars. Did Richard make a spaghetti sauce which everyone liked, then it became Richard's Finest—none better in the world.

We were, I suppose, a sad and pathetic lot. Some of us had helped bring down a president; now we were reduced to glorifying the most trivial things, seeing triumph in the kinds of mundane affairs ordinary people take for granted.

Ray's imagination gave us a common myth, but it didn't get the wood in or the house prepared for winter; that and other necessary chores got done in fits and spurts by a small nucleus of people, one of whom was me. During this period, physical work had a low priority in the overall sense of what had to be done; or the then reality of the farm, as defined by Ray, didn't leave enough space for it. This was terribly frustrating to those like myself who were accustomed to defining ourselves on the basis of our work. For a long time I remember waking early in the morning bursting with energy, ideas, and plans for things I wanted to do during the day only to have the day end in rage and anger because there was no one with whom to share my enthusiasm and because all the things I wanted to do were new to me and there was no one to either teach me or share my mistakes.

My reality, as it usually is, was based on the immediate world around me, what I could touch, see, hear, identify, define, understand. To Ray, the woods were magical. To me they were trees—maple, birch, ash, oak, pine, hemlock, cherry, beech; I wanted to learn them all, to know their uses, and to use them well. But they were new to me. I had to learn about them from books and walk among them, cut them, split them, run my hands over their surface, examine their grain, so that, in time, I could say, by the feel of an ax, that this log is a birch, this a maple, and the log with the grain entwined that does not fall away easily when split is an elm. That was my reality, then, and a mighty shaky one it was. Ray could give his reality to the farm; it was all fantasy and existed in his imagination. I had nothing to offer but my ignorance. If the farm could have only one reality and that reality was the web of Ray's words, then I was left out. I suppose others felt that way, but none of us was secure in our own worlds enough to compete or, as it turned out, add to the blend.

It wasn't a matter of competing, of course, there was room for all. I think Ray was the first to understand that there had to be room for everybody's reality on the farm or there would be no farm at all. If Ray was our "leader," it was only because we defined him as such. He refused to lead. He carefully defined what he would do on the farm and left a lot of space for us. As we learned and became confident in the things we wanted to do, we filled that space. There was certainly room for all. But it took a long time. Some of us were afraid to assert ourselves, others were fragile and their realities would collapse at the slightest squeeze. Ray became then a magician, a juggler of our different personalities, always there at the right moment to give someone a lift when he felt that he or she was about to fall.

Once I had political visitors to the house and one of the ladies, because politics at the time threatened her reality, threatened her idea of what the farm meant as home, freaked out. She did everything possible to drive them away, but Ray stepped into the breach (I was stunned into helplessness) and, despite the lady's admonition that he was a traitor to her, played the perfect host and eased their stay. Later, Ray told me that he was not really concerned about them. It was me he was trying to boost, trying to assure me that there was room for my political world on the farm, that I need not ever fear being shut out. This was one of the lessons Ray taught us before he left. He may have had the strongest reality at the beginning, but he learned to leave room for us and, like a magician, create whatever space was needed to allow us all to be.

But now I am ahead of the story. The lesson about the many realities came later, and then only after much pain. The first year, as I said, was miserable. Raymond rapped and we held on. I sometimes wonder why we did hold on and why, as so many other communes have done, we did not give it up as hopeless and go our separate ways. Maybe it was pride that kept us going. We had been quite public about leaving politics and moving to the country; there was a lot of heavy ego-satisfaction at stake. Possibly, it was our ignorance that held us together. For once our initial preconceptions were shattered, we became like newborn babes reaching out to the world for the first time. Everything we did was a unique experience; the world around us may have been beyond our understanding, but it was there, waiting for us to touch it and learn. Remember, also, that this was 1968. We, along with our sister-farm in Gonamute, were the only two communes in the area. Sunrise Hill, nearby, had already failed and we weren't yet aware of Byrn Athyn (now Rockbottom Farm) to the north. In addition, the ecology movement which would give our back-to-the-land instinct a political underpinning had yet to begin and no one knew, least of all us, anything about organic gardening, natural foods, etc., that would give our experiment standing in the community at large. In a way, our isolation worked for us. We had nothing with which to compare ourselves, no expectations, no obvious goals, and, most important of all, no sense of our own ignorance. The only direction the farm could go from this nadir would be up.

Though no one had the forthrightness (or the stupidity) to state it, I think we all quietly understood that we had gotten into this thing way over our heads and that our community was fragile, very fragile indeed. Potential disaster always pulls people together and so this, our common vulnerability, helped create communal bonds. It was as if we all realized individually that a single breakdown in any of us or, worse, a single violation of the many tacit understandings that defined, though minimally, what we each could and could not do, would cause the community as a whole to collapse. So we moved gently about one another, treading softly around bruised and tattered egos, careful not to say anything or do anything so harsh or final as to burst the bubble that Ray's genius for words had so finely made.

For a long time I felt that we were being less than honest with one another. I had come to the farm with expectations colored by movement experience. I expected everyone to confront each other directly, and the farm to become an ongoing encounter session until all our differences were straightened out. I had a very arbitrary and elitist attitude. Those who couldn't make it, who couldn't deal with what I considered forthright honesty, would just choose to leave. I didn't know much about process then and I didn't understand the importance, in Ray's phrase, of having tolerance beyond reason, or about letting things flow naturally.

We learned this the hard way: that the rhetoric of communal living has no place in our reality or in any reality. Like all rhetoric it separates words from their meanings, deludes us into perceiving situations that lack substance. You can't force community in a night, a day, or even a year. Love is not all you need; to claim to love everyone fully and equally is an insult to their individuality and is not to be believed. It took me years to get to love everyone who lives on the farm and I suppose if I had to I would learn to love anyone who came to live here; but not right off and not on principle; love, like anything worthwhile, takes trouble and time. And honesty, too, is not a value to be trifled with and assume comes automatically on a commune. It has many levels and takes different shapes. Love, honesty, patience, tolerance, and the ability to take an incredible amount of shit and let it all pass are among the qualities required to forge a community. It ain't easy.

I've seen communes, especially just beginning, O.D. on honesty and destroy themselves in the process. I've watched while friends have sat around a kitchen table hours at a time making kamikaze attacks on each other's egos and their own, leaving emotions raw and psyches shattered under the delusion that in being honest and open with one another they were creating stronger communal ties. In the long run, I've felt, such deliberate encounter sessions become dangerous verbal games with participants striv-

ing to outdo each other in personal confession or in being out front without regard for the consequences. Who needs such *tsuris?* Living together is tough enough without inviting trouble. Confrontation might work on a weekend encounter marathon or a group therapy session among strangers who have a home to flee to when the session is over. There's no such escape valve on a commune where everyone lives all day and every day under the same roof.

We usually had the instinctive good sense to avoid such naked honesty.

We never got together in a group to expose our emotions. Nor did we ever delude ourselves into thinking that just because we lived as a group on a commune we were, in fact, a communal group. That's process again. Everything in its own time. I wish I could delineate a specific chronology of events to mark how we managed to pull ourselves together and become a "working commune." I can't except to say that it crept up on us in fits and spurts, most of the time when we were not looking. I remember a few isolated events that marked its coming. Sitting at dinner at the very beginning (dinner was our first ritual, we always ate the evening meal together and it was always a culinary production) and going around the table, each of us, telling our parents' first names. A trivial matter, I suppose, but a linking of our individual pasts to our collective presents. Also, family acid trips that brought us closer together. This was a form of "psychic roulette." We'd risk our individual egos, throwing them all into a psychedelic mix, and hope at the end we'd come out a better blend. We usually did. Or the few times we worked together, long human chains carrying wood out of the forest, filling a spring-box ditch (and imagining we were patching the Ho Chi Minh trail), painting the house, and busy autumn days putting up the harvest.

Slowly, very slowly, we came to learn each other's weaknesses and strengths, where our areas of sensitivity lie, who is particularly vulnerable and to what, who responds to humor and who criticism. It was an uneven process. I learned about different people at different times; some I know better than others; others I trust to know and understand me. As we came to be comfortable together, we came to trust each other. Our guards fell. We learned that we could trust the others to treat us with care. In this way we accumulated a solid layer of love so that no matter what came between us, the love was there to cushion the hurt. Our friendships became strong enough to withstand any personal strife.

This is when we started to shed our egos and assume the burdens and the pleasures of being, in part, everyone else on the farm, so that within each of us there became space in our heads to hold the essential understanding of what it is to be everyone else. Late in the second winter, Ray came up with the phrase "No more me, no more you" to describe this particular state of mind. At first I thought it was just another of Ray's glib phrases (he was and probably is full of glib phrases and usually they end up making sense) until I realized that I was carrying a whole farmload of people around with me wherever I went and that I was no longer sure where I stopped and they began. This terrified me (and still does when I'm foolish enough to try to peer into the future wondering how far this path leads and will I eventually, yee gads, disappear?). Sometimes it becomes a burden; just the weight of being a dozen or so people when it is difficult enough just being myself. Most of the time, however, it's a real goof. What a relief not always having exclusively to be me, but to be free to perceive and react the way the others do, especially since everyone on the farm is so crazy and unique. Always, I am astonished that everyone else on the farm seems to be staggering under the same load. John Lennon described it best: "I am he as you are he as you are me and we are all together."

This summer I first started to realize how well the farm was working. It was weird because even on the worst of days, when everything seemed to be going wrong and everyone seemed to be conspiring to frustrate me, even on the kind of days that used to send me away from the farm, I was undeniably happy, as if the basic strength of the farm was sufficiently strong to bear me up under the greatest of difficulties. We seemed, finally, to have attained a strong group consciousness, a consciousness that gave each of us individual strength and the assurance that, no matter what minor obstacle might get in our way, the good feelings of the farm would go on. Thus, where we used to keep silent rather than trounce on somebody's feelings, we now fought and criticized each other at will (and also with a certain amount of flair—some of us really did it up in the grand style).

It amazed me, looking back, how strong and unflappable all these once fragile egos had become and how, also, the nature of our egos had changed. I could no longer think of myself in the first person singular; though I maintained my individuality and the privilege (which we all insist upon) to be out of step when I felt like it and bopping away to the beat of my own private drummer. Nor could I think of myself within the confines of the communal "we," because the privilege of being one alone was something I needed and, more importantly, saw no reason to give up. So I am stuck with an identity that lacks a pronoun. I see it floating in space, an "I" in flight, in continuous motion defined or circumscribed by a framework of the communal "we."

—MARTY

·135·

·BLOOD IS THICKER THAN· ·WATER·

BEING A NICE JEWISH BOY, from a good Jewish home kept plentiful and clean by an all-suffering, all-giving Jewish mother, family was the Friday evening meal of chicken soup and roasted chicken, ginger ale (for the gas), and heated and alienating arguments around the dinner table which inevitably provoked heartburn and the departure of one or more members of the "family" to one of the shared bedrooms, to the accompaniment of slammed doors and peeling enamel. Or extending the family further, but nonetheless tightly, there were the summers at Uncle Sam's and Aunt Alice's rented cottage by the lake, where both sides of the family would congregate to ski or swim or gossip, and eat hamburgers and hot dogs cooked on the barbecue grill as the sun went down. But the family was most apparent and complete at those weddings and Bar Mitzvahs which always drew out even the most distant cousin to sit around the tables, where the seating arrangements were impeccably planned, for God forbid Uncle Hyman should sit next to Moe—they've hated each other since childhood— the whole smiling shebang recorded on fading Kodacolor slides for the unwritten family chronicles.

To be in the family was to be aware at a very early age of what my mother has never tired of telling me: "Blood is thicker than water." No exceptions. Your friends, your lovers, even the more distant family, could never be entirely trusted to sustain you or give you the unremitting love you'd need to remain alive and healthy. For after all, what was there to bind you but the transitory affinities or attractions that water can create for water, whereas blood was of one source and unalterable current which would always lead you safely home.

And we were special. The neighbors' habits were often incomprehensible, and at times positively "cheap." The unwed mothers, and troubles with the law, or "problem children," or runaways—the scandals—were always next door or down the street. We would remain invulnerable if we stayed close to one another and learned to make the unspeakably important distinctions between ourselves and the neighbors and friends, and even lovers. If we called home when we would be late or had a problem, if we brought the girl home for a nice home-cooked meal, if we remained at home even though there was a rumble inside of us which signaled the time to move on, the family would keep us eternally happy and bear us through. There would be little the outside world could offer. Blood is thicker than water.

This is the point where, before writing this, I thought to dramatically reveal the changes that have occurred for me and the farm in the meaning of family. But, in truth, even though the faces around the dinner table have changed, and the alienation of the evening meal has dissipated, much remains of that solidarity and identification, and even speciality, that was such a part of growing up. It is that spirit of proximity and kinship, learned and suffered through back there in the genetic neighborhood, which transfuses the belief and reality that we, here on this Total Loss adventure, are bound heart for heart by ties of kin, so that we indeed refer to ourselves as a family, and to this place as home. Indeed the family, very much like those of our blood, is broken down into the inner core, and the nearby and the distant. And instead of Uncle Paul or Sidney in California or Spain, it's Ray or Schweid who send letters home to assure us of their safety and health and familial love. And though the place cards have disappeared, every now and then a marriage or a birth or some other excuse for celebration and reaffirmation of kinship draws the family together from near and faraway to dance and toast our bonds. And all around us the visitors or friends or strangers assure us that they've come from or are about to return to the family, without a surname, back home. And there is a growing network of communication and hearsay which brings either letters or scouts to the farm bearing news and introductions of the desires of the scattered tribes to keep in touch, and meet.

I would venture to presume that this is a phenomenon of both our day and the very ancient past. For it seems to me that what we are living through now is simply the attempt to reach back into a time of our lives when the value and need of banding together in small and lively groups was painfully apparent. That's how and where we began. But we lost both the need and understanding of that process in the diaspora of industrialized civilization, and the only remnant was, and still is, the abiding life of the hearth, even when that became the electric heat of a Manhattan tenement or townhouse. The isolation of the factory and the streets of cosmopolis, vitiating the functional necessities and rewards of group labor and hilarity, unable to completely destroy the primordial instinct or accident of family bearing and rearing has, however, engendered the desperate need to quickly break the family bond and seek further isolation, so much so that the family of blood and marriage today seems to be crumbling all around us. One escapes the isolation of family, with its clinging heritage of solidarity and hanging-on, to seek further isolation in the streets or in the repetition of the syndrome: marry, work, produce offspring, await their often painful departure, and make ready to survive or die alone.

To reach into a past which thrived before this is to ally ourselves with the "barbaric," earth-wandering tribes of planters and hunters who, in the image of the fire they had discovered, learned that the warmth of close living, blood relations disappearing into the fostering and blending of the tribe, could bring about the efficient and comradely quest for food and shelter. In such a place, isolation rescinds into communality, family becomes the spirit and energy of the group, and the feelings which must endure are the buoyant ones necessary for tribal accomplishment, which lead in turn to celebration.

The movement of the centuries away from that has led us here. And although we believed, all of us, that we had matured in the modern way of leaving both the isolation and suffocation of family behind us, we find ourselves in the midst of a family life as ancient and pragmatic, albeit less obligatory, as the sons and daughters of Eve and Adam. For us, who are now a tribe or family, the same bonds of love and labor and responsibility exist, transformed in the alchemy of friendship without bitterness or regret, because it is neither a place we were born into or had thrust upon us, but have deliberated upon and found.

There is a certain sadness as well as promise to all of this. For I recall several Thanksgivings and Passovers ago telling the family whose last name is my own not to set my place at the dinner table because I would be here celebrating with my family. It was painful for all of us. For the distinctions between rejection and extension were difficult to understand, although it is true that all of us here, since finding one another, have come to respect and understand the families we've left to a greater and richer degree. And it now appears, after four years and the short and amusing visits of all our parents, that they too begin to realize, perhaps hesitantly, that the farm is a family, even though my father, when I tell him I'm on my way to the farm, always asks *Why?* . . . and the "blood is thicker than water" rushes through my ears. The promise, of course, is apparent. For the roots which bind us all to whatever bush or tree in this human dream are now beginning to be rediscovered, and the water which floats every loving one of us is heading toward its mark.

—RICHARD

·HUGH BEAME'S SEASONS·

I AWOKE ONE MORNING in the early dawn. Red Antares still held court in the paling sky and the moon, crouched above her, sang a song well-known to many of my sky-minded friends.

A run down the old farm road and a dip in the beavers' pond washed the last thread of dreams from my eyes. Then a slow, contemplative walk home and a leisurely breakfast of yogurt and honey gave me ascent to the day. Ah! The spring's a grand time.

Outside, propped up on younger second cousins, was a grand log straight from the forest. With the axed ends neatly cut off with the crosscut, it reposed eight feet long and an easy foot and a half through at the butt, which is that end nearest the ground when the tree is standing. This log was soon to become a beam of heavy timber. This beam, when properly finished, would stand in the hall, workroom, bunkhouse, or three-in-one room; its foot to the side of the hearth, its head supporting the great hickory beam that runs east to west where the windows look out on the garden and the hills beyond.

My mind played with the beam, determining how best to use her girth to my advantage. Then I drew a line on each end of the log where I deemed it proper. These lines, preliminary guide lines, were on a level perpendicular to the pull exerted by earth's gravitational field.

The guide lines are connected from one end of the log to the other by throwing chalk lines. Somone, or a nail, holds the end of the chalked line to a point where a preliminary line leaves the end of the log for infinity. The other end is held to the corresponding point on the other end of the log. Then the string is plucked so that the chalked line will leave a mark along the length of the log. For accuracy it is best to pluck the string so that it will fly in the direction of the other line, thrown from the other two points. To ensure an even line, it's often necessary to hew off obviously excess wood where the tree bowed out in its growth, or the swelling around some large knot.

Though broad axless, I soon hewed down to the lines with my cedar ax so as to leave a flat plane on one side of the log. Cuts are made every eight inches or so, depending on the type of wood (closer for hardwood), the length of the log, down to the plane represented by the chalk lines. This I usually do with my ax, though I have found that a crosscut will do an admirable job. It makes it easier to shoulder right up to either side of a knot. This helps alleviate the pain of bothersome grain when chipping off the wood that lies between the cuts, which is the next step, and, I think, self-explanatory. Old-timers with their broadaxes sloughed these off with a vertical cutting stroke. I chop off the top.

This was one side of my beam, rough cut, ready to be smoothed off, if I so chose, with the adz. Croaking frogs marking time, the other side lent itself to my rhythmic strokes. Then the third and fourth sides lent themselves to the blessing of my steel blade. A few hours, and a support was born, as well as a huge pile of chips, the greater good fire wood, the lesser acid rich mulch or compost or what have you.

I made short work of this white pine beam, nine inches by twelve when finished. Hardwoods, naturally, take a bit longer to work.

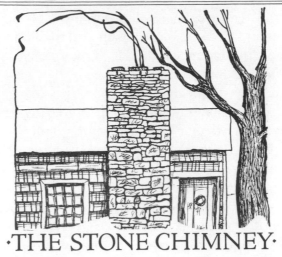

·THE STONE CHIMNEY·

Later, the great maples that guard the fornicarium allied with the wind to fill up the flues as I laid up brick and stone for the chimney. I might add that there's nary a place that can match the colors of our autumn.

I first apprenticed myself to the mason in the sky the fall before, when Luis and I dragged the mammoth stones for the foundation down from the hilltop in the stone boat, made from an old car hood. In the mouth of the old garage I set them in a hole deep enough to hold the massive weight of the fireplace in proof against upending frosts and the sinking mud of spring.

Now the work stands well up beyond the edge of the roof and, though freezing weather put an end to my finishing the last eight odd feet, a stove-pipe extension gives it the height to pass Bob's dormer and get sufficient draw or smoke suction. Carrying stones, some of which weigh well over two hundred pounds, up the scaffolding and placing them was quite a trip. I laid up this fireplace in such a way that it would hold together even without the mortar, by tying it all together or overlapping stone over stones like most brickwork you might have noticed. With a little sand cement and lime it should stand for a long time and see many children's faces; if the Russians don't bomb us.

This chimney has three flues: one for the fireplace, another for a forge in the future, and the third to provide suction to stoves connected to it from a few adjoining rooms. The marble linteled firebox, forty inches wide by thirty-two inches high and eighteen deep, could have been safely built about twice as high as it was and would have been more efficient heatwise, following the principles set down by a certain notorious count, but I was well beyond this stage before I came upon his rum-fed teachings; besides,

I'm led to understand the man was a fascist. Anyway, a lack of flashing, which keeps rainwater from running in twixt roof and chimney, and lack of a floor, keeps me from utilizing it too much, and yet this monolithic pile of stones serves as a good anchor against frequent flights the building is wont to take when winter winds and summer thunderstorms come howling, funneled through our high notch.

A few cloudy boats sail overhead, their home shores farther west, gray boding cliffs rear in the azure sky. A storm, I thought, but only a few lonely flakes swirl around the house and settle in to wait. Crops are in, beans are binned, winter quickly closes in.

In the leisure of winter one has time to be busy. Old ideas ferment and come up anew, a tangy beverage for new thought. New ideas come up like spring's sprouts and ask to be watered with a little action. A new set of spoons cut from wood or dried gourds. Graven images carved of linden command veneration or ridicule. Gifts for loved ones; let the heart have control. Doors, windows, a hundred household articles, new canoe paddles for that proposed trip in the spring.

Getting around becomes a favorite occupation with me. *Skiss, skiss* say the skis to that warm yet frozen landscape. The breath trails like ghosts or streams on ahead like a clipper's pennant. Fuck the snowmobilers coming up the hill: I'll take to the woods. The paths between the trees are good enough for me and I know old trails where the beelers never go. During the week after a snow even the roads are navigable for hours, sometimes days, before the town plow or too many occasional vehicles make them hopefully just a little less so.

Uphill and down for miles around, my skis, like magic wings, only ask to be waxed and put on. My wax, though sometimes paraffin, is a little less necessary to skis than gas to a snowbike. There's times when I've pulled myself to the top of some steep grade solely through the power of my arms with their steel pole extensions for lack of that stuff of proper skiing ease. My skis are old downhillers, cut down in size by friend Michael, who took a similarly worked pair away with him to Colorado. I wish him luck and good skiing on those mountain powders he once told me about. Perhaps I'll try them myself someday. I've spent weeks logging ten to fifteen miles a day (sometimes more), preparing for a race I'm pretending to enter.

·FIREWOOD: SAWS AND AXES·

Back home there's wood to be sawed and split. I believe in the old smokeless way of going about it, save of course that vapor from the lungs and that (poetically) that rises from the cut made from a well-plied crosscut. My crosscut is old and the teeth are short in the middle from many sharpenings, but it provides many hours of ruminations warm and out of doors. It's not particularly fast nor does it provide the foul fumes and hellish din, not to mention danger to the ear, flesh, and spirit, that I associate with the chain saw, or the cord saw that fortunately lies defunct in the shed, that cousin germane to the chain saw already under mention. I must admit I have used the chain saw and may again, but I dislike it and the circumstances. If we did not have it no one would be tempted to use it by its offers of wood in a hurry for a lot of trouble. (Ha! As of rewriting this, that devil saw has died.)

There's a certain reverence for each round cut with a handsaw that is lacking in those cut by machine, and I stack it all carefully, a place for each piece. For couples (this can be quicker) there are a number of, may the sexists excuse me, two-man saws of various ilk, both peg-tooth (every tooth cuts) and the type with a clearing or raker tooth between every two cutting teeth. The reason for these two types I'm not quite sure of. The clearing tooth scrapes out the dust made by the cutting teeth, eliminating any clogging and leaving a free surface for the cutters to work on. Perhaps over the years these scrapers were found unnecessary, due to the cutters doing both jobs. All my peg-tooth saws are new, whereas the old ones are marked by that double-footed enigma. Were the old saws designed at the desk of some woodless practitioner? What's the skinny? Will somebody show me an ancient peg-tooth crosscut? Surely those old sawyers knew what they were doing, but then again, they cut all our trees down.

Saws have a set to them. When you hold one aloft and look down that row of teeth they aren't straight on, one after another, but are slightly bent alternately first to one side then to the other, like a "V," the arms being edged to the outside. Thus each two blades cuts and chips out a small groove, like two blows of the ax when starting a cut. Many of these teeth properly set and well-sharpened will cut off a round in two shakes of a lamb's tail. The teeth of my usual tool are set close, best for hardwood. The saw does not cut softwood like linden (the local basswood) or our white pine very well; the soft fibers bind the saw blade. The teeth are usually set in a wider "V" for these woods. Setting is a quick and easy chore on my old anvil. A single light tap of the hammer is just right for the set I want.

Frequent sharpenings are a drag: they symbolize reduced life for the saw. I avoid knots, particularly hemlock, and am always careful to split off dirty bark, sand, etc., which will do quite a number on the blade if they aren't eliminated. In these old pasture lands it's well to have an eye open for signs of old barbed wire in the wood. I once met a man who had sawed a horseshoe in half, grown deep into the heart of an old tree, but that was at a sawmill.

Splitting wood is another joy (though a tedious writ). Splitting axes are not felling axes. Felling axes, particularly the double-bitted variety, are piss poor for setting those two pieces on opposite sides of the chopping block. A thin sharp blade will sink into a piece of wood and stick there. A good splitting ax is sharp but broadens out quickly from the point so as to spread the grain of the wood. For those knottier problems or those big rounds, the wedge and sledge are used to good advantage.

I've seen people swing the ax in such a way that, if their strength were great enough, the ax would have entered the round upper horn first, passed on through the side of the same, and traveled on through thin air, hopefully between their legs. Usually strength isn't needed: almost anyone can split wood and live to tell about it. Just be careful. *Think where the ax blade would go if there were nothing in the way of it.*

When I was a child I had a small hatchet my father had given me. It was very small and very dull despite my attempts to bring it to a razor edge. This was fortunate, for I whacked my knee with it many times. Happily, one of the lessons it didn't teach me was how to walk with a crutch. Now I bring my arms down with the blade, so when it passes through the round it ends up in the chopping block or, if anything should abort, at most in the ground.

·THE WOODSHED·

The woodshed itself was made of a lot of the work that goes on inside it. The framing (those studs and timbers that support the roof and siding) was constructed entirely of thinnings from the pine forest. By thinnings I

mean that, to preserve the health of the trees in that overcrowded former pasture, the dead and dying trees, as well as many live ones choking the growth of their brothers, were cut out so that the remainder would have room to grow and flourish, perhaps some day to become like the giants of the past. The majority of these thinned trees were from four to ten inches in diameter. Some I hewed flat to take siding or roofing better. Others were used in the round. The roof is tin of a type still used on many barns around here. The logs were spiked together, though it would have been nice to have lashed them together, perhaps with rope made from the bark of the basswood tree like the Indians did years ago.

The sides, though I've left them open for nearly a year now, I'll cover with hickory bark that I flattened out under the sun with the weight of stones. This will cover the side that faces the house. The side that faces me is old boards with two arched openings side by side providing a means of egress: in all, a pleasing and sturdy building, though the sills need creosoting. But the insides of our stovepipes are rich in that, and will go a long way in preserving those important members so close to the ground from the rotting effects of moisture.

Another shed close by is much the same in construction. It's entirely open on one side and has a single pitched roof slanting back and down from the front. The roof is much stronger in construction. Its flat surface is apt to hold a lot of heavy snow and the roofing material itself is heavy indeed. An old conveyor belt cut into three-foot squares for easier handling by one man. Each tile of this ultra-heavy-duty roofing weighs nearly thirty pounds. A six hundred and eighty pound roof better not fall on somebody's head. Perhaps a sod roof next, but I'll have to look further aforest for trees that can be taken righteously, my conscience being what it is. For we all know that trees are getting rarer these days. And those lumber magnates saw on, seemingly oblivious to the balance of nature. And a man cuts down his redwoods to reduce his taxes.

—HUGH

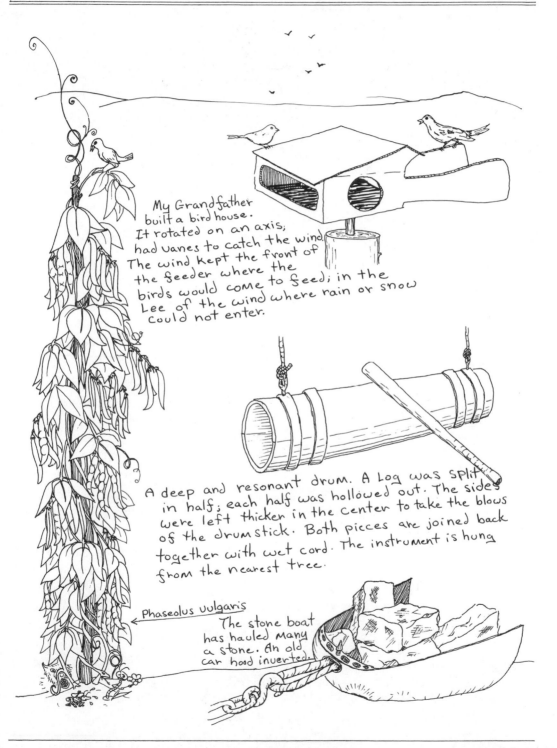

My Grandfather
built a bird house.
It rotated on an axis;
had vanes to catch the wind.
The wind kept the front of
the feeder where the
birds would come to feed; in the
Lee of the wind where rain or snow
could not enter.

A deep and resonant drum. A Log was split
in half; each half was hollowed out. The sides
were left thicker in the center to take the blows
of the drumstick. Both pieces are joined back
together with wet cord. The instrument is hung
from the nearest tree.

← Phaseolus vulgaris

The stone boat
has hauled many
a stone. An old
car hood inverted.

·TOTAL LOSS ECONOMICS·

ONE EVENING we sat down and tried to estimate our monetary expenditures for the average year. Our records are chaotic. We have no treasurer and have never bothered keeping books to detail income and expenses. Money is spent as it comes in. Sporadically. Sometimes we've got thousands of dollars in our checking account. Other times you can't even find loose change under the cushions of the couch. The checkbook is accessible to all and we trust each other not to make unnecessary expenditures. But what's an unnecessary expenditure? We tend not to get petty about the outflow of petty cash. Anarchy isn't completely successful, however. Some of us are more reluctant to dip into the common checking account than others. But we're learning gradually that there is no need to be shy. Money's never caused much of a problem. People earn whatever they can, some earn nothing at all, and that's OK, too. People who earn money usually take out pocket money before depositing their checks into the common account. That's OK. Anyone who goes out and makes a wage deserves a hamboogie or two on the sly.

We live on between $8,000 and $10,000 a year. We tried to inflate this figure because it seemed too low. But we can't. That means each of us has a per capita income of less than $1,000 a year. Not bad.

Our major expense is the mortgage. It is $2,700 per year for ten years paid in monthly installments; $3,500 with taxes. We owe the mortgage to the woman who sold us the farm. We're her major source of income so we can't miss a payment. We've got six years to go on the mortgage and have always met the bill.

I doubt if we spend more than $15 a week on food. And we feed anywhere from six to twenty people a day—probably averaging ten for dinner any given night. If there is anything we do well on the farm it is eating. We really eat.

Vegetables, dairy products (milk, cream, butter, eggs), and fruit (pears, peaches, apples, various berries) are home produced. So are some herbs, a little meat (beef, pork products, tough old hens), corn meal, and some maple syrup. We also make various kinds of wine, home brew, and hard cider, but not enough (as yet) to keep us in full supply.

We have to buy such staples as salt, sugar, cooking oil, most spices, pasta, tamari, different kinds of grains and baking flour, brown rice (in one-hundred pound bags), and stuff like sesame seeds and cashew nuts to meet gourmet tastes. We also crave cheese, and have to buy all our fish and additional meat.

We heat and cook entirely by wood. The first year we broke a lot of ax handles, but not anymore.

Animal feed runs to about $10 a week. The hens, horse, goat, and cow all get their own grain. We make hay with the help of neighboring farmers. We also have to call the vet often.

Our constant expenses are propane gas for the hot water heater, electricity—which runs one stereo, the water pump, light bulbs, and amplifies an occasional musical instrument and that's all—and gas for the tractor, chain saw, truck, and the one and sometimes two running cars.

Vehicles are a major expense. There are no mechanics on the farm. Our road is notorious as a car-killer and we usually make do with third-hand wrecks. Only in the past year have we had any luck in buying good used cars. We're especially wary of sweet deals on good, used American cars and pickup trucks. VW's seem to suit us best.

Capital equipment is our other major expense. Our agricultural implements, the tractor and its various accessories, are probably worth about $2,500. We could use a cart, a manure spreader, an old-fashioned thresher, and a new chain saw. A hay rake and baler would be nice, too. Bessie, the cow, cost us $225. Cheap. We'd like another cow. Then we'd be fixed for cheese. The other animals cost us maybe $100 combined. It would be nice if we had some sheep.

We do most of our building for the price of hardware and nails. We've had to buy little lumber, but more probably than we actually needed. We tear down old barns, sheds, and buildings. Sometimes we can sell selected beams and boards. Mostly, we get to keep the lumber and the old-fashioned brick. Initial building costs were high. Fiber glass insulation and Ashley stoves. But even with the cost of these basic goods we get by for less than $10,000 a year.

We probably could live cheaper than we do. Another cow, the sugaring operation, honey bees, more grain, and additional livestock for meat would get us closer to self-sufficiency in food; but probably we could never make it all the way. Someday we'll have a fish pond and a windmill, too, and cut our expenses for protein and electrical energy. And the more we learn about animals and machines, the cheaper their upkeep becomes. We're already pretty good at handicrafting useful tools out of wood.

We rummage old attics for clothes; boots and winter garments cost some, but mostly we wear the same funky old clothes. By the time you read this, we may be at the height of style.

There's usually enough money to finance vacations and trips, which may last a day or a month and take us to California or to a neighboring town.

Our income has come mainly from books. As we get royalties on some, they are:

> *Famous Long Ago* (Beacon) and *Total Loss Farm*
>   (Dutton) by Ray
> *Burnt Toast* (Knopf) by Pete
> *The Body's Symmetry* (Harper & Row) by Verandah
> *The Food Garden* (NAL) by Marty
> *Living on the Earth* (Random House) by Alicia

Also, if you should come across some funny-looking peddlers with manure on their boots hawking *The Green Mountain Post* it could be one of us or a friend. Buy a copy. It's pocket money for a movie or a boogie.

The fact that we make most of our money through literary efforts makes our economic situation somewhat unique. But a dozen people, even if they are all functionally illiterate, can easily earn enough to meet communal expenses. We haven't always been dependent on milking the media. One and sometimes two people teach at the university level. Their income helps meet day to day expenses, though they have commuting expenses of their own. At different times, we've worked as a nurse's aid in the hospital, laundress at a mental institution, dishwasher at Filene's in Boston during the Christmas season, dispatcher at Yellow Cab, baby-sitting for various neighbors, and sugarmaking and haying for local farmers. Only in the first year were outside jobs vital to our existence. The fact that some people still feel a need to work probably means that our open checkbook still doesn't work in actuality as it does in theory. Or sometimes people have immediate expenses that the farm can't meet. The situation should improve with time.

This essay, remember, refers to Total Loss economics. Economic theory doesn't take communal situations into account. And there is hardly

a place for us in the capitalist scheme. I can already hear some academic fart saying, "What about labor, they haven't taken into account the cost of labor." Well, if we did we'd be theoretically bankrupt and in debt to ourselves for thousands. We work, quite obviously, for slave wages. But as there are no masters, there can be no slaves. Our garden, for instance, cost us about $100 in actual expenses (which we make back selling our surplus) plus about six months of varying degrees of physical labor. But the labor comes free. We've got nothing better to do with our time but swim in the beaver pond, visit neighbors, travel and make hay, and we get to do all those things and still have a garden.

Economically, then, communal living makes sense. And you don't have to live as we do to make it work. Any kind of cooperative sharing cuts expenses at greater than an arithmetic progression. Two can live cheaper than one, but four can live cheaper than two and eight can live cheaper than four and possibly almost as cheap as two. Whoopie! Talk about revolution. What would happen if lots of people started living this way? Worked only at socially useful jobs and bought only the necessary things they couldn't make themselves or scavenge from industry's bountiful wastes? There'd be a depression, yes; but that's only another way of saying that people would lead simpler, less materialistic lives. And there'd be unemployment, or a lot of people freed from meaningless, boring, and socially useless jobs able, finally, to do things that they always wanted to do: like plant a garden, write poems, make pots, tinker with old engines, or play a lot of handball. Of course, there are implications that should be faced. The Gross National Product would tumble and put a lot of economists uptight. And we'd no longer be the richest, most powerful nation on earth. But our people would be a helluva lot happier and so, too, might the Vietnamese. Think of that. End of rap.

—MARTY

·LEAN PICKIN'S OR·
·SOMETHING FOR NOTHING·

AT FIRST GLANCE the average person might wonder where we hide the food in our kitchen. In fact, we've wondered about that very thing ourselves from time to time. But, no matter how bare our shelves may appear, we always manage, "as if by magic," to come up with the now famous something for nothing dinner.

Learning to perform this feat was no easy matter. For a long time we assumed that if we had rice, everything else would take care of itself. After all, rice is a perfect food. However, unless you're on #7, rice alone, night after night, can be a painful ordeal. When we were young and foolish and very broke, we often sat down to things like rice a la oleo or rice and potatoes. For months Verandah and I shared a secret ingredient which we were

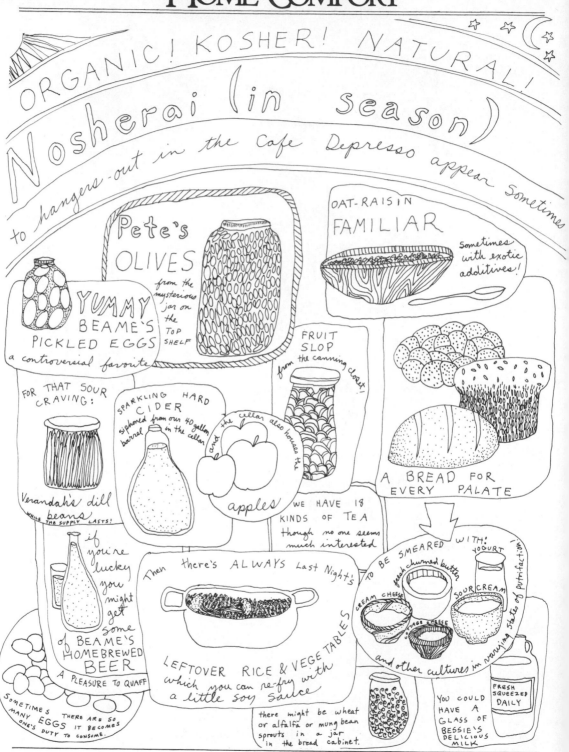

ORGANIC! KOSHER! NATURAL!
Nosherai (in season)
to hangers-out in the Cafe Depresso appear sometimes

Pete's OLIVES from the mysterious jar on the TOP SHELF

OAT-RAISIN FAMILIAR
Sometimes with exotic additives!

YUMMY BEAME'S PICKLED EGGS
a controversial favorite

FOR THAT SOUR CRAVING:

SPARKLING HARD CIDER
siphoned from our 40 gallon barrel in the cellar

and the cellar also houses the

FRUIT SLOP
from the canning closet!

Verandah's dill beans
WHILE THE SUPPLY LASTS!

apples

we have 18 kinds of TEA though no one seems much interested

A BREAD FOR EVERY PALATE

if you're lucky you might get some of BEAME'S HOMEBREWED BEER
A PLEASURE TO QUAFF

Then there's ALWAYS Last Night's

LEFTOVER RICE & VEGETABLES which you can re-fry with a little soy sauce

TO BE SMEARED WITH:
YOGURT
CREAM CHEESE
fresh churned butter
COTTAGE CHEESE
SOUR CREAM
and other cultures in varying states of putrefaction

FRESH SQUEEZED DAILY

YOU COULD HAVE A GLASS OF BESSIE'S DELICIOUS MILK

SOMETIMES THERE ARE SO MANY EGGS IT BECOMES ONE'S DUTY TO CONSUME.

there might be wheat or alfalfa or mung bean sprouts in a jar in the bread cabinet.

sure made the whole meal: a heavy dose of poultry seasoning. Things were bad.

However, we've learned that man does not live by rice alone so we now attempt to keep on hand at all times: sugar, kasha, lentils, soy beans, chick peas, dried salt cod, dried shrimp. If you have these on your shelf you'll always feel secure when dinner time rolls around. The amount you should keep on hand depends on the number of people you usually have for dinner. We seem to average around ten so we buy in large quantities. These things aren't expensive and you can do amazing things with them. Dried salt cod is fantastic, it goes a long way and makes you feel as if you are eating really well. A good protein rush. Dried shrimp is good for group morale.

We're fortunate because we can count on Bessie for milk and cream, the chickens for eggs, summer fresh fruits, vegetables and herbs, and winter preserves, canned, frozen, or dried. If you don't have any of these things, try hard to get them. If they're really out of the question and your shelves are empty, try your local supermarket. It's a far cry from picking things right off the tree but you can get food there for free. Go to the produce department and ask for any "rotten" food; often they'll be glad to give you many incredible things for free or for very little money. Eggplants, avocados, tomatoes, and other fruits bruise easily and have to be thrown out. Be friendly and they'll be more inclined to save you things. It's worth it. Go to the meat department and ask for dog bones. They make great soup stock. Of course anything you rip off is free. Just don't get caught.

If you live in the country try to locate a grain mill. We've found one near us that grinds its own animal feeds without adding chemicals. We buy fifty pounds of soy meal and fifty pounds of cracked corn every couple of months for the kitchen. We then grind it up for corn meal or soy flour for a whole lot cheaper than we could get it at a health food store. Just be sure to ask about additives. They put all kinds of awful things in animal feeds these days that you wouldn't want to eat, or feed your animals for that matter.

—PEPPER

·HOME·COMFORT·

·LIVING WITH THE ANIMALS·

THE HENS ESCAPED from their roosting room in the barn on the day I started reading an essay by Virginia Woolf. I had just finished the part of *A Room of One's Own* in which the author relates how women writers were denied access to experience outside the sitting room and the home, which made them bitter and strident, or at best limited their range, when dusk drew me to the barn. The hens, a particularly brave and inquisitive group in our experience, had pushed open their door, improperly latched, and were exploring the grain area, scratching the floor for food. Eight or nine of them were in the cow's stall, in the manger, and even outside in the snow. They were all busy and happy, not afraid of me at all as I shooed them back to their quarters. *Freedom must be good for the girls,* I thought, admiring their spirit and coveting their eggs.

As these hens, who came to us as five-month-old pullets, matured and reached a peak production level of twenty or twenty-one eggs a day from two dozen chickens, I have become aware of their growing consciousness. A number of bolder hens, who at first merely pecked at your feet and approached you with interest as you knelt to take the eggs from the nests, gradually escalated to pecking the collector's hands, the eggs, or the collector's backside. Many more hens have joined this movement. In addition, there has been increasingly sophisticated sabotage, from covering a nest full of eggs with straw, to pushing eggs and straw down behind the roost, to laying the eggs in a corner of the adjoining pig sty. I must clarify that it was the pigs on the other side, Dolores the big sow in particular, who made the holes in the chicken wire above the wall, both large enough for their greedy snouts and for a hen to fly through. The egg stash, which Joan suspected for a week before it was found, is behind where the pigs actually live, in a corner of sawdust, scrap wood, and cardboard boxes. Thus both species cooperate to outwit the oppressor.

After a meeting in which we each read aloud what we had written, Peter told me that my attitude was entirely too negative, verging on harmful, since chickens respond to human expectations. I admit to an overly subjective view. Although I may interpret a hen's flying at my face while others scurry through the door as soon as it's open as a sort of jailbreak, it is true that those actions are the hens' only way of saying their feed trough is empty. Pecking at eggs is a sign of calcium deficiency, a request for oyster shells or limestone. Peter boarded up the pig wall higher, the hens lay only in the nests, and we understand each other better now. We keepers are careful to give them all the grain, warm water, space, and light they might want. The kept give up their eggs. As a rule, they are alert, curious, and content rather than hostile, scheming, or resentful. I have struggled to correct my thoughts and am no longer afraid or defensive when the hens bite my hands at feeding time. They are eager, inquisitive, even affectionate. Above all, they are Just Chickens.

It is a delicate matter to distinguish one's projections from the livestock. No day goes by without someone reporting one of the animals' views on life or the cosmos. Bessie the cow says, "I bin waitin for dat bus a long, long time," as she chews her cud in the barn. Mama the white goat blurts out, "Oh, I'm so lonely here, let's go for a walk, let's go visit that nice big Toggenburg, we hardly had a chance to talk . . . oh dear, Windy's going to take my grain again, I just know it." Flora says, "I'm all dressed up, but where's the party?" Max says, "You want me to kill myself, don't you?" The calf says, "Hug me!" and Dolores and Long John say, "Oh boy, rancid wheat germ again! And whey and squash and rotten pears and moldy tomatoes and dried-up oatmeal and a few brussels sprouts and fermented rhubarb, and . . . hey, it's all gone. We want more!"

Pepper, who takes care of Windy and rides her, is very clear that

Windy is a horse. Others are not so sure, and Pepper, like everyone but Marty (and Connie who's in Arizona), knows that Becky, Packer, and sometimes Noodle are not Just Cats, but monsters. There used to be great Cat and Dog factions when we had large numbers of each, but one by one the pet population has decreased. From five cats this fall, one died of bad vibes and ague, another sought and presumably found better quarters after three weeks of homemade cat food. Of the five big dogs, one was sent to a doting artist's home in Boston, one was shot by hunters right nearby, and the mother-to-millions rode off with her mistress very early one morning.

The cats now live pretty much in the barn, from milking to milking. Noodle, the greatest hunter, eats birds around Hugh's bird feeder, and Packer must eat mice for he has grown big and solid enough to have been mistaken for a puppy on at least one occasion. Becky is a small cat, inheriting her grandfather (and father) Packer's chronic eye disease, with little to recommend her, in my opinion, but her tenacity. Flora is the only True Dog left, Max the Irish setter being more dybbuk than dog (see Verandah's moving essay). Flora barks at approaching objects, goes for all walks, rolls in the snow, and plays all the time. Her bushy black tail wags so hard it takes her whole rear end with it. Unlike her brothers, she has both wits and instincts. Unlike her mother, she is spayed.

The geese and the ducks are untamed and unnamed. It's true I call the Chinese couple Madame and Generalissimo Chiang, and often shout to them in what little Mandarin I can remember, at which they draw themselves up and stare. But when, from the hills opposite the barn, I hear their weird high calls in the late afternoon, I know they are a species apart, great birds with teeth and tongues. It is their nature, not their personality, to be bossy, protective, vocal. The Chinese geese and the two sets of ducks, two mallard and two white Peking females, lived all summer without a pond, and all winter without a barn, their only shelter being a doghouse Bob built for the puppies before the dog kennel became the barnyard. Despite occasional suggestions that we roast the noisy and useless fowl, all hail their fortitude and spirit. Christmas Eve found us toasting their health with, of course, Cold Duck.

—ELLEN

·FRITZ AND THE BOYS·

GODDAMN THIS SMELLY OLD TRACTOR ANYWAY, ought to get a pair of workhorses. Well, personally, I never got on very well with horses, they're nervous, but always dug the idea of oxen, like in "Sweet Betsy from Pike." When Marty and I were sugaring for J. and R. Clark last spring, we came into the barn one morning and there was little Emmet, still wet behind the ears, among all the heifer calves and Lucius the Angus. He was so shy and pretty I said, Rod, what do you want for him?

Well, he's worth fifty bucks, says Rodney, but why don't you keep your money and help us fix fence and spread shit when the weather warms up?

Okay, I said, now I guess I better find another one to go along with him.

So the word went out and pretty soon Shorty Clark came down and said, sure enough, he had a bull calf, did I want it.

Better have a look at him, I said; so up the road we went and there was Perley; you couldn't ask for a better match, in markings anyway, but it's hard to tell about size at that age.

I'll take him. How much?

Oh, says Shorty, you come and help me fix fence for a few days and he's yours.

So I did and I've been fixing fences and shoveling shit ever since.

Had to get them home—I was at Tree Frog then—so Daniel and I stayed up till ten o'clock one night building a calf pen at the back of the shed where Harry keeps all his ridiculous lawn mowers. Next morning we loaded them both in the back of the Land Rover and brought them up the hill. I bought some hay, calf grain and milk replacer, and found myself in the cattle business.

Things went along pretty good, except that Emmet started throwing his weight around now that he was the big guy and there was no Lucius to pick on him. He knocked Perley away from the grain, until I started feeding them from separate dishes. But then Emmet would wolf his down and then go for Perley's. He was strong even then and Perley was no help, dawdling over his food trying to pick out the parts with the most molasses on them. I ended up tying Emmet until Perley was done eating.

Everybody whose advice I asked told me something different: castrate them young; don't castrate till they're six months old; start training them now; wait till they're older; do this; do that. So I said the hell with all of you, I'll do it my way. I took them out every few days, one at a time, and led them around on a rope to get the feel of being handled. Once Emmet got away from me and ran twice around the house at top speed, but then he couldn't figure out where to go, so he let me tie him again and lead him back to the barn. He's always been the more rambunctious of the two of them. Perley would just as soon cooperate if he could figure out what I wanted him to do.

I gave Harry a ten-dollar bill to buy hay but he came home with a training yoke instead, so I yoked them up and they dragged me all over hell's half acre. We did that a few more times during the summer, usually when I was hung over, wanting to pick a fight with somebody. They didn't pick up the voice commands, but at least it got them used to the yoke.

In July I moved to Michael and Annie's house and put the boys out to pasture over there. It didn't take them long to start breaking out of the barbed wire, so I got an electric fence, which held them for a few weeks until Emmet discovered that it only hurt for a second. He wouldn't go very far, though, because Perley stayed inside the fence. After a while they both started getting out. They would wander around, making trouble all over the neighborhood; I had to chase after them twice a day after they discovered Sid Gaine's young heifers, so I figured it was about time to cool their passion.

Maynard said he would come and castrate them, but he never got around to it until long after the boys and I moved down the road from him. I had got a stronger fence charger that held them for a month, but pretty soon they got a whiff of his cows and started raising hell down there. By that time, Emmet's playfulness had developed into the characteristics of a bull, so it was a relief when Maynard pinched his balls off, even though it hurt me some, too.

Since then they've been as good as gold. They stay home most of the time and their biggest kick is standing in front of the rabbit hutch watching the bunnies hop around. We walked all the way up to the Corners and back last week, to the surprise of those who said I would never get them trained, and they even enjoy the yoke. We all love each other, me and the boys, and I wouldn't swap them for any dog in the world, except maybe Clambone, who I guess is gone forever, anyway.

—FRITZ

·163·

Max plunders. Max wonders. Verandah wanders with the cows.

·MAX AS METAPHOR·

WET WOOD smoldering smells of creosote. Open the damper. The acrid odor seeps from the room. On the stove a kettle roars, moistening the air so that the dog won't keep me awake with his snoring. I never meant to live with dogs. I rescued cats from coffee houses. Each of us maintained an orbit, had our love affairs, or stalked our prey, meeting only for moments when one of us would say, "Well done, Sloth cat," he having fanged a rat in the hallway of the house in Somerville which was called, for reasons obvious, The Hovel, five years and three cities ago.

Once there lived a man named Marshall Bloom, two cities and a farm ago. His body was always in motion, what with itches and allergies, trips to the store, to the Coast. Marshall was one of the last great vaudevillians, a Jew in show business. Everything executed with a flourish, including finally his body, which, I reckon, is inching his way east as an earthworm.

Now Marshall had a double who was locked for this lifetime in a dog-suit, to his endless humiliation. And that was Max. Max dropped out of Boston society shortly after the farm at Gonamute began. They met and could not be severed. Max was a Jewish setter like another Irish Bloom named Leopold. His ribs were skinny as a washboard. His coat matched Marshall's mane in summer, when the sun, relentless over the cucumber fields, burned it red. Setters are bred to point and fetch, but Marshall was all that Max stalked. They ran rings around each other in a pas de deux, heartbreakingly awkward and graceful. They crept and leapt and rarely touched ground. If Marshall was a knight, then Max was his escutcheon.

There is a narrow, boulder-treacherous road to the dooryard where caravans of snowmobiles come. No one used it the years I'm thinking of, but Marshall in his green Triumph. The road was his runway. We called it the Bloom Highway and nailed a plaque with that inscription on the old tractor shed. Marshall and Max would explode from the car like popcorn. Some called him a scarecrow or stormcrow, because he often bore sad tidings of the flat lands, the death of loved ones, or just trouble in the kitchen at Gonamute. He was proud and easily insulted.

Max was a mime. He punctuated Marshall's sentences with his outlandish and suggestive postures. If Marshall left him standing for the duration of a trip to the outhouse, Max would be scratching on doors, chasing his shadow, or simply arranging his face into masks of torture and grief which seemed to become him.

A visit from Marshall and Max was always a delight to me. Always, not because he brought me gifts of clams and sherry, or exotica from his travels, and not because he made love to me, because he did not. He was possessed of an elegance of mind which gladdened my tiny house as the kettle boiled over as it does now. It was not the sherry sipped that changed the air, but whims and tales—suddenly Paris, or Bloomsbury, though chickens once were slaughtered here, and their blood and feathers filled the house before I did. Max would curl like an island between the civilizations of our rockers. His vertebrae rippled in sleep.

Marshall sought to keep the lamp of the mind burning, alive and in secret on our farms. Someday people would be interested again in, say, the influence of the diction in Yeats' translations of the *Upanishads* on the plays of that period. Then Marshall would rise to the occasion, his mind full of such confections. He was a shipwrecked anachronism. Marooned with his sensibilities and a logbook full of lists, illegible in his fine squirming print.

All the while, his body fidgeted in chairs, tractors, pacing in shower thongs the kitchen floor before morning. And Max prowled forever after, or led him further on through woods, worlds beyond fields planted or in pasture, or to ponder in a graveyard. He might have changed his body for the dog's. Max would clear his throat to call the vultures off the door.

"Parting is all we know of heaven. And all we need of hell." Verandah, why don't you write like Emily?

When Marshall Bloom died, he siphoned the light from November. No word he left spoke more eloquently of pain than the wraith-like specter of Max whose sole form and purpose was parody. Months passed like a stitch in time. Max sired puppies, fought in the dog wars, and tried to follow many a reluctant master.

One January I was dog-eared enough to take him on. He sensed in me courtship and romance. Max shunned the company of our four robust husky dogs, whose names alone were a catalog of dreams, to sit at my feet, ride by my side, sleep in my bed, lead me away from my suitors, growl at friendly footsteps past my door, wait anxiously as I milk Bessie, or disappear into the depths of the forbidden hen house. He reads to me from Omar Khayyam as I lounge in the tub.

How could I know what tricks he held in store for me? The Suicide's Dog, Great Caesar's Ghost, Fang, and Flame. These were but a few of his incarnations. My virtue, my dignity, and my solitude, all gone.

Winter hung in abeyance. In March, we tapped the maples, and dropped down to the Carolinas. Max folded himself into the back pocket of a Volkswagen. When it warmed up, he tiptoed over the mulch in the garden, rarely bending a vegetable or weed. We hitchhiked to the sea at Portsmouth. Max sat at attention at the edge of the Atlantic (by some quirk of genes, he cannot, will not, swim), terrified that I might cross or drown. Sometimes I tantalized him into the waves, and he floated back to shore on his fleas. Later that night he swooned to the bow and unerring strings of Frankie Dodge's cello.

Entering an early dotage, Max is graying at the temples. He suffers from chronic indigestion, giving rise to foul winds. And spells of depression, somnambulism. I feed him geriatric vitamins and oil for his paltry coat. Strangers say I'm lucky to have such a handsome dog. A man in Boston offered me a hundred dollars. I could see Max in the back seat of a limousine, smoking a cigar and driving a hard bargain. A shopkeeper said, Sorry, no pets. Should I wait outside and let him do the marketing?

Max and I stay mostly in the mountains. How can I complain? It was a marriage made in heaven. Good night, Marshall, Max, my haunted hound.

—VERANDAH

The Interesting Adventures of
Marty and The Skunk

A skunk came up from Don and Phoeb's
Trotting ahead of Willy the Jeep
Hoping to find some goodies to eat
In the compost heap at the farm.

But the fertile mound was covered with snow
So into the roomy red barn did he go.
The little red hen scurried to and fro
Crying cut cut come help save our eggs.

Just then Marty arrived with some corn feed and water
He looked at the hens and cried "What is the matter."
Then, "Don't worry ladies I'll set things in order."
And sat in a rocker to think:

"If I try to banish that skunk from the room
He might send out a blast of his famous perfume
And sweet Connie would sigh and fall into a swoon
From my odor instead of her ardor."

Just then Laurie arrived with a tall can of beer
Marty cried "Eureka, I've got and idea."
All the ladies asked, Marty said "Just wait here".
And he vanished to master the task.

Moments passed, all at once a bang came from the barn.
So loud that the ladies cried out in alarm.
The skunk emerged cursing "Foiled again, Darn
I'm no match for this human technology."

"Be gone, oh be gone skunk and don't come again",
Quoth Marty assuring the shuddering hens,
As he entered with eggs I reached out for my pen
To record the momentous event.

Now the hens are so happy they sing as they lay
And the kids are so glad they declared it a day
For rejoicing because the foul skunk went his way
And sweet Connie gave Marty a kiss.

Thus passes, kind reader the tail of the skunk
And how we got through it without getting stunk
If you think that this history's nothing but bunk,
Just ask *Old Tidewater, she'll tell you.

— verandah

*Tidewater the hen was a gift from the Dodges of Portsmouth,
the first "farm animal" to arrive on the scene.

·GIVE ME THE WILLIES·

FIRST IT WAS FLOYD the rooster, a huge white leghorn test-tube bird, rescued from the anesthesia, who never got on well with the hens. One day he developed an awful rot around the tail and all agreed his number had come up. Raymond strode down to the hen yard with the splitting ax, only to be followed an hour later by Michael, who, as an emissary from the kitchen, came to see what was up. The ax was propped against the wall. Ray was rapping to the chickens about this and that. Michael lobbed off Floyd's poor head. We buried him and that was that. It was 1968.

Or sickly kittens with convulsions drowned in a burlap bag, buried, their meowing heard in sleep.

Fritz was swinging at the block the day we did in some of the fowl. It was hot summer and the yard was full of flies. I, watching from the porch, tried to convince myself that "it is important to know where dinner comes from," a sentiment as essential as the barn is red. . . . Fritz strove to be nonchalant. I could not help but flinch at their death spasms, although I had cursed them by name, and warned them of their fate.

Or the deer the dogs brought down the first spring, butchered the same night in the yard, and served as stew for lunch. I saw the deer fleeing in terror with every bite. Are we the dogs, I wondered.

Or the sheep that Buzzy slaughtered in Portsmouth and brought to us. I knew her myself, recalled her grazing beside the horse and hen who formed a trio. I ate her with gusto, but several abstained.

Yet the people were crying for meat, especially in winter, though some more urgently than others.

All of us are instinctive pacifists, some ready to be jailed rather than to maim or kill, others prepared to involve themselves in whatever chicanery necessary to flee from battle. Not to kill.

We lived on tuna fish as much as anything. Tuna was a treat in the old days. Tuna grew in cans that came from the other side of the world. The bigger the tins, the cheaper, and it tasted worse than Calo, the tuna of Angola. Or sometimes there was tinned pink ham or chopped meat from weekend guests.

He came in a burlap bag, jostled in the trunk of a car from Wendell and the huge black sow, newly weaned and unsexed and frightened and hungry, little Wilbur the piglet. He had black pants and a white shirt and he wasn't much bigger than a football. His skin is a bristly drum now. His trotters, a pair of castenets; his ears, a silk purse.

Michael and I held him on our laps and scratched his belly. When he got an abscess, Michael gave him shots and cleaned his wounds. He grew in girth and appetite and great care was taken with his meals. Here is a sample of a hot lunch.

·WILBUR STEW·
Fit for a Pig

2 quarts whey
2 bags of zucchini or New Zealand spinach (least favor-
    ite vegies from the freezer)
a spill of brewer's yeast
table scraps, but for coffee grounds and citrus fruits
sprouted potatoes
molasses
rotten apples
supermarket garbage
handfuls of soy meal
wild greens in season
Simmer in a caldron, cool and serve

Often weekend guests had to be discouraged from sampling these concoctions on the stove.

We knew we were going to kill and eat him, but we didn't know how

or who. He was having such a pleasant life, scratching his bristles against the fence of his run and getting a sunburn, begging below the outhouse window, squealing as if he were starving. He was friendly when not ravenous. Finally he began to look like a hog. It was hard to believe that the sweet dear the ladies wanted to dress in babyclothes had grown so quickly into a beast of slaughtering age.

That morning in June it was sweltering even at dawn as I milked Bessie and fed the animals. No food for Wilbur. He should have been rampaging for food, but he was silent. Are we really going to do this to you? Is this what you were born for?

We waited for Terry, who had learned his skill from a government pamphlet, to come with his dead eye and butchering knives. Trying to be levelheaded. There was no way, waiting through the waning morning. We borrowed a revolver and a block and tackle, set up a long table on the porch to receive the carcass.

By the time Terry and the lovely Margaret arrived, the day was hot enough for a lynching. We shut the hungry dogs in the house. They knew something was up. Then the fetchers were sent for Wilbur.

See us then. It is unutterably still, windless, and seething. Wilbur trusts us. We bribe him with food to the scaffolding, his nose always close to the pail. We bind his legs, and the moment comes when he is squealing with outrage.

See, then, ten people, partly naked, aproned and sweating, all frightened yet full of terrible purpose, as if in the midst of some rite of passage (learning to kill), standing in the farm yard by the scaffold. Wilbur is frantic. Terry straightens his arm, his face is completely impassive, and fires. I hear a short scream. Later someone tells me, it was I.

Wilbur is down, a perfect shot between the eyes, it was. We cut his throat and say good-bye and Godspeed. A relief, so profound it moves some of us to tears, changes the edge in the air to ease. It is over so quickly, so little pain and fear. We move again, as in a dream. Pierce the Achilles tendons, hook, and hoist him up, catch his lifeblood in a basin, sever the head, and start ever so carefully, to peel back the skin with knives.

Our neighbor, Ralph, pulls up on his motorcycle. He heard we were doing our pig today and came to offer his help. All are blood-spattered on bare skin, yet relaxed. Willie's trials are over. The rest is our labor. He chuckles, "You kids will undertake anything." He is amused and approves.

He used to slaughter his own meat until his son, who is slightly younger than we, protested on behalf of the animals. Nothing in the spectacle seems to shock him, the near naked women, the pig in surgery, the general state of chaos around the farm.

The skin is off, salted, and rolled up for future use. Terry painstakingly slits open the body cavity. Far from gruesome, it is a revelation. It is beauty. I have never seen such color, each organ in its evolutionary place, and perfectly formed. We empty miles of intestines, and sever one by one the organs, careful not to break the bile sack beneath the liver. I take each lovingly in my hands, no longer afraid to touch and know them.

Luis fills the bladder with water. Like a translucent balloon covered with networks of veins, it shines in the sun. We inflate the lungs *in vitro*. They are birds. They have not lost their power. The heart, a muscled fist.

Of one another, we may know the mind, the heart, one might say, the soul; of some we say we know or love the flesh. To love the body we embrace the skin; the rim or rind of the myriad systems which support us. We enter, never touching, never approaching the source of life itself.

Some kill the body to stop the torments of the mind. The body never wants to die. The body cries out against such cruelty, the heart, the lungs, the liver. I picture Marshall sometimes, his body quaking in the vanishing air of his tiny Triumph, that November morning, his cells protesting the carbon monoxide, while his mind, impervious, betrays the urge to keep on moving.

This is the lesson Wilbur taught me the day we killed him. The lesson I remember with the taste of his muscle, which gave me the energy to fly around these hills. Eight months later, a few packages in the freezer mark the end of his earthly flesh. John made a drum from his bristling hide to mark and measure times of celebration.

—VERANDAH

One-eyed Packer
moose patrol.

Swirls of moonlight
Idle woods.

It's more important to pat the Packer.

Aanu

·WHERE BARF BARF IS·

I KNOW WHERE BARF BARF IS, Ray; where he was shot and where he is buried. There is a granite outcrop there that marks the spot. Once you know where it is you can't hardly miss it. You can tell it's The Rock because there are two trees rising out of it. The first tree is a dead birch with two forked branches extending over it like a bowsprit of an old sailing ship. Behind it is a huge silver birch. The roots of both trees have split the rock where they emerge from the earth. They remind me of jockey's legs, the way they are dug deep into the flank of the rock, high, hard, and urgent, as if spurring a horse down the homestretch. The roots straddle the granite and form two arches above the outcrop. The trunk of each tree rises at the apex of its arch. The silver birch looks to be the tallest tree in the area.

It's pretty strange that I, of all people, happened upon this rock, the rock where Barf Barf is, and learned his secret. I mean, you know how I feel about dogs. They're not my favorite animals and I'm not into them at all. As a whole, I find them unctious, ingratiating, overly dependent on humans, and annoyingly underfoot. I do not like it when a dog clambers up all over me and slobbers in my face.

Now cats are something else. I really dig cats and would rather be telling you a story about one of the cats we know. Like the story of Noodle and his journey into the peach orchard. Remember when he disappeared for six weeks and I gave him up for dead and then he returned unexpectedly, scratching at the front door on Halloween Eve, meowing to be let in? Or I could tell you the story of the beautiful, black, long-haired Ariel, who visited us for a few days two winters ago, or of the Wild Black Kitty of the Woods who lived in the barn much of that winter and, like Ariel, hasn't been seen since. Or the story of the little sick kitten, one of Bratislava's litter, that you and I drowned in the stream and how it wiggled in my hand just before it died. For days afterward my hand felt cold and lifeless, like a metallic appendage, a gun perhaps, which I had no use for but couldn't shake. Then there was my own sweet Lady Jane, a little gray puss who ran away the first day we moved here. The last time anyone caught sight of her was two years ago in the yard of the old Kiraly place, before Myron moved in. I often think of her when I'm walking in those parts, hoping to catch a glimpse of her hunting in the brush. But I doubt if she survived the first winter. She was a house cat, raised in an old tenement on the Lower East Side. What could she know about cold, snow, and winter?

You see? Of all the people who might have something to say about a dog, I'd be the last one you'd expect. Sure, Barf Barf was special. I'll even admit that. It took time for me to get to like him, and that happened more through his efforts than by mine, but we did become friends. He used to follow me on jaunts through the woods and he was beautiful to watch bounding up the meadow at full speed. Still, I'm not one to be telling stories about dogs. That's why I take the story I'm about to tell you so seriously. I really do know where Barf Barf is. It would never occur to me to make up a story about a dog unless the truth of it was so pressing that I couldn't bear to hold it in.

Let me tell you how I came upon the spot. A lot of the places along the route will probably be familiar to you. You won't have any difficulty finding it alone, but someday I'll take you there if you wish. It all happened one autumn day, a warm Indian summer day when the leaves were just beginning to change color, but about a week before they reached their autumn peak. I guess it was sometime in the early eighteenth century when it happened, at least that is what it felt like. I didn't bother to guess the precise date, because time changes so rapidly around here that it is impossible to keep track. You know how it is, Ray; each day is a totally new experience, a new adventure, a different time.

We wake up each morning with the sun and the history of the Planet before us. It's our choice, really. The number of options are infinite. Some days we frolic in the past. Other times we are rushing so carelessly into the future that I often haven't time to put on a shirt. Some days we even live in the present, at least according to calendar time, if that means anything to you. But that's the least interesting time of all. Mostly it means putting a working vehicle together from all the automotive scraps and pieces that are strewn about the yard. It means leaving our hill and going into town. What an illusion! To get into a car and expect it to take us some place. Where is it that one should ever have to go? Whatever is of value will eventually make it to our front door. It always amazes me the extremes humans will go to in order to get some kicks.

For myself, I'd much rather follow Uncle Luis back into feudal times and enjoy the life as it exists on our manor. Serfdom has been abolished, of course, and our friends and neighbors are all M'Ladies and M'lords. Except when there are potatoes to be dug. Then we all become peasants and live in thatched huts. It's also fun to follow the Fen of Wick into the woods like lumberjacks in days of old. First we breakfast on buckwheat cakes with homemade butter and maple syrup and wash it all down with strong black coffee brewed on our wood burning stove. Then it's off to the woods to chop down towering white pine with the heavy steel blade of a double-edged ax. The wood has many uses. Verandah is cutting shingles from the short, straight pieces that have no knots. There's also a woodshed and a sugar-house to be built and Pete is making a chair. Not one board foot of our lumber goes to the King. The British Navy is stuck in port for want of our white pine for its masts. Bengal tigers and wise old elephants with ivory tusks still roam through India. Africa remains a civilized continent. Bantus, Hottentots, and Watusis (remember them in *King Solomon's Mines*) live there, along with antelope, giraffes, lions, monkeys, apes, and black and white striped zebras. We're very careful about which trees we cut down. We've seen the way lumbermen abused the woodland in logging days of the past, and we're careful not to repeat their mistakes.

The time I like best, however, is when we are early eighteenth century yeoman farmers, rough, hardy, proud, independent folk, living close to the land at the edge of the woodland frontier. Iroquois are our neighbors and are free to hunt and trap game for food and hides wherever they wish. There are no fences on our land and we used the deed to start a fire one damp, chilly autumn night. We give them vegetables from our garden in exchange for meat, and often we sit around the campfire together smoking a pipe of peace. We also freed the slaves, but that was a long time ago, around the time we decided to free ourselves. One night some Indians and black people came around to play some music. Luis brought out his big conga drum and Richard made up a chant. The rhythm made the dark rain clouds disappear and the chanting caused the moon to shine. Things like that go on around here all the time. We hardly ever miss a good sunset and almost every night we get to watch the stars shine.

Sometimes when a stranger comes walking up the road, I wonder if we are not to be visited by de Tocqueville or some other earnest traveler. I would like to show him how prosperous our homestead has become. There's always food to eat and cider, peach wine, beer, or milk to drink. We make it and grow it ourselves and there's always enough for one more setting. There's a roof over our heads, wood for the stoves, you've built a porch, and there are no more holes in the barn roof. What more could one ask? We really do live well and I know he'd be tickled to see how times have changed and how much better it's all become since he last wandered through these parts.

On this particular day, the day I found where Barf Barf is, I began my walk in the juniper bush atop the hill across from the cemetery. I often come here because there are no trees and one has a clear view out over the Hollow. The juniper bush is one of my secret spots. The woods around here are full of secret spots and each of us has one or two of our own. This is what keeps us here, I think, and why no matter how far we stray we always come running home. Once I walked up to the waterfall near the site of the old sawmill up beyond the sugarbush. This is another of my secret spots and I thought I was the only one who knew of it. I didn't see Pete and he didn't see me until we bumped into each other. Then we hemmed and hawed a bit and I commented on the weather and he agreed that it certainly was a fine day. There was nothing much else we could have said to one another that would have been as clear to us as what we left unsaid. Besides, we were both embarrassed (and happy) to find we shared the same secret. It's kind of like when you make love with somebody and it's good and there's nothing that need be said afterward (you both lie staring at the ceiling) because you both know it was good, yet you think you ought to say something, anything, if only as a means of acknowledgment because, after all, it was a shared experience and it really did happen.

But I was telling you about my walk. Let me continue. From the juniper

I headed across the ridge toward Mt. Muste. I have another secret spot there, a ledge on the Western slope, just below the summit. You can sit on this ledge high above the forest floor and dangle your feet over the treetops. The view's toward Owl's Head and the Green River Valley. It's the best spot I know of to watch a sunset or to follow the darkening path of a thunderstorm blowing in from the West.

At the point where the juniper gives way to woodland, I picked up the trace of an old wire fence, most of which was buried under the accumulated leaves of autumns past. It's so natural to bury the past; easier to bury it, in fact, than it is to carry it around with you all the time in a rucksack on your back with a change of clothes and a toothbrush. I don't mean that we should abandon the past. That's something else entirely. The trick is to just let it lie quietly under the weight of new experience. In time it'll compost and become humus. The fertile seedbed from which new life springs. How easy it becomes to begin life anew. Each moment an act of creation. Acorns falling from the sky come crashing through the leaves and hit the ground with a thud. Some will be gathered for winter feed by chipmunks and squirrels. Others will sprout new oaks and the life cycle will be repeated. Forests seem to grow despite the best efforts of humankind to destroy them.

The woods are remnants of ancient ecological civilizations. Giant ferns, cedar, and chestnut grew where maple, beech, and ash grow now. The woods are so teeming with life that you have to be careful where you walk. Have you ever watched what goes on in a square inch of dirt? Insects of all shapes, sizes, and colors, bopping along paths of microscopic roots and decaying matter. On important missions, I am sure. The survival of their species is dependent on the success of their journeys. Life is everywhere, if you know where to look. Most people are so busy going places and doing things that they never take time out to look. Many of them even forget that there is such a concept of "life" and that they themselves are alive. But we're the lucky ones. We've no place to go and not much to do. We've no goals or careers or jobs or ambitions to distract us from our pursuit of life. We see it everywhere. We know it's there.

I mean what else is one to do on a day as splendid as the one in which I took a walk and found where Barf Barf is. Should I have been working in a bank, sitting at a desk, driving a cab, arguing a suit, giving an order, or shooting a gook instead? That's nonsense. Better to be taking a walk, jawing it up with the neighbors, shingling a house, or making apple cider, as

Fritz and Luis and Luvie were indeed doing that day. I could hear them pounding the apples with mallets and baseball bats, beating them into a soft squishy mash. Then Luvie would hold a bucket to the funnel of the press. Fritz and Luis would circle her, turning the press as they walked. Cider would flow out ready to ferment in the old whiskey barrel Fritz got from a nearby farmer; enough hard cider to get us through the winter.

There were other things that could have been accomplished that day, equal in importance to the task of making hard cider. When you are working for yourselves, when the produce you produce by your labor is survival, there are an endless number of things you want to do. I, for instance, might have been out in the field picking the winter squash or digging the potatoes. But it was still a few days before the first frost. The weather was warm and there were no signs of change. They could wait a day or two as most things can. When you work for yourself it is important to do things only at the proper time.

So I took a walk. All sorts of adventures and discoveries happen when you take a walk. For instance, shortly after I lost trace of the fence that was buried in the leaves of autumns past, I came upon a knoll where the novel is buried. Fiction as a literary form is dead, as you probably know. For if everything I told you so far is true, what is left for fantasy? If our life, as I have described it, is real, then what is left for fiction? Are we characters out of some moldy, Utopian novel? Is this the news from nowhere William Morris once wrote about? Did he expect it to ever be true? I don't know, but obviously it is.

Consider my own situation: Once, when I was still in college, I had a discussion with my father about the future. He wanted me to choose a major and pursue a career. I had nothing in mind, so I made up a story. I told him I wasn't interested in a career or money; oh, maybe just enough to live on but not much more, and that I expected to spend my life doing whatever it was that appealed to me. But of course I was only kidding. No one lived that kind of life when I was going to college. No one ever even thought about it. It was nothing more than a piece of whimsy that went flashing through my mind (I had to say something) and neither of us took it seriously.

After college, I started a career. Journalism and advertising, made a bit of money, and never got to do the things I wanted. But I didn't complain, because that was what everyone else was doing those days. I rode the subway to and from work every day and wore an olive green suit always with the same tie, the only one I had. And here I am today telling you about walking in the woods, digging potatoes, and making cider, and insisting it's just a typical day. Except for a few nails and some carrot seed from last spring, my pockets are empty. I carry no money or identification, and I'll never ride the subway to work or wear an olive green suit again. In a month I'll turn thirty. If I didn't know any better, I would think that I was a character out of a children's book. Fiction, of course; you are Owl, I am Eeyore, and our home is like the House at Pooh Corners. It's all true, our fantasies have become reality. What fiction could we imagine that would be more fantastic than the life we are living. The novel is dead. Everyone knows that but the publishers. Poor old Alfred Knopf; he actually thinks that *Burnt Toast* is a novel. My God! Does he really believe that Pete made it all up, that it didn't actually happen to him just as he says it happened?

The trouble with most people is that they're always prepared to think the worst of a stranger. Tell people a story and the first thing they want to know is if it's true. They think that people have nothing better to do with their lives than go around telling lies to one another, making things up. But that's foolish. I mean, if you tell me something that you think is true, I'll certainly believe you. Why should I doubt? If something is true for you, then it is true for me. If I want it to be true, then why shouldn't it be? All I have to do is think about you, and think about what you are telling me; then merely think about what you are telling me as it pertains to you and *voilà* it is true. Would I lie to you?

Well, the knoll where the novel is buried is one of the more interesting landmarks on the way to the spot where Barf Barf is. But just past the knoll, on the slopes of Mt. Muste, is the spot where I discovered the secret of my shit-eating grin. You'll want to pass by here and explore a while. For the past three years, ever since we moved up here, I've had this shit-eating grin. Not the sheepish kind of shit-eating grin one gets when others catch him embarrassed with his pants down, but the kind of shit-eating grin one gets when, so caught, he invites them to join in. You've probably seen it on me anyway and know what I'm talking about. It stands out from time to time, plastered all over my face, especially in the wake of the usual disasters. Nothing fazes it. It won't ever go away. Friends die, wells run dry, houses burn, trees fall, loves are lost. But still the grin; smack dab in the middle of my face, a huge shining arc filling the void between my nostrils and my cheeks. It was here on the slope that I found out the secret. You see, I've escaped. We've escaped. No matter what befalls us, we'll never have to go back.

Not that it was an easy escape. For some of us, it was a pretty close call. We could have been Harvard dons, wealthy ad men, builders of bridges, business execs, wheelers and dealers of the first order. But the state trembles in our absence. Corporate decisions go unmade while we sit in the outhouse reading R. Crumb. Memos go untyped, commercials do not jingle, bills pile up on desks, quarterbacks toss silent passes to lonesome ends who are nowhere to be found. And who, having found them, would want to return for to tell. Yes, we've escaped. Maybe you heard me in the woods that day, telling it to the trees and shouting it to the wind. We've escaped!

Here now, as luck would have it, my route took a fortuitous turn. I had intended on climbing up to my ledge near the summit of Mt. Muste, but the discovery of the Secret of the Shit-eating Grin left me too exhilarated to make a slow, tedious climb uphill. Instead, I turned downward, on the run, through brambles and a grove of pine, over a small ridge, down into a bog (got mud in my boots!), and up onto some dry land. That's where I saw the rock with the two trees growing out of it, the spot where Barf Barf is. It immediately caught my attention and I stopped to examine it closely. I ran my hands along the roots and felt their strength, climbed the top of the rock and jimmied up the live birch to determine my location. Surely, I was thinking, this is another one of those wonders the woods hold in wait for us, another secret spot worth returning to. I began exploring the area for landmarks so I could find it again.

As I said, once you know its approximate location, you can't miss finding the rock. Directly to its front is a small hemlock, rising a little taller than

I BEGAN TO THINK OF BARF BARF AND TO FEEL
THAT I HAD BEEN HERE BEFORE.

the rotting forks of the dead birch. To its front, and on a direct line toward the rock, is a large maple and directly in front of that is a pile of rocks out of which a spring flows. I figured that if I followed the course of the spring water, it would lead me to a stream which, grown in size, would eventually cross the road. Then, by retracing my route, I'd always be able to find the rock with the trees growing out of it.

I followed the spring to where it became a streamlet and finally a full-fledged stream, and I thought about a name for it. I thought of all the possible names to describe the stream and then settled on the most obvious one, the expression I used to describe the rock at its source when I first happened on it. "Far Out Creek," I called it and you'll understand why when you see it.

I still, however, had no idea as to my location, as I had left my sense of direction back on the knoll where the novel was buried (knowing that no matter where I walked I could never be lost). Gradually, however, I became aware of a strange sensation slowly creeping over me. I began to think of Barf Barf and to feel that I had been here before. The landscape began to look familiar, though I could not recognize anything in particular. Then a great silence swept the air. I could see it blow through the trees till it all but engulfed me. The sound of the stillness was deafening to my ears. Yes, I had been here before. This was the spot where, last April, I had last seen Barf Barf's tracks.

Remember the morning Ed had come into our yard with a shotgun to tell us that Barf Barf had killed seventeen (or eleven, we always argued this point) deer and that if he ever caught him running deer he'd kill him? Well, Barf Barf was already running loose that morning, so I started off toward the Lohnson Pasture, hoping he'd be there, and that I could get a leash around him before Ed got him with his gun. I followed Ed down the road, past the tree and up toward the Golger Pasture. Do you know where the shortcut through the roads to the Lohnson Pasture comes out on the road opposite the foundation of the old Golger House? Ed walked right by it toward the Lohnson Pasture, but I noticed dog tracks heading into it so I set out to follow.

You know the trail I'm talking about. At first it's very wide, like the remnants of an old carriage road. Then it crosses a stream where there is a tree with a sign nailed to it saying "Water." Well, as it turns out, this is the stream I named "Far Out Creek." It comes out at the road, crossing under it, just above the T. The shortcut, of course, continues as a path through the woods, coming out on the road up by Harry's. But there is an old logging road that forks left at the water sign and heads up a hill in the direction of the stream. I followed Barf Barf's track up this hill and in a short time came to the carcass of a baby deer. It had obviously just been killed. Its flesh seemed to be quivering, its stomach was torn open and its innards lay uneaten but askew over the blood-splattered snow. It was a real young deer, Ray, with big wide eyes and a soft fawn's nose. I suddenly became very angry with Barf Barf and with us for letting him run free at this time of the year. Had I beaten Ed to him I'd have killed him myself. But the snow was very deep. I followed his tracks as far as I could, up toward the source of Far Out Creek, but couldn't get much farther. At a point which must have been very near the rock with the trees growing out of it, I gave up the chase. His tracks headed in the direction of the rock.

We never saw Barf Barf again. And now I was standing near the spot where I had last seen his tracks, close to where I had found the dead fawn, just above the sign by the water which crosses the shortcut to the Lohnson Pasture. A second powerful stillness overcame me and I felt compelled to return to the rock, which was taking shape in my mind as a landmark for where Barf Barf died. I started running toward the rock. My heart was beating wildly and my mind was in a frenzy, spiraling toward something central, a kernel of understanding that heretofore had been lost somewhere in the void. Then everything stopped and an image of Barf Barf, the great Border Collie in the sky, was before me. He was reaching down toward me, with his paws, as if to rest them on my shoulder. My God, I thought. I am seeing God and He's Barf Barf and He's right here before me.

Then I blew it. Remember, Ray, how I was describing our life, telling you how we had freed ourselves from all the burdens of the past, and that we have learned to transcend time and to work with whatever reality we choose. Well, I wish it were true (and someday it will be true) but that was all just an exaggeration. We've gotten rid of a lot of the load, the bottom of the barn is full of trunks filled with this kind of junk, but bits and pieces of the past still remain. The intellectual in us, for instance, that's still there, in me anyway. The stubborn insistence that nothing happens for its own sake, that everything must have cause and effect and a whole mess of attributes for us to define, articulate, compare, and to play the usual intellectual games with. Well, it would have been enough that I had seen God as Barf Barf, accepted what I had seen, and left it at that. But no, being an intellectual, I had to place my vision in a context to give it meaning that visions of the supreme should never much need. "Aha," I said to myself, breaking the trance. "A religious experience. I am having a religious experience." And then I thought of a file card in a library's card catalog. It read:

RELIGIOUS EXPERIENCE, VARIETIES OF
See James, William

And the experience passed me by.

Confused and ashamed as I was, I continued to head toward the special rock. There, I thought, I shall get my bearings. But in my anguish I had lost the track and was no longer sure of the direction. I seemed to have been walking in a circle, crisscrossing the path and following the water flow of other streams. I stumbled through the woods some more, hoping to see something familiar until I heard a shot. Later, I realized that people had been shooting at the nearby rifle range all day, but this was the first shot that caught my attention. I stopped in my tracks and looked all around me. Right in front, in the direction of my line of walk, was the rock with the two trees growing out of it. This is where Barf Barf is and where he was shot. I know it for sure. To get there follow the fence hidden by autumns past to the knoll where the novel is buried over the slope where I learned the Secret of the Shit-Eating Grin. You can't miss it, Ray; it's at the source of Far Out Creek.

—MARTY

·HEMORRHOIDS IN PARADISE·
TO DMC (1946-1964)

THE TWO ADVANTAGES OF SELLING OUR MAGAZINE, *The Green Mountain Post,* over, say, the *New York Times* or the Cambridge *Phoenix* are these: you get to take the entire purchase price (from 8¢ to 50¢) and spend it immediately on a Big Mac and you get to talk to people about how it feels for twelve friends to live in a communal way on a subsistence farm; otherwise known as The Life. Skeptics who doubt that the life we lead is different from that led by the friends and relatives we left behind should listen to the questions I get asked. What do we eat, do we all eat together, where do we sleep, do we all sleep together, where does the money come from, who makes the decisions, who does the work? Eating, sleeping, working, fucking; these are the basics. That's just the sort of things that anthropologists want to know about the primitive societies they study, some of which, so I was taught, may have less than a hundred members yet speak a language uniquely their own.

Look, I'm not trying to tell you that we're a different kind of people at the farm. It's true that we are developing our own dialect, of Kajamunyan, our own myths (cf. *Burnt Toast* and *Famous Long Ago*); that we eat, sleep, work, and fuck in ways a bit odd; and that such a thing as the group mind exists and is growing. But underneath it all we're no different from our American friends than they are from Eskimos. Way down deep, I mean.

Buying this book is like buying our magazine. You pay either in money or in as much curiosity as it takes to remove it from a friend's bookshelf and we eat hamburgers for a while.

You get Verandah's poetry, Pete's drawings, Marty's stories, and all the rest just like in *The GMP* and you also get to have the guy who sells them on Eighth Street and Sixth Avenue tell you what it's like to live in Vermont. I can't answer all your questions. I can't stand above the group mind and tell you about it. Since we've yet to bury any of us in our ground and since our first child is a few months from being born, I can't tell you how we bear our children or bury our dead. Of what's left over, I think I'll tell you how we dig wells.

First of all we had to decide whether or not a well to supply the barn with water should be dug, which was not easy in a situation like ours where there is neither monarchy nor democracy, but rather anarchy. Especially in view of the fact that work is not a value in and of itself. Thoreau was speaking for us communards when he said that there was no greater bungler than a man who used both his forenoon and his afternoon in the getting of his living. Sleeping to eleven, climbing Mt. Muste, riding Windy, swimming in the Beaver Pond, eating peaches, and sunbathing on the peach orchard hill, visiting Gonamute and Wellden are what The Let's Live Decent Lives Movement is all about. Weeding the garden and paying the bills come under the heading of what we have to do. Thus the question is: do we have to have the well?

Fortunately the question answers itself because at the farm anything that has to get done will get done. This principle has a corollary which adds that very little really needs to be done. On the one hand this is self-evident, for had we left any necessary thing undone we would not be here. On the other hand it is descriptive of the kind of people we are. I've been at the farm over two years and have observed in my own coming and the coming of others to stay what it is that separates the five or ten visitors who would like to stay each year from the one or two who do. Sometimes it's a question of space, of course, but assuming that it's a time when there's room for one more it's primarily one's ornamental value that is most important. This one is funny, that one is beautiful, another draws, and some just have a talent for enjoying the peach orchard hill. That's what gets you in and that's what makes you want to stay and what makes you want to work when you have to.

If it has to be done it will be done. What an admirable dictum. It prevents excessive worry about unfinished tasks (we've been trying to build a sugarhouse for three years now) and reminds us of our right to do nothing. What about the well? I could apply my slogan in its first sense and state that having done without a well for three years it could not be called necessary. Thus, why dig one? However, there was something about watching Ellen, Verandah, Pete, or Marty all last winter carrying two five-gallon buckets of water four times a day from the house to the barn fifty yards away and down an icy trail, falling as like as not, which made me vow to see to it that there was water in the barn next winter. It didn't make me vow to help carry the buckets, mind you, for I'm not a cow person. I mean, for some unclear reason (perhaps it's dislike of routine tasks, although I'm sure there are sicker motives involved), I don't feed the animals much. Others of us have similar quirks. What I am, however, is precisely the sort of person who will take on a project that has a beginning and an end (although nothing is ever finally finished and keeping the electric fence going, for instance, becomes almost a routine) and that will eliminate a problem. I am, in short, a well person. Not everyone is. But everyone thought that a well on the peach orchard hill which would supply the animals with water in the winter was a good thing to have. And one day last summer Pete, Marty, and myself picked out a good spot, with help and advice from Bob Brigham, the county water resources agent, whereupon I turned over a spadeful of sod.

There is for me as for other primitives an obvious, if little understood, connection between the small and the large, between willing and getting. In a former life I lived in a five-story walkup on the corner of Lafayette and

1. The site chosen

Grand in New York's Little Italy. I was working for world peace at the time and was discovering that it wasn't enough to want world peace to enjoy working for it. You needed a talent, a calling; you had to enjoy working for world peace.

I remember an interoffice obituary that was stuck on the bulletin board at 5 Beekman Street, which was where most pacifist groups in New York hung out. Mr. Frackert, the man whose obituary it was, had worked there for thirty or forty years and as he became older he limited his office activities to helping put together peace packets in which articles reprinted from *Win* and *Liberation* magazines would be collected and sold. Usually this would be done when the reprints began to take up too much space. He was known, and this is what bothered me, as Peace Packet Frackert. He might as well have gotten a gold watch. But, after all, if what we said was true, that the war in Vietnam was not an abberation but rather the result of the basic economic substructure of America, and if it was true, as we also said, that the willingness of one man to kill another at the order of the state was not an abberation but rather the result of that man's psychological substructure, why then peacemaking was a career with a future. So I went to work for Wall Street. I was muddled, quite obviously.

I began to think about living on a hippie farm. But how do you get from the city to the country? You can save money, find like-minded friends, and search for land. All this was too slow. I had to start immediately. I had to start growing vegetables now. Using wood from the pallets and skids which litter the warehouse district of New York, I built a box 4½ × 2½ × 1½. This was to be my farm. I put sheet metal under it to catch leaking water. The box was filled with as much dirt as it takes to fill six garbage cans two-thirds full; all of which was brought in from a friend's house in New Jersey and carried up five flights of stairs. Three 48″ Grow Lux fluorescent bulbs provided light and the whole thing was covered with chicken wire to keep the cats out. Finally all was ready and I planted onions, leeks, spinach, lettuce, radishes, and catnip. Four months later I put a sign up on the *Win* bulletin board announcing my desire to move to the country. A month after that I was invited by mail to come to the farm and see what happened. Do I think that I am now living there because I grew leeks in Little Italy? I do. Did turning over a spadeful of earth mean that there would be water in the barn? To me it did. I felt that after that it was just mopping up.

Now that the well had to be dug and now that we had our spot, we had to decide whether to dig it by hand or to rent a backhoe. It's true that funds were short but even if they had been available we should have dug it by hand (although I can assure you that subsequent wells, if needed, will be done with backhoes). It was this first one that had to be done by ourselves. We are just playing at farming, you see. That's why we dig wells by hand, hew beams from great hickory trees with an adz, make our own furniture, build stone chimneys and make our own clothing. We don't have to be efficient because we don't have to undersell anyone. It's just that when you walk in Vermont you see all these stone fences and you wonder what sort of people made them. Some of these stones are too big to lift. Then just for the hell of it and because you've got plenty of time you try it yourself. Soon you're thinking of ways to make it easier and after a while you're good at it. But it's merely play and we don't do it fourteen hours a day as did the original stone-fence builders.

Some reader who yet hopes that the thousands of hippie farmers are not lost to the earnest task of reforming or revolutionizing society may applaud such play as being conducive to the development of the problem-solving muscle. At our deaths he will say of us as Emerson did of Thoreau, that:

> "Had his genius been only contemplative, he had been
> fitted to his life, but with his energy and practical ability
> he seemed born for great enterprise and for command;
> and I so much regret the loss of his rare powers of action,
> that I cannot help counting it a fault in him that he had
> no ambition. Wanting this, instead of engineering for all
> America, he was captain of a huckleberry party. Pound-
> ing beans is good to the end of pounding empires one of
> these days; but if, at the end of years, it is still only beans!"

How little Thoreau was understood by his closest friend. How little we are understood by our fathers and teachers. We are not serious. I, one of many, intend to still be playing farmer when death comes. Perhaps my epitaph will be: "Still only beans."

What's it like to dig down fifteen feet into the ground, how do you get the rocks out, how fast does the water come in, what's the soil like down there, just how did those fucking pioneers do it? I was digging as much for the answers to those questions as for water. In view of all the above declaim-ing, I suppose the fact that Harry, the local Ashley Automatic Thermo-static Wood Burning Stove dealer, used his bulldozer to get us down the first yard or so will seem to have been cheating. I suppose it was. We also made use of the finest plans the Department of Agriculture could provide. To give you an idea of the Platonic vision of a well that we had in our heads as we dug, I offer the following diagrams:

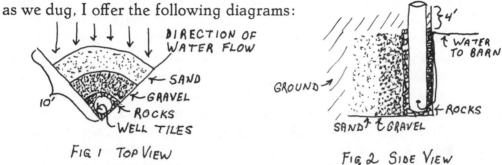

FIG. I TOP VIEW   FIG. 2 SIDE VIEW

So, at three feet down I started digging, using Mayday farm's shovel and Don's pick as I couldn't seem to locate ours; an utterly typical experience. I began at the point of the right angle and worked back, describing quarter circles from the left side of the well to the right. I threw the soil as far as I could. After a bit I decided to start saving the larger rocks against the time when I'd need rocks to put underneath and alongside of the well tiles, which are concrete cylinders. I therefore set aside an area where I threw all the rocks I saw. To keep them from scattering too far, I aimed them at a large box, open on the side facing the well, which I had made using planks and stakes. I dug down two feet, at which depth it became more difficult to throw the dirt far enough so as not to have it slide back into the pit.

Easy to fix. I pounded stakes about a foot and a half from the edge of the hole, laid planks against the stakes and threw the dirt over the planks thus pinning the planks to the stakes in the manner illustrated below:

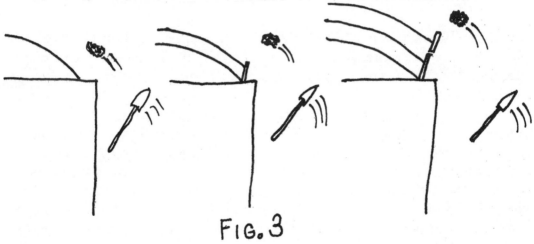

FIG. 3

This proved satisfactory for only about eighteen inches of digging. By this time the soil was very moist and the weight of the soil pressing against the planks forced the stakes to act as picks, thereby threatening to cave in the sides. For a bit, I would dig the soil from behind the planks, then descend and fill up the vacant space just created. But it was no good. Puddles had begun to form, making the dirt too sticky to throw out of a seven-foot pit. It was with mixed feelings that I told my friends that I had gone about as deep as I could alone. I was pleased that we had chosen a spot with water even in the driest season just then coming to a close. I was distressed because I didn't know how we would proceed. Then, too, I was tired.

A way had to be found to get the water out of the hole. Fortunately, I'd seen enough movies about ancient Egypt and peasant China to know what the water extractor should look like. Simple enough in theory. You merely stick a log not quite the size of a telephone pole in the ground some two feet from the edge of the pit. Thanks to Hugh there are always lots of small telephone poles lying around the farm. Then you stick a twenty-five-foot pole (marked B in diagram #4) on top of the aforementioned log (A) in such a way that the second is free to swivel both up and down (to raise the water out of the incipient well) and sideways (to carry the water to the runoff slope).

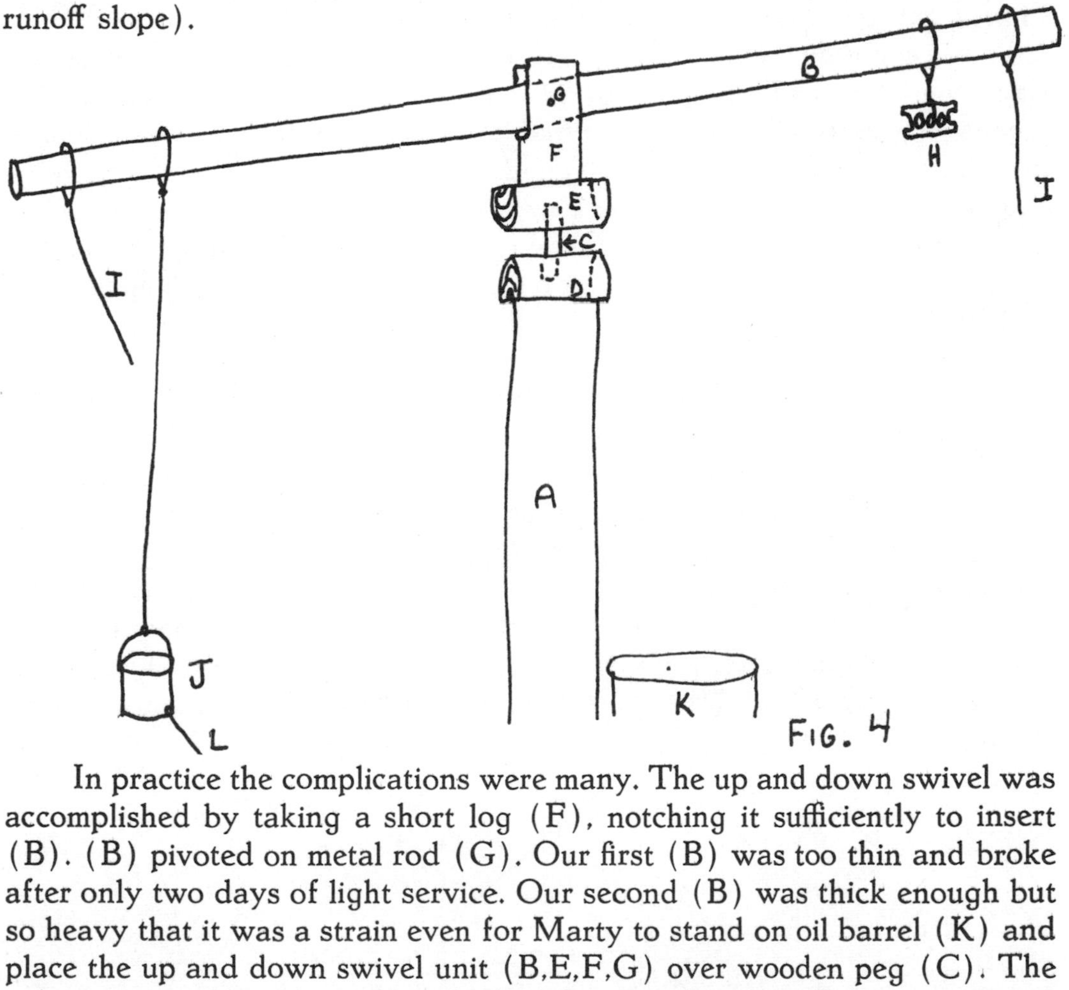

FIG. 4

In practice the complications were many. The up and down swivel was accomplished by taking a short log (F), notching it sufficiently to insert (B). (B) pivoted on metal rod (G). Our first (B) was too thin and broke after only two days of light service. Our second (B) was thick enough but so heavy that it was a strain even for Marty to stand on oil barrel (K) and place the up and down swivel unit (B,E,F,G) over wooden peg (C). The sideways swivel was accomplished by having the up and down unit turn on (C) which was inserted in a hole cut in a short log split in half (D) and nailed onto (A).

What, the technically oriented reader will ask, are the purposes served by (E) and (D)? Why not have (C) connect (A) and (F) directly? Alas, no amount of pressure would induce our peg auger to drill into the butt end of a log. Uncle Luis designed the arrangement of ropes and pulleys so that one man in the well's bottom could—by pulling first on this rope and then on that one, all the while keeping his foot on a third—empty out the water by himself. Later it was found that three people made extracting simpler.

So, there was our prototype. During the next week everything that could screw up on it did. The nails holding (E) to (F) pulled out, (E) slipped out of (C), (C) slipped out of (D), (D) pulled out of (A), (G) fell out; each time the up and down swivel unit would come crashing down. Each time we would change something and, thinking it was for the last time, struggle to put it back up until, about the seventh time I think it was, the whole accursed swivel unit fell on my head. It was then that I discovered a method whereby three men using two forked poles could easily and safely replace it. Finally, by using blosts, by replacing nails with bigger nails, and then when even the biggest nails didn't hold replacing them with metal rods, and by replacing our first (C) with a larger hornbeam, the machine was perfected.

After all that—and believe me when I say that I haven't conveyed the least part of the bother that the water extractor caused me—it was used for a total of five feet and then had to be abandoned for insufficient efficiency in dealing with the flow of water at that depth. It still stands next to the well it helped to dig; a monument to one hippie farm's recapitulation of well-digging technique from the Stone Age to the seventeenth century.

For the moment, however, we were down seven feet and having provisionally solved the water problem we had to find the solution to the problem of getting sopping wet clayey muck out of our hole. The solution is shown in diagram (5).

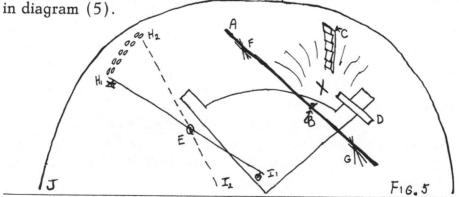

FIG. 5

What you have here is a top-view outline of the well. The soil excavator (K) consisted of a 25-foot 4" × 8" beam suspended over the hole from tripods (G) and (F) with block and tackle (B) (borrowed from a local hog farmer) hanging from its center. The area shaded red was some three feet lower than the original ground surface and X marked the spot where the bucket hauler would stand.

From seven to nine feet down the procedure was as follows: In the morning three of us would empty out the night's accumulation of water. The person in the hole would pull down on his rope and fill the bucket with water. The person at (H-1) would then haul his end of the pole down and walk to point (H-2). The third person would grab the bucket thus presented to him and dump it into a ditch heading away from the hole. When the water was out, one of us would go away and the poor devil in the hole would begin filling maple sap buckets (with holes punched in the bottom to let the water drain out) with muck and hooking them onto the block and tackle. Someone would stand at X and haul them up, climb up the stairs (C), and dump the buckets somewhere on this side of ditch (J). (J) was dug at this time to prevent the surface runoff from the September rains from filling in our half-finished well.

Up to this point we hadn't spent a cent. However, looking ahead, we knew we were going to need sand and gravel to fill in around the well tiles and that meant buying it from Brookstowne Sand and Gravel. We priced the stuff over the phone. Well stones were $3 a ton (stones approximating an inch and a half in diameter) and $1.80 a ton for gravel (everything from sand to rocks a foot across). Not too dear, we thought. However, just as I was surprised to find out how small an acre was, I was surprised to learn how small a volume of sand and gravel it took to weigh a ton. Our truck could carry three tons of the stuff and it only covered its bed about a foot. By the time we had finished, we had made six trips, spent $45, and never did get enough to satisfy me.

At nine feet my health broke down. In *Eyeless in Gaza*, Huxley has one of his characters complain that there is a profound untruthfulness in even the greatest of novels. He decries the "... almost total neglect of those small physiological events that decide whether day-to-day living shall have a pleasant or unpleasant tone. *Excretion*, [my italics] for example, with its power to make or mar the day." Of course! Without a doubt!

Constipation, in a word. Which in turn caused my latent hemorrhoid condition, a legacy of my years in college, to flare up (to erupt?). It took over my life. I would work hard one day, fail to shit the second (you don't mind me telling you this, do you?), recover on the third, and work again on the fourth. It got so that unless I had a decent shit I couldn't concentrate on anything else. My body was like a V-8 running on seven cylinders. As long as I didn't want to go above thirty mph or up hills I was all right, but when for the first time in my life I pushed the accelerator to the floor (which is what I did as I wanted nothing more than to dig from morning to night in the well), I stalled.

Well, I'm nothing if not obsessively methodical. How to become healthy for the first time in years; in decades? I asked everyone's advice; I consulted the *Encyclopedia Britannica* and *The Merck Manual*, I ate bran, apples, pears, and peaches. I ate prunes. Then I discovered Adelle Davis. (Can you ever forgive me, Joan, for driving you up the wall by compulsively repeating in my every conversation the nutrition esoterica I had read the night before?) I mean it's all true about vitamin B-6, about not cooking eggs without a cover, about rancid oils, about folic acid, about big breakfasts, about cholesterol, about the evils of refined flour and sugar. But you're sound as a nut and it's only to be expected that you didn't want to hear about it all the time. This is not to say that Joan in particular or the farm in general disapproved of my spending money for yeast, lecithin, B-vitamins, and other obscure nutrients. Everybody's entitled to his or her addiction, be it cigarettes, alcohol, or health. But for God's sake, shut up about it.

Be that as it may, I tinkered with my gastrointestinal system in the same trial and error manner previously used in working with the up and down swivel unit and with much the same results. I was back on the job, however precariously.

At ten feet it began to rain. Or, as Alan Watts has said and as the Hopis have implicitly stated for centuries, there is no "it" which rains; therefore, it would be better to say raining occurred. Raining occurred for two days and when letting up happened (ah the hell with it) there was eight feet of water in the hole. We tried emptying the water with our trusty extractor but it was beyond its depth. It could handle two hundred gallons, but we had fifteen hundred in the hole already with two gallons a minute pouring in. What was worse, parts of two sides of the well had caved in to the tune of maybe three cubic yards. We weren't to see the bucket we had left on the bottom of the hole the night before it rained for over a week. Furthermore,

2. *The plan discussed*

the ledge we stood on to haul up the buckets was so undermined that it would no longer hold us. Despair!

The rain also caused the telephone situation to go out of control. We don't believe in telephones, you see. We believe that telephones, like newspapers in which we also disbelieve, only serve to plug us into the bad news network which makes it difficult for people who use them to feel emotions other than guilt, hate, and fear. Our long-suffering neighbors, Tom and Allison Hannon, pay the price for our hypocrisy. In the course of that September, I must have made ten well-oriented calls, each time invading their privacy, spending a dime, and trying their patience. Only I could make the calls. Of the twelve people on the farm, nine were not deep enough into the project to know what information was being sought or orders being placed. The two others besides myself who were so informed were more eloquent in pleading their hatred of phoning. Then, too, I wouldn't have been happy unless I was personally getting a busy signal, or no answer, or no dial tone, or being cut off by static; each of which happened at least once. Vermont's telephone system seems to be fully as bad as midtown Manhattan's. The whole telephone ped-X reminded me of the one attempt I made to do some antiwar organizing, as distinguished from antiwar witnessing which I was good at. It was a meeting and there were three variables: time, place, and speakers. Do you get a place and then the speakers, or the speakers and then the place? I made dozens of calls and never did figure it out.

But now it was September, 1971, and I was calling Peter K. Loomis of Putney. I was telling him that due to the rain he should not deliver the four three-foot in diameter well tiles the next week as we had previously arranged. Earlier calls had been made to change the original order of five two-foot well tiles to three three-foot ones, to order a well cover, and to give him directions to our place.

For two days after the rain I told myself that three weeks of labor and a broken body were a small price to pay if two centuries hence a farmer ignorant of the history of his land should hand dig a well on our spot (it's the obvious spot) now filled in and grown over, and find our bucket ten feet under. Perhaps he would attain enlightenment.

On the third day—it really was the third day—I thought that a siphon might work. Pete had been telling me it would work for two days, but it took me that long to stop mourning my beloved water extractor. Because of our maple syrup dream we've got a lot of inch-diameter plastic tubing. Plenty to cover the two hundred feet downhill to get to a point below the bottom of the hole. Now the only problem was to get the siphon going, given only such tools that are lying around the farm. We could only think of one way (I have since been told of another) which would either work or not. Stupid as it sounds, with Pete holding the funnel in the pipe's upper end, and Ellen holding the bottom end closed with a cork, I tried to fill up the pipe by pouring the water in quart by quart. It's a sickeningly slow job to fill a pipe with a funnel, but finally we gave it a try. Standing on the ladder we used to get in and out with, I waited for Ellen to shout that she had uncorked at her end, whereupon I unstoppered my end, waited a bit and watched the flow begin. Very nice. Three hours later, there was between one hundred and two hundred gallons of water left in the well, so we reassembled and with split-second timing, which was essential to preserve the prime, we plugged both ends of the pipe, making it ready for the next day's draining. The humble extractor again proved useful in getting out the last foot of water and in periodically emptying the water accumulated while digging.

3. Bob in the hole

But how to dig when X is out of the question. Build a wooden platform an inch above X and stand on that, of course. I spent a sleepless night and the better part of the next morning trying to think of a way of supporting a platform from the floor of a hole that was being deepened. As a matter of fact there were several ways, each incredibly cumbersome, but not impossible, given the state of the art. Then it struck me! Why not suspend the platform from the beam? Eureka! I exulted. Then, a second later, I came crashing down with the thought that it had taken me quite a while to think of the obvious solution. I felt somewhat sheepish. I have since come to feel that I was too harsh on myself with my second thoughts. A result of a once automatic, still powerful self-denigration reflex. Suspend the platform; an obvious enough solution in retrospect perhaps, but can you be certain that a night and a day would not have passed before it occurred to you? After all, the discovery which prompted history's most famous "eureka" and even Gauss's prodigy were not the less obvious once seen. These occasional piddling discoveries were my greatest joy during the project. Their absence in digging future wells, since we now know how to do them, is the ultimate reason why I'd never do another by hand.

Now that we once again had a place to stand, we could begin to move the earth. At this depth it was a job. There was Brandeis University professor Dr. Luis Ellicott Ygleisas, stripped to the buff and ankle-deep in mud, filling buckets. There was Ellen, newly pregnant by Pete, taking these buckets of muck (which must have weighed twenty-five pounds) and hooking them on the block and tackle. There was Pete, celebrated author of *Burnt Toast,* hauling up the buckets and placing them in the middle of plank (D) (fig. 5). They too were naked. Every time I looked at the three of them I thought that Flash, Dale, and Dr. Zarkoff had been captured by the Clay People, who forced them to slave in the muck mines of their abysmal realm. Can Bobby save them, I wondered, or was he on another television program? Anyway, back at plank (D), there was myself, invariably fully dressed, staggering with the bucket to point (K_1). (K_2) replaced (K_1) outside the perimeter of the ditch as the mud dump after the latter was exhausted. We had achieved a three-bucket operational state and it was surely a pleasure to have everything humming.

Eleven, twelve, thirteen, fourteen feet we descended. I ordered another well tile. At fourteen feet we uncovered three large rocks. By dint of great striving we managed to remove two of them. The third one, however, turned out to be as large as our dining-room table, which sits twenty. I canceled the extra well tile. What a drag, only two more feet and I would have been content. Not true. I was so crazed by that time with the need for a really big well (maybe it could supply the main house in the summer, seeing as how it will have the sweetest water, I thought) that I never would have been satisfied so long as there was loose soil on the bottom of the well. But now even I, much to the relief of the others, had to admit that that's all there was.

Three days later, Mr. Loomis, who makes his own well tiles, showed up to put them in. I'd like to encourage all of you people thinking of digging wells in the vicinity of Putney, Vermont, to patronize Mr. Loomis. He sells his tiles for a third less than anyone else that I found. He came twenty miles with them, getting lost for an hour trying to follow my bum directions. He brought his wife because she wanted to see the fools who would dig a well by hand. He spent another hour using his truck to place the tiles, which weigh at least a thousand pounds, properly in our hole. For all this he charged us a crummy ten dollars over and above the price of the materials.

4. *The Egyptian Machine in full swing*

When he and his wife left with our check, peach preserves, and thanks, I felt that henceforward it would be downhill.

Downhill from the well to the barn. That meant filling in the hole with the sand and gravel we had stockpiled to within three feet of the surface, digging a trench three hundred and fifty feet long and four feet deep, laying the pipe and then covering the pipe, sand, and gravel with dirt. None of these things asked any questions. There were no obstacles to digging a trench that called for a deliciously simple new way of looking at things. It was just digging was all; an activity we were all thoroughly sick of. So after shoveling in the store-bought fill, we spent forty dollars and had a backhoe come in and dig a suitable trench to within fifty feet of the barn which was, owing to the terrain, as close as it could get. The pipe was placed and our friend's bulldozer filled in the trench as well as the remaining three-foot depression around the well tiles.

I hand buried pipe for the final fifty feet to the nearest corner of the barn, hitting the chicken coop as it happened. Not particularly wanting the water outlet to be in with the chickens, Pete and I ran the pipe along the chicken floor and under the chicken door to a point halfway between the coop and Bessie's stall. We stuck a faucet on the end of the pipe, put a fifty-gallon barrel sawed in half under the faucet, and stepped back. This was in the nature of a tense moment, for we were a step away from success but we had no confidence that the funnel method would be·sufficient to make the water flow. It was true that it had worked before, but now the pipe was three hundred and fifty feet long instead of two hundred feet, with the additional one hundred and fifty feet being uphill. Our nonconfidence was well-placed, for the funnel failed.

This time it was Harry's turn to stand on his head and be inspired. Instead, he said, of trying to pour water down the length of the pipe, why not push it from the bottom up? Pursuing his thought, we attached a length of hose from the would-be barn outlet to the main water system and turned on the main house's outside faucet. Pete, up at the well, gave a yell when water flowed out the pipe's upper opening. Richard then turned off the water at the house while I closed the faucet at the barn. The temporary hose was removed and the barn's faucet opened. A hiss, then a gurgle, then a dribble, then, lord almighty, an actual ten-gallon-a-minute flow. We had turned over the first shovelful of sod during the summer dry season and now there was snow on the ground, but we had our water.

I wish that I could report to you that we still had our water; that all a cow person need do is to dip his or her bucket into an ever-full barrel half. In fact, however, there is a certain reluctance to complete projects which we all share. The roofless sauna, the stone chimney just short of its projected height, the still temporary greenhouse, the barn's ninety percent paint job, the uncovered insulation in the living room, the not quite big enough wood-pile, and now the frozen water pipe are examples of our tendency to falter at a task, be it never so brilliantly conceived, boldly undertaken, and determinedly carried through, when it is one, or two, or three days from completion. Usually when you get that close whatever it is that you're working on is usable after a fashion and the Good Enough is more of an enemy of the Good than the Best.

By which I mean that when it became clear that the barrel half would freeze from time to time, causing a flood in the barn, Pete and I should have replaced it with a sink. Instead we merely bypassed the barrel and had the water run outside. Good enough, we thought. Last night it was ten below and the water stopped.

5. *Extracting a boulder*

I would have liked to have been able to end this reminiscence on a positive note, an up as it were. But then, we don't call our approach a total loss for nothing.

—BOB

·THE WELL·

WATER IS OUR WINE, our milk and eggs, our vegetable garden, and our balm. Early this spring we had six sources of water for people, animals, and plants, but one by one they dried up as the summer wore on. The Upper Well, in the woods near the southern boundary of our land, used to supply all the needs of the house until our whole family and the animals began to draw on it all the time. We alternated with the Lower Well, in the marshlands between the old tractor shed and the garden. When we weren't using it, the frogs were, until Bob built a permanent cover. Marty rigged up a shower there, where a person could douse him or herself with a couple of bucketsful of cold water poured by a friend through a sieve-bottomed pail at the top of a tripod.

For the garden and the new apple trees near the yard, we dipped buckets into a hole that Hugh Beame had dug between the lower well and the tractor shed. The hole, about four feet across and five or six feet deep, was intended as a well or fish and duck pond, but it boasted only a fine family of frogs who floated lazily on some small planks, sinking lower and lower toward mud-bottom through July and August.

Away from the house were the water sources for the animals, the orchard, and the newly planted herb garden and fruit trees on the rise at the bottom of the hill between the raspberry patch and the basketball court. Bessie and Windy would amble down to the trough in the pasture below the barn every day until the end of July, when we had to run a hose from the house to a trough in the goat pen beside the barn.

Halfway up the peach orchard hill, west of the pasture, is an old stone-lined well beneath a yellow apple tree by the blueberries. It's a long haul with two buckets from there to the orchard where the new apricot and peach trees live, but drawing water from that well gave refreshment to the carrier as well as the trees. The air underneath the apple boughs was cool and sweet in the summer, the water seemed fresher than anywhere else. At the bottom, rocked each time by the bucket's splash, lay something round and white, just beyond recognition. As the water dried up in August we found the fragile skull of a deer. Because of a quiet awe that came over a person stopping there, we called it the Magic Well.

The Magic Well is the uppermost point on our land of a series of underground springs running downhill through the raspberries to the small spring box at the bottom of the hill which channels the flow into the barrel for the large animals. Turning right, or east, from there, the springs go underground again, joining the stream along the road as it flows through a beaver pond, some raccoon fishing holes, and a shower of waterfalls, under a culvert where once there was a wooden bridge, and out into the flatlands to water Maynard Squires' magnificent cows.

Meanwhile, back at the raspberries, the sixth source gushed from a rut that Marty made getting the tractor stuck in last October's mud. The rear wheel left a depression that filled with water, right near the newly planted plum and pear trees on the rise. A bucket would fill slowly on its side there while a person could wait in the balmy air, lulled by the shadows of sumac leaves in the breeze and the faint hum of bees in the goldenrod. By August that place, too, dried up but it left behind its signal of the underground springs. When Mr. Brigham of the Conservation Service came to consult with Luis about a pond in the marshlands, Peter led him away to the rut by the raspberries where, the experts agreed, a well could be dug.

As he has described, Bob began the well himself. It was not until the project had reached major proportions, requiring more advanced technology and a larger work force, that I began my connection, my immersion if you will, in the new well. Like the proverbial frog in the bottom of the well who thought the whole world was a circle of sky growing light and dark above him, my view of the well project was conditioned by my position on the crew.

I started in the pit. While Luis shoveled globs of clay mud from the bottom and sides, I handed him empty buckets, thrown by Bob from the western rim with a shout just before the thick cold splat. I would also pull down the rope on the pulley as Peter let it out, hook on a full bucket, and yell up for him to haul away. From the wooden platform on which he and the block and tackle stood, Pete would hand Bob his mud pail, which Bob would try to catch in mid-swing and carry over to the growing mound of gray sludge in the bushes, returning in time to toss the empty down, careful to miss my cringing form, before picking up his next load.

I would like to put in a word about the equipment used. The buckets were old sap-collecting pails with improvised wire handles, battered out of shape by their new routine. If they had been any smaller they would have held next to nothing, allowing for dents and clay sticking in the bottom; if they had been any bigger they would have been too heavy to lift all day. Typical efficiency on Bob's part, I thought, and, besides, it was all we had. Apart from the water bailer, the block and tackle apparatus was the most imposing feature of the plant. The pulley itself (first borrowed from Mark Kramer to hang up our first pig at slaughter and finally returned to him for the same purpose at his place) hung from a sound beam over the pit, resting at each end on tripods of hornbeam poles lashed together. Lastly, the siphon, unimpressive in repose, indispensable in operation, was a length of black maple sugaring hose full of water at all times. Except in use, the well end stayed corked in a bucket of water, while the other end, down by the water barrel in Bessie's pasture, lay corked, covered, and clamped, screwdriver by its side in readiness for the daily emptying of the well.

An alert reader will have noticed that the siphon is the second piece of maple sugaring equipment mentioned at the well. A real maple sugaring operation has been Marty's dream ever since he first learned to identify the sugar maple and noticed that there were a lot of them on one part of our land. It's a dream we all share now, and this was to be the summer that the sugarhouse got built. Could we have read the signs in the well this September we might have seen that the well was taking energy, not just equipment, from the sugarhouse, so much so that by the end of October, after taking down an old barn for materials, everyone was too worn out to begin construction. But we had a long list of summer projects and energy to burn, and what came next didn't matter yet to those who worked in the well.

It was Bob who got us up in the morning and who blew the whistle when the sun went down. He was not exactly the foreman, and was hardly comfortable giving orders or suggestions, but he had the plans and he knew what had to be done. He was, as Mrs. Loomis on the well-tile truck saw right away, the engineer.

Peter joined the crew as a boy who had always loved digging holes and finding water, although his private dream of the well was a smaller model, hand-lined with trapezoidal flat stones, something like the Magic

Well. As it turned out, Pete's jobs were as strong-arm man on the pulley and as truck-driver, hauling a total of twenty-five tons of stone, sand, and gravel from the pits by the Connecticut River.

Luis saw the well as both a practical necessity and as an art form, recapitulating all the stages of man's struggle to channel water and earth to his needs. Nor was he unaware of the therapeutic effects to both mind and body of some hard physical labor.

I would have worked on the well solely to guarantee water in the barn all year around, but I had just learned that I was pregnant, and needed an activity to center my head and keep me in shape.

It was August when we formed the well crew, the driest part of the year and also one of the busiest. The kitchen stove burned all day as the tomato-canning, corn-freezing marathon went on, with smaller campaigns on the broccoli, cauliflower, peppers, and New Zealand spinach. There was wood to be trucked home, stacked, and split for winter. Marty was beginning to prepare the pasture for disking, liming, and winter seeding. Hugh was hauling stones from the woods for his fireplace and chimney. Whenever the need arose, especially toward the end, Marty and Richard in particular gave their help cheerfully and unsparingly.

From four feet down to ten feet down, we were pretty much the same people at the same posts for the better part of a month. From where I stood, ankle-deep in mud, swaying to avoid Luis' relentless shovel, flying buckets, and the bees calmly gathering water from the wet sides of the hole, it seemed unseasonably cool and decidedly unreal. The variations, such as lifting out huge rocks, repairing whole sides after rainstorms, and other heroic efforts are all memorable, but for me the lasting impression is a dreamy sameness. As I warned, these are only the croakings of a frog at the bottom.

Each morning after a breakfast featuring Adelle Davis Pep-up I would walk through the sunshine out to the well site, where Bob would be sitting on the lower end of a ladder stuck in the pit with a hose between his legs. When the siphoning was done, we would fill the five-gallon pail on the Egyptian bailing machine until the bottom was dry enough to show rocks, shovels, and bailing cans, and the frogs began to scurry up the sides to pools in crevices. Then I would take off my clothes and slip gingerly into the pit, where both Luis and I soon exchanged our nakedness for an uneven coating of clay.

About midmorning, with the rhythmic groaning, shouts, and splashes, we would always have the distinct feeling that we were in some undiscovered circle of Dante's hell, suspended in time, cut off from the living world. Looking up, I would see Peter, naked and muscular as a Greek statue, pulling the wet rope in hand over hand in an endless motion. He would be red-faced and sweating in the sun, while we shivered in the dank below. Then there was Bob, wearing the white hat Peter's mother brought back from Trinidad the time she went to sprinkle Pete's father's ashes on the sea. Bob also wore a T-shirt, dungarees, kneeboots, and gloves, no matter how hot it got, remarking only once that the crew seemed to be getting more and more naked. Although clothed, he was no less bizarre than the rest of us, no less muddy, trudging back and forth in the slime with his slippery, gritty pails.

Seeking an image of Normality, I could usually catch a glimpse of Bessie in the east, grazing imperturbably, Windy not far behind, on the peach orchard hill. From the orchard itself, Joan or Verandah or Richard might come with peaches for us all to eat. Visitors came, too: Fritz put in several days' work near the end in exchange for help getting a sawmill to his new home in the hollow. John Anderson came one day with the drum he made from Wilbur's skin. But no one ever came with a camera. Diana once made an attempt, but the camera broke on the spot.

It's not that we were gluttons for publicity, but only that photographs might be an image less subjective than memory of our experience. The quality Raymond had of glorifying our least achievements, of making, as Verandah says, a walk down the road a parade along the Great Wall, may have accustomed us to more applause and attention than the average construction worker, well-digger, or hydro-engineer expects. But I think it's fair to say that we each did the job for its own sake, from some personal need (Richard labeled the entire project "compulsive") or from merely being caught up in its rhythm and development. Besides, none of us had ever done anything quite like it before and we just wondered what it looked like.

On the last day, Mr. and Mrs. Loomis came with the three cylindrical well tiles on the specially equipped truck. From the hydraulic winch on the back of the truck, they lowered the concrete pieces one by one into the hole, where we had previously shoveled tons of wellstone and sandy gravel for drainage and filtering, and hung black plastic around the sides. (Bob asked not to be questioned on this last practice—it was recommended in the pamphlet he had read.) On that morning we solemnly threw all the startled frogs onto the mud and grass at the top. The bees had already swarmed away from our hive, so were not part of the well population. Swami Satchitananda, whose magazine portrait had radiated from the west wall, had slid down into the bottom along with great slabs of the well, only the day before. Marty, Bob, Peter, and Fritz worked overtime past sunset that day digging and hauling out the collapsed clay before it set overnight in rising water. It was the last great effort on the well, the last heroic act, Pete's and Marty's climbing onto and into the well tiles to straighten them as they hung from the truck notwithstanding. As the concrete cover scraped into place the saga of the well ended.

More work remained: refilling the hole, digging the trench to the barn, laying the pipe and covering it with enough dirt to prevent freezing. Bob has written of these things, as he had again a major part in all of them. What he has not written is the Triumph, the actual Achievement of a Goal: Water in the Barn. Water in the barn means an end to our treacherous water-hauling operations of previous winters. I myself used to swear quite loudly as the buckets of hot water sloshed into my boots or onto the ever icier steep path from the house down to the barn. While my behavior was more a reflection of my mental condition than of the task itself, still my nightly performances accompanied by dramatic sighs and tears even before leaving the house may have contributed to the general feeling that water in the barn by winter was a priority.

So this winter there is water in the barn, running all the time to prevent freezing. Of course, once it did freeze up, bad, so that we had to pour salt water into the pipe when we could no longer defrost it with hot cloths. That was the night that Bob had planned to finish his story of the well. It was Fritz's idea to let the salt work overnight, but when Bob went to bed (after we relieved him of all instruments with which he might harm himself) the pipe was still frozen. By morning, water ran again, Bessie and Windy drank deeply, Mama slurped daintily, and the chickens bobbed up and down at their water pan.

—ELLEN

·MAPLE SUGARING·
·OUR FINEST HOUR·

OUR FIRST GREAT AGRICULTURAL SCHEME was to produce maple syrup as a cash crop to pay our local taxes. It started the very first autumn when, with Grimm's *Guide to the Trees* in hand, I sallied forth into the wood lot and learned, after much initial confusion with the ash, to identify the sugar maple tree (*Acer saccharum*), which is the most common hardwood on our land. About the same time I read Helen and Scott Nearing's *Maple Sugar Book* and was properly inspired. Here, at last, was a moneymaking venture, a cottage industry if there ever was one, as honorable as it was honest, and decentralized to boot. The Nearings, after all, were red-blooded radicals, tried and true, who had pioneered homesteading in Vermont thirty years before. If they could make a buck from the sugar maple, why couldn't we?

So, with pencil and notebook in hand, I ventured out once more into the wood lot to survey the trees. In all, I counted six hundred good-sized maple trees, close to one another and convenient to tap. Most of them were in a sugarbush on top of our hill at the far end of a logging road. The others were alongside the road and most of those were fat. I figured we could hang about a thousand buckets in all and, in a good year, produce a couple of hundred gallons of syrup which we'd market (didn't I once work in advertising?) as "Vermont Gold." I envisioned a great cooperative effort by all the people living on the hill (they had trees, too) and we'd share the work and split the profits and have ourselves one fine time. Ray, being Ray, immediately drove off to town and had a rubber stamp made with our name and address. Total Loss Maple Producers Cooperative. We were in business.

Later that year we bought the contents of a sugarhouse in West Hawley, Massachusetts, which contained everything we would need to produce our liquid gold. Spouts, buckets, covers, gathering tanks and pails, a 3′ × 14′ arch to hold the fire, and evaporating pans to boil off the water from the sap. This was the winter of 1968. We figured to build a sugarhouse the next autumn and go into production when the sap began to run in March of 1970. For some reason, which I can't remember, we always operated on the notion that autumn was the best time to build. The harvest would be done, the wood collected, and the days cool enough for carpentry. In the autumn of '69 we dug holes for the foundation, but it rained, Marshall died, I had split, and the holes filled with snow. In the autumn of '70 with Fritz leading us on we poured cement for the concrete arch foundation, but then a cold spell hit and it started to snow. Later, we decided we had chosen the wrong site, anyway.

1971 was to be the year of the sugarhouse. It had top priority. But early in the summer we decided we needed a new well. That was fine. Everyone into sugaring was also into the animals and no one enjoyed lugging buckets of water in below-zero weather down an icy hill from the house to the barn. So we dug a well. At the time the hole was finished, our neighbor Hugh Sloan arranged for us to tear down a barn. Here was all the wood we'd need for the sugarhouse and then some. One autumn weekend everyone on our hill assembled in vehicles and drove in a long procession to the sugarhouse in Hawley to pick up the arch. This, the legendary March to the Arch, got everyone enthused about sugaring. The cooperative in action. So we trucked the arch back to the sugarhouse site, where Bob and I had already laid a cement foundation, and set it on its new home. But the barn was slow coming down, the well wasn't hooked up by pipe to the barn, a lot of cordwood still had to be hauled out of the forest, I started to winterize my house, and we all suddenly got a craving for apples and apple cider.

The arch waited on its foundation, beams and siding were piled next to the site, I fixed up my house, Hugh built a fireplace, we cut some wood, picked a lot of apples, made more than a barrel of cider, and Bob worked

GATHERING THE SAP

like the devil with Verandah and Joannie to help get the pipe from the well to the barn buried before winter. We were all plenty tired and some of us were becoming manic about work.

One day I decided to say "fuck the sugarhouse." It was my finest hour. First I told Pete; said, "Hey, Pete, the wood isn't in and it's getting on toward winter and if we want to have a really fine sugarhouse we'll never have time to do it."

Now Pete wanted a very fine sugarhouse. No hammer and nail construction for him. Each beam mortised together with hand-carved wood pegs. A sitting room on the side, a huge steam vent on top, a sturdy old-fashioned weathered board sugarhouse to recreate the very essence of Vermont. But Pete was exhausted from digging the well and from taking down the barn and from driving the truck back and forth hauling wood. Besides, he had spent the last week picking apples and making cider and had probably drunk too much.

"Let's see what Bob thinks," Pete said. Bob, after all, is nothing if he is not rational.

We found Bob shoveling dirt at the bottom of a three-foot ditch.

"Hey, Bob," we called down. "We've decided to fuck the sugarhouse and not build it."

Bob didn't believe us and climbed out of his ditch to make sure we said what he thought he heard us say.

"Suppose we forget about the sugarhouse this year, finish up the wood and whatever else we have to do, and do a really good job of it next year?"

"You feeling all right?" he asked, sensing that some major catastrophe in a vital area of our personal lives had frustrated our ambition, for what else could lead us to abandon the farm's oldest, most cherished dream?

"Never felt better," we chorused, and this was close to true, "and we've no plans to start hitching to the Coast tomorrow," I added as reassurance. "Better to take an objective view of the situation and act from a position of strength than to throw ourselves into a project we obviously can't finish and then have to admit defeat," I said, fancying myself some battle-hardened general, MacArthur perhaps, glorious in retreat.

Well, Bob was all for it. He wanted to fill in the ditch, hook up the pipe, build a garage for the truck, and do at least six other things before the snows came. Let's go tell Ellen the good news.

Ellen didn't believe us. She had never heard any common sense coming from any one of the three of us. We were obviously out of our gourds. But we explained. Blah-blah-blah this, and aw fuck it that, and on the other hand and furthermore why not just forget it and say *mañana*?

And so, as three Mexican guitar players crooned beneath the outhouse roof and Carmen Miranda clicked castanets off in the west, four liberated wetbacks, freed from the burden of the last most difficult task, went tripping across the meadow to enjoy the fading autumn light.

So we didn't get the sugarhouse built last year. Next summer, perhaps, or maybe *mañana*. In the meanwhile, Fritz and I will spend another year apprenticing with John and Rodney Clark, as we did the year before.

We'll set about fifteen hundred buckets and another five hundred taps with plastic tubing. We'll wallow through the snow—hopefully, this year it won't be up to our waists—gathering sap every day for about a month, hang out in the sugarhouse, have a few laughs, and maybe learn something more about sugaring by helping Rodney boil down the sap. Hopefully, too, we'll improve on last year's record of destroying five gathering pails under the tractor and crawler. Rod said I should put that in for the sake of factual accuracy.

Back at the farm, the gang will also be making syrup. We'll set about sixty or seventy buckets on the trees closest to the house and boil it down over a wood fire in the front yard, a slow, tedious process that produces a thick, dark liquid somewhere between Grade Y and Z. Some of us believe that the darker and thicker the syrup is the better it tastes. In this way we'll make about twenty gallons which, combined with our cut from John and Rodney, will give us enough maple syrup to stuff ourselves with pancakes for a month or two and get good and fat before starting to build that illusive sugarhouse again.

—MARTY

- Fall -

A Nervous Appraisal

ONE OF THE MORE TRAGICOMIC IRONIES OF OUR LIFE rests in the ambiance of men and women relationships, or what Verandah once called the eternal revolutions of the "male and female saga." And of course it is just this quality of our lives which provokes more curiosity and innuendo from the outside world than any other. Tell someone you live on a commune, and in the briefest possible time the conversation will turn to subtly or not so subtly formulated questions about the ratio of men and women, sleeping arrangements, love affairs, group sex or marriage, who sleeps with whom, etc. Much more interesting than the questions themselves is the shock of disbelief which registers in the eyes of the interested party, like three plums rolling into place in a one-armed bandit, when the quiet truth is out.

For the most part, intracommunal love life is as chaste as the driven snow just falling outside my western window. There's the irony. Here, in the midst of a love energy which oozes or radiates from each of us toward the others, and at some time is held supremely insular in the grip of winter, and at others caught in the febrile potency of spring borning all over the front yard—in the midst of all that—no orgiastic endeavor to stay warm, no idealized communal rolls in the spring meadows, no inspired bounding into one another's arms. For the curious and often paradoxical ways of love, it seems, have not created that here. And this failing of farm life to fulfill that need and passion, which has exiled some of us to search the city or other farms like this—some finding what they wanted and returned, others never again to return—is the sorest lack of all, and the most apt to provoke departure. For there is always, I think, for most of us, a lingering sensation of pain and disappointment or resentment brought on by the inability of the place to make our lives passionately complete. And every now and then, one of our limbs is severed, in pursuit of its other half.

The essence of the irony is, of course, not that here is a group of beautiful and loving people who, unfortunately, are not sexually attracted to one another, or that the proximity of our lives here is so close and frequent and tight that it diminishes any possible desire for each other beyond the bounds of work or domestication, but that the process of the place which has made our lives one for one so vulnerable to the others, so naked in a sense, cannot sustain the general closure of simply two of us caught up in each other. In a way it demands that we are friends facing one another in the minuet that moves this place—comrades, colleagues, dancing partners —never lovers.

The history of couples here testifies to the truth of that irony. And I've changed the imagery of group love to couples because the reasons why the halls or fields were never filled with orgying communalists is quite simple. For although moving to the farm can and does effect great spiritual and mental changes in the lives of each of us, it has not, to my knowledge, created any remarkable individual psychological alterations. The excessively educated, and (at least at some point in most of our lives) highly neurotic temperament which the farm has attracted was not, and probably never will be, ready for the stagy complications of love à la mode. Living here has certainly not made the psychology of any one of us more prone to jolt the sexual superego demands of one-to-one intimacy out of its seeming rightness and comfortableness. The desire for coupling, however, has always been as full-blown and eager as anywhere. Yet the circumstances have engendered a new set of mating and courting dances which have proved more difficult and painful than expected.

The problem briefly stated is this: How, in the midst of all the demands and, perhaps, obligations of love and attention which the farm demands can two people simply create a solitude and intimacy necessary for lovers to grow in and discover each other? How is it possible in an environment in which all business is for the most part public, inclusive of the emotional ups and downs, hesitations, frustrations, etc., of each of the persons involved, how it is possible to create and live that special secret sharing which defines lovers—that ecstatic need to find the two as one, separate, and alone, and plugged in? (For it has always seemed to me that lovers must fall out of the world and time together in a way which allows them to realize their love by realizing the distinctions between *us* and *them*, by making their space and time set off from the pragmatic movements of the crowd, etc.)

We obviously have not found the answers. And the possibilities for such relationships, in cynical moments, may be dubious at best. For every couple that has at one time or another grown or thrived here, all but one has met with either doom or exile. And the only kinds of coupling possible on the glass hill are either, two who live here who try to make it, or the kind in which the long tall stranger wanders up the road, it's love at first sight, and he or she has to move in or constantly come a-calling. Limited possibilities. And they just don't work. And that's a serious problem. One has to ask himself if he is indeed living in such a way that the love of man for woman and vice versa which stirs the cockles unrelentingly and makes a body warm and glad all over is impossible and/or untenable. That's pretty serious, and rather frightening. While we've asked ourselves this, two of us would have fled on some early rainy Saturday morning desperate for love, and unable to say good-bye. Or Jack would be moving out of Jill's room, and looking around for a new room friendly to his broken heart. Must it be that way, and why?

There was just recently the case of a young man who wandered up the hill to settle in for some time with a solitude-loving neighbor of ours. A rare occasion. And bang. The heart of one of the ladies was stolen right away. He was hesitant. Why? Because, he said, a love affair with one of the ladies here meant for him a love affair with Total Loss Farm. He wasn't ready for that kind of commitment or vulnerability. He had come to the woods of Vermont to be more or less alone, and the looming possibilities of falling into the center of attention which a love connection here was bound to promote—the family eager to know if he would care for and cherish the lovelorn daughter—frightened him. It made the possibilities of what could have been created in some other time or place less likely. We were forced to be bound together in commiseration rather than in the celebrations of love. And it had happened before.

Is there then some tidy theory which one can make about all this? It is true that Ellen and Pete, having met here and fallen in love, are still growing and loving as ever, and are in the process of bringing the newest member of the farm into our lives by way of the umbilical cord. But their abiding love for each other is hardly an overwhelming record for the success of love relations on the farm. And although they represent in a way the knowledge and recognition that two people can survive in the turmoil of love and life on the farm, one is more apt to draw foggy and cynical conclusions about the blossoming of love here than happy and promising ones.

The only answer which I can presume to give is that the energy which it takes for a dozen or so men and women to discover and embrace one another high on a hill in nowhere as yet cannot foster the milieu that is necessary for the mysterious, private process of falling in love. I wish I could be sure whether or not the sad interpretation that I've brought to all of this is a correct one. It would be perverse to have had such a perception completely unfounded. And if what I've written is true, then what are the possibilities for the melody to change, and for the marriage dances to make themselves apparent and possible?

Perhaps that will come soon when all of us have become so secure and mellowed in our knowledge and love of one another that we can finally begin to draw the energy of good loving away from ourselves and bring its strength and endurance to those others we'd love to love.

Postscript:

I am happy to report that this spring discovered the explosion of wonder-working love; my cynicism diminishes.

—RICHARD

·QUEEN TILLIE'S NEEDLE·

LONG AGO, IN THE DUST OF HISTORY, in an age when heroes thronged the teeming streets of Kajamunya, Queen Tillie ruled over her people with the wisdom and beneficence which were her regal heritage. Her beauty and gentle manners were lauded by poets and citizens alike as surpassing even the most beautiful sunrise that had ever lightened Kajamunyan skies. And, above all, the queen's talent as a spinner of fine fabrics, was on the lips of all who had seen or heard or benefited from her astounding gift. For, by some cloudy chance or circumstance, Queen Tillie had come to possess a spinning wheel which, when set to work by her hands alone, could spin golden threads from straw. No one knew where the wheel had appeared from, and it was rumored that Queen Tillie herself had never dared to ponder its origins, but had graciously accepted the gift at her coronation, and without words had begun to spin. She discovered the wheel's efficacy one morning when some stray wisps of straw which clung to the newly shorn wool she was spinning had turned to golden threads. Believing that the gold was a sign of the richness that would fill her reign, the queen sent word to all her people to bring straw to the wheel, and the golden threads filled the palace sewing rooms where Kajamunyan maidens set to work weaving garments for every man, woman, and child within the realm.

Twice yearly on the appointed day, all of Kajamunya would don their golden garments and join the queen in the great banquet hall, designed by the brilliant Borimini, to offer up celebration and prayer for their good luck. The Feasts of Luck, as they were called, were the happiest and most reverent days that ever passed in Kajamunya. Great lines of Kajamunyans danced hand and hand within and without the palace, gold gleaming in sun or candlelight. It was at the Dance of Gold where lovers found each other, and new songs were sung, and Kajamunyans reaffirmed their love for one another and the land of Kajamunya, which celebrated not the value of the gold, but its shimmering beauty.

Many years passed, which found Queen Tillie every morning from sunrise to noon spinning threads for her people. Yet one fateful morning the queen awoke from a foreboding dream in which the sun had refused to rise, and there was endless darkness. Quickly dressing, she ran to the room which housed Dorinda, the wheel, and found that the precious needle which never tired of spinning was gone. The palace was immediately roused to search, and as day broke word went through the land that the needle of Dorinda had disappeared, and all of Kajamunya climbed to the palace to join the hunt. The needle was nowhere to be found.

With the remarkable clarity for which the queen was known, Tillie summoned the knights of the realm to the court and requested that each of them set out to seek for Dorinda's needle. To the knight who found the needle she offered the opportunity to court the beautiful princess Responda, who eagerly agreed.

On the fifth of April, as it is told, in the early hours of a morning which stirred with the promises of spring, ten of Kajamunya's most gifted knights set off from the court with their queen's prayers and blessings to search near and far for the gold spinning needle. Hopes and fears of unknown adventure took root in the hearts of each of the men. And there too the beckoning image of Responda blossomed, whose beauty and grace were like that of a swan gliding silently over water.

The knights rode together one day's journey to the edge of the great forest Ubanima. Here they departed from each other, each man to forge his own path through the untamed woods. Among them was one Iachimo, a tall and handsome knight whose face and stature had beguiled many a Kajamunyan lady, but whose heart, from childhood, dwelt on the princess Responda, who having brushed against him one starry evening on the terrace of the National Library, was immediately taken by his charms. A demure and tender relationship blossomed between the two, and now Iachimo as well as Responda knew that it must be he who found the needle, and so consummate their love. Destiny must have meant their fates to entwine. For only Iachimo, whose name meant "I call" could justly suit the fair Responda, whose name meant "I answer."

I remember listening to this story told to me by my great-grandfather many years ago. It was here that he looked at me intently with the warm and clear eyes of age and wisdom and said, "Ah, you must wonder how it

came to pass that knights would ride to the forest to seek a needle that had been lost in the palace many miles and a day and night away. But you are young yet, and so distant from that magic which once dwelt in the bottom of the heart of Kajamunya, which brought our people to that very mountain, and filled their lives with constant surprise and fascination. For, in the times before you or I were born, that very magic which brought Dorinda to the coronation of Queen Tillie was always sure to bring about the strangest of events. No one ever knew what might at any time be lost or discovered on this mountain of their dreams. For the mountain itself, and you know this, was magic, and all those who came to live there were heirs to that mysterious power which allows all things to be born and to die and to be born again, which can change time and place into nothing, or make the moon stand still, and the heart gasp. And it always was that those who set out on some fanciful or ambitious quest—in search perhaps of the place where the dead go to, to look one last time upon the face of one who was loved, or perhaps to solve the mysteries of love or time or being—always traveled into the depths of the Forest Ubanima where, it was said, the powers of darkness and light sited together through the towering oaks, and made all moments one."

Embracing his comrades in farewell, Iachimo set off into the forest astride Kniebal, his dashing stallion. He rode two days, stopping only to sleep, his eyes always expectant for some clue to the whereabouts of the lost needle. On the third evening of his journey, Iachimo was awakened from a dreamy sleep by the rustle of someone approaching. Rubbing his eyes of sleep, he noticed a gloomy beam of light piercing the darkness. In a moment, an ass emerged into the clearing, followed by the indistinct shadow of a gnarled and stooping figure. The horn of a unicorn was planted directly above the nostrils of the ass, and it was from this very horn that the gloomy light was emitted. Kniebal snorted, and pranced like a frightened dancing bear. Iachimo, trembling with wonderment and fear, soon found himself face to face with the most wrinkled and soured countenance he had ever looked upon. The ancient woman reached out to caress him. Iachimo sprang back with revulsion and disdain, and in the most courtly of fashions asked the woman to identify herself.

"Hagus is my name, and you are the vagabond Iachimo who is about to become my lover."

Iachimo was forced to laugh at this awkward information, and protested that even though Hagus knew his name the remainder of her words were mistaken. The woman persisted in her attempts to fondle and caress the knight, assuring him that indeed if it were he who was to find the missing needle, they would make love there in a clearing of the Forest Ubanima.

Abruptly changing her disposition she told Iachimo this: "I will tell you of the mystery you came to undo, and of the power of the wood to make men quest and discover answers within its bounds, and of the secrets of wood and water and the needle, for it is I who have the clues, and one is yours but for your love."

And so it was, born of his desires to please Queen Tillie and to hear Responda answer, that Iachimo with hesitation and revulsion yielded to Hagus' promise, and accepted her embraces and embraced her, assured that on the morrow he would have one clue to the needle's weherabouts. In their embraces Iachimo imagined that he was lying with the most beautiful woman he had ever known and, curled around Hagus, he drifted into sleep.

As dawn broke, and the sun streaming through the trees awoke the sleeping knight, he was shocked to find Hagus sitting and smiling beside him.

"I am beautiful, am I not? And you thought me old and ugly," and her haggard laughter rang through the woods, frightening the birds into flight. "And here is your reward. Mark these words, where there is water, you are; fish and find trout." With these words the woman and the ass vanished, as if they had never appeared.

Convinced that he must have dreamed the evening's saga, Iachimo shook his head and pulled his hair as hard as he could to make sure he was awake. He realized that indeed he had not been dreaming, and the haunting beauty of the woman who had beguiled him to test the courage and endurance of his quest lingered within him, and moved him to be quickly on his way. Calling for Kniebal, who had disdainfully wandered off during the night, Iachimo found the horse nowhere within sight or hearing. He began to walk, following Kniebal's prints.

The day wore on, and Iachimo arrived at a brook where fishes leapt into air as if the sun were bait. There too was Kniebal, wistfully drinking at the bank's edge. Excited by the promise of a long, cool drink, and the possibility of a lunch of fish, Iachimo bent down to drink, but sprang back as if a hand had beckoned him to enter. For there in the clear water was reflected the image of an old and bearded man, stooping to drink. Iachimo

knew the reflection must be his, for the old man's image was of an Iachimo years in the future. Instinctively Iachimo felt his face. There was no beard and pulling a hair from his head he found it brown and unchanged. He stooped once again over the brook and once again the image there was of a bearded and aged Iachimo.

Here again my great-grandfather interrupted his tale, and gazing into my eyes, said pensively: "You see how youth must turn to age, how we wear our skins like seasons which tear away at all the time we desire to possess, like water over rocks in the brook, or the faces that we meet. You may think that Iachimo's story is a dream or a tale told to you by your old and doting great-grandfather to wile away an afternoon. But the forest of Ubanima and all its magic is where men grow old and turn to winter, their shoulders bending like the boughs of great trees laden with the weight of snow. I, too, will go there soon, and you will meet me by a brook some cloudless day, and stoop to drink, and find me there. That will be joy, and a little pain."

Too frightened to move or think, and unsure whether or not he had experienced some hazardous transformation, Iachimo lay down by a tree whose roots grew to the water's edge, and fell once again to sleep. He dreamed that he was by a mountain lake casting out for fish, when suddenly the image of himself that he had seen in the brook walked toward him and said: "You see, you *are* me, and I you, and now I will take you to the Hellespont to swim a race with me. If you reach the other shore before me, an older man, you will know more of the mystery. But, ah, remember, you swim against yourself." And there they were, in the dream, swimming toward the other shore, Iachimo always laps ahead, and behind him the echo of an old man's laughter.

On the other side, the old man spoke: "You have swum and reached the other shore, and perhaps now have learned how I am always behind you, a bit slower but never far off. Soon enough we will meet, perhaps by a stream in Ubanima, but until then, it's fish for lunch. And hurry."

Iachimo awoke, his dream clinging to him like an overcoat. He felt discouraged, for once again it seemed that hovering about him were the clues to the end of his search which had now somehow come to entail more than Queen Tillie, the needle, or Responda awaiting his return. Hungry, and recalling that twice he had been admonished to fish, he snapped a young bough from a nearby tree, sharpened one end with his knife, and began

haphazardly to spear the water with the hope of catching one of the beautiful trout he had seen leap into the sunlit air. Soon, a squirming fish was at the end of his spear, and Iachimo with pride and excitement severed the head from the body and, slicing the fish in two, found the lost needle gleaming within the fish's side. Amazed by this unexpected find, poor Iachimo dropped both the fish and needle on the bank; both rolled as if bound to each other, and returned to the brook.

Iachimo could only think of following after, and leapt in. Spying the needle below him, he dove to the bottom, grasped the needle in one hand and, surfacing, found that the current of the brook, which had seemed lazy, was pulling him rapidly downstream. As the current floated him away, he heard at his back a vague and distant laughter which seemed to mock all of his travails, and the words fading upstream: *"So you found the needle . . . needle . . . needle; we will meet again . . . again . . . again . . . you know me . . . me . . . me now; never be afraid . . . afraid . . . afraid.*

As the echo died away, Iachimo felt the current leading him toward the shore where, lifting his head for a moment, he saw Kniebal grazing peacefully on the bank. The needle held tightly in one hand, Iachimo pulled himself onto the bank and, lying in the sun to dry, fell blissfully to sleep.

Iachimo awoke as the sun was setting, ignorant of where or who he was, an old man or a young man, a dream or the flesh and bones of waking. Slowly remembering all that had passed, the needle still clutched in his fist, he mounted Kniebal and reined in a direction he thought was home. On through the night he rode, and as the moments and hours passed, the evening wind wafting against his cheeks and chilling him to his toes, all of the images and events and dreams of his journey sifted through his memory like sand in an hourglass. The woods of Ubanima seemed more haunting and disarming than ever before. He felt his whole life had passed by him there, and that some secret of destiny had beckoned to him, and offered what no man could bear to know. Iachimo rode all night, and as the sun began to yawn over the darkened woods he saw that he was riding over the very path he had made on entering Ubanima. It seemed so long ago, and tracing Kniebal's prints back to the clearing, he realized how simple and silent his journey had been.

"So there you are," my great-grandfather said to me, "a Kajamunyan story. And of course you can guess that as Iachimo approached the palace, there was Responda calling from her turret window, 'Iachimo, Iachimo.'

Iachimo looked up, holding the needle between two fingers, and with only the slightest bit of sadness in his voice called, 'Responda.' Oh, my boy, it's a rough magic."

—RICHARD

·How I Was Absorbed From· ·Afar into Farm Universe· ·And Of· ·The Irresistible· ·Nature of Human Osmosis·

Three years ago when I lived as a quiet simian minstrel right in the gurgling canyons of the California Coast, something seized me and made me manifest it on the physical plane. It turned out to be a book; so long as I worked on it, I was comfortable in the palm of the Creator; whenever I stopped, misery rained in buckets. Such a force, I knew, would get itself published and make itself known, so long as I did not entertain any notions that *I* was writing it. Sure enough, a small unadvertised edition was released in Berkeley.

Right after *Living on the Earth* came out I got my first fan letter (from Vermont—the other side of the world!):

I immediately sent them a card:

dear raymond &
sneaky pete
I love you both
fully & in
different ways—
alicia

dear raymond
I have taken
Alicia bay laurel
to bed. It had
to be.
your brother
sneaky pete.

dear alicia:
you have no idea what
a soft warm light your
book has shed upon our
winter hearts love - raymond

And how could I have known that it is true? That osmosis had already begun?

From this grew a lovely correspondence, filled in with some letters from Stevie Diamond of Gonamute and a copy of *The Green Mountain Post*. I studied the pictures, treasured the letters, wanted to touch these people and see their eyes. I became quite restless at Wheeler Ranch with the prospect of going East. The first emissary from Farm Universe came the night a pyromaniac burned down Wheeler's studio (it was early spring, when the hysteria blooms). Pale, luminous, and warmhearted, John Anderson bespoke a life of long white winters and close communal families.

Meanwhile, the book was sold to a New York publisher by the Berkeley folks. Innocent of the ways of corporate publishers, I accepted an invitatin to meet the media in New York, thinking it an easy way to get to Vermont. And surprise—Raymond had reviewed the book in the *Times*. So began my maiden voyage to the East Coast. Somehow I upended in the Chelsea Hotel, where Ray and Stevie appeared in a misery of young love, black magic, and self-imposed exile. I loved them at once, heard their stories, licked their wounds, shared their misery. The media is a nightmare funhouse mirror; I saw myself billboard size with my fat middle painted fluorescent pink.

Peter Simon drove me through the tender yellow woods up to the hill, where I collapsed in a little puddle only to find myself in yet another déjà-vu dream meeting Richard and Verandah.

The next day Peter Gould and Ellen, who are in love, walked me up to the peach orchard, where Pete gave a discourse on birds by saying nothing.

Verandah magically produced my quintessential dress. My toes caressed the soil of Vermont. Everything here is very, very old. Sometimes you have to part the spirits like curtains as you pass, they crowd about so thickly.

I brought a lot of Clear Light, pure and strong as a dose of truth, the drug that had made telepathic musicians of us at our Sunday church suppers at Wheeler Ranch. Only a few people here cared to try. Everyone was turning the soil in the garden, or maybe just afraid. Margaret and Terry looked like two centaurs in the tall grass. Richard and Verandah and I discovered the outer limits of pain. The primal scream: no more acid for this kid.

The next day I left for New York to ped-x the calendar I had been asked to do by my publisher.

Soon I will be home in California, I thought with relief. I had had plenty.

But it had only begun. I roamed the boundaries of my universe—all along the Coast from Carmel to Eureka, working intermittently on children's books and my calendar, but not particularly possessed and very disoriented. Ray and Stevie danced through San Francisco. The last months of summer and some of autumn (you can tell it's autumn in California when the poison oak turns red) I spent in an abandoned cabin overlooking a huge canyon and the blue Pacific, writing letters to Verandah, trying to touch center.

A Boston TV show asked me to come East. It was a bad reason to go; a bizarre scene at best, but all the farm folks swept me up and we left and laughed. The farm had changed much since spring. The fruits of the busy planting were already in the freezer. Joan had joined the crew; Luis and Luvie were leaving. I had lots of fun becoming Jewish again.

It's not easy for a hermit to join a family scene. I am used to spending most of the time with leaves and constellations, walking at least a quarter mile for human company. And housekeeping used to revolve around two dishes, a salad garden, and no obligations of any sort. California weather made it possible.

But the joy and whimsy of my new family more than compensates for losing the luxury of solitude. Last night while trudging through the snow to the outhouse I saw two people hugging each other in the shadow of the barn. It turned out to be Windy the pregnant horse, looking like two vaudeville tap dancers in a horse suit.

—ALICIA

·ARRIVALS AND DEPARTURES·

INEVER UNDERSTOOD WHAT LEAVINGS MEANT until that summer in Scotland with Pete and Luis and Diana in a cottage by the loch. We received a letter from the farm which let us know that Dale, one of the first of us to move and groove on the farm, was heading for California with a young man who had ambled up the road one evening, and had now ambled off with Dale, and in love.

The afternoon of that day, we had all gone to town for provisions and, inspired by the sights and smells of the small shops, I decided to cook Richard's "Famous" (an interpretive rendition of macaroni and meatballs). Pete bought the fixings for strawberry shortcake, and we headed back to the cottage high on the expectations of good food and drink. It was when we returned that we read the letter, and all of us felt pangs of pain and disappointment at Dale's departure.

I was the most vociferous in expressing myself, but was quieted with assurances that "Oh, she probably has just gone on a summer fling and will have returned by the time we do," or "You know that Dale could never really leave all of us," or "She knew her happiness was in some other place, and if we loved her we'd accept her departure joyfully," etc.

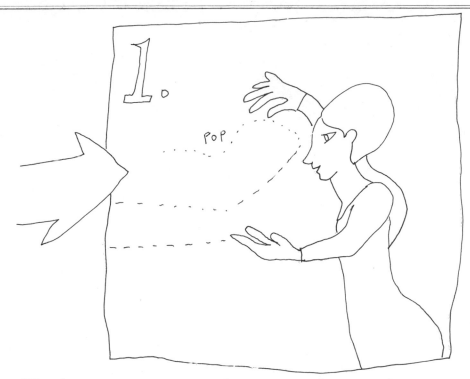

The day was moving on, and we were so happy with our prospects of Scottish Scotch, and the pie and the meatballs and ale, and perhaps a late night visit to the pub, that we quickly shelved the issue and got down to cooking dinner.

In checking over the ingredients, I suddenly realized that nowhere in the house was any form of spaghetti, noodle, elbow, wagon wheel, or fettucine to be found and that our dinner was in the throes of compromise. Luis came to the rescue by suggesting that there was still time to get to town, buy pasta, and return before darkness and hunger could inundate us all.

But what about the burn? You see, the cottage was situated on the bank of a tidal loch, and the only access by vehicle (ours was Sylvie's decrepit but faithful deux chevaux Ondine) was at low tide when the loch receded from the small inlet which separated us from the mainland. Because we had many packages that afternoon, and no plans to go anywhere without our feet, we had brought the car directly to the house at low tide. We all agreed, some of us who knew the situation better than others, rather hesitantly, that the tide was still low enough to make the crossing.

Luis and I bounded out of the house on the pasta mission, got into the car which neither of us had driven before, and although the water level had

risen higher than we expected, gamblers and pasta lovers as we were, we assured each other that we should carry on. We almost drowned Ondine. She came to a waterlogged halt in the middle of the burn, and nothing we could do would make her go. Luis went to get the others to push, while I determinedly, yea obsessively, ran to the pub/hotel to inquire after spaghetti. They had two antiquated boxes; noodles are not a favorite in Scotland, and we pushed the car with great effort and drenching to the other side of the burn. Phew.

Back at the cottage, Luis and I began to prepare dinner while sipping Scotch and adding it here and there to the sauce. The more than ample dinner was declared the best I had ever done. And between the ale and the Scotch all of us were more than ready to spend a quiet, stationary evening by the fire, ruminating, sipping, and telling stories. In my excitement and pleasure and booziness and overeating I found it hard to contain myself, as it were, and agonizingly slipped or plodded out of the house to give back what I had so excessively taken. Feeling much better, I joined the mellow vigil at the fire.

It was a talkative and animated evening, and quite later the conversation turned to Dale's letter. For some reason, I think it was the drink, I became painfully sad and bitter over Dale's leaving. "How could she do that to us?" and "How will the farm ever grow into stability if people can feel no obligation to stay and dedicate themselves to creating a permanent life

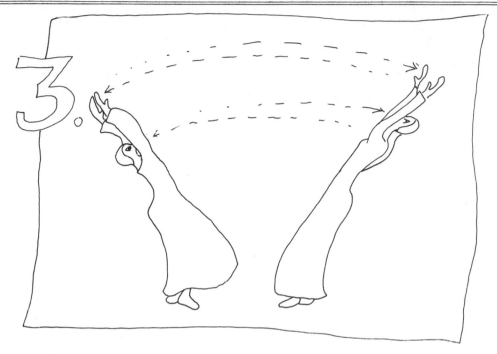

there?" The more I thought and spoke about how I felt, the more exasperated and morose I became.

Luis, because he felt I needed a lesson, provoked me; the discussion, flamed by his assignation of my position as puerile and ignorant and inexperienced, flared into outright choler. Luis told me then and there that leavings were goings, that departure was not death, and that the farm could never survive if it imprisoned people and made them feel guiltily obliged; that a home was a place where people could come to rather than always be. And though I called those sentiments callous and cruel and rationalized, because they were foreign to me, alien to my charting of other people's emotions and movements according to the schema of what I wanted and expected from them, I awoke the next morning hung over with the realization that Luis had taught me something overnight which I had always refused to acknowledge or understand.

Dale has never returned. But I came to discover that she had left here some benign ghost of herself which, although never seen, pervades all of our lives.

The lessons I learned from Dale and Luis were, I think, already known by most of us. And although there is the sorest pain when one of us leaves the farm, and it hasn't happened often, there is also the feeling or vibration

or knowledge that this place could never be home if a body couldn't leave
to discover that that indeed is what it is: a place to hang your hat or shelve
your books or plant the expectations for your return, or at least leave your
ghosts to help fill the drafty holes. There is no severance really. For, you
know, if you've watched the seasons do their dances, watched the death and
transfiguration of everything around you, you know that it all comes around
again, and in the next revolution or the next you'll be back to where you
started from: past Go. Home Free.

In point of fact, there have been very few exits from Total Loss Farm.
Ellen left first. She stayed away for over a year, came back, and fell in love.
Then Dale. Then Marty, who came back, waited around for two years, and
fell in love with a lady from across the hill.

But you might have already become curious about how people get here
in the first place, and how they come to stay or leave. Is there some point in
the career of each citizen at which they stood on the kitchen table to hear
nominations for their permanent residence, with votes to follow? Or secret
meetings, when you've stepped out for a walk on a summer's day, which
decide your fate when your back is turned? That's not quite it.

The way people get to be here, in what is considered to be a family and
a home which would be foolhardy to extend, is to arrive by suggestion or

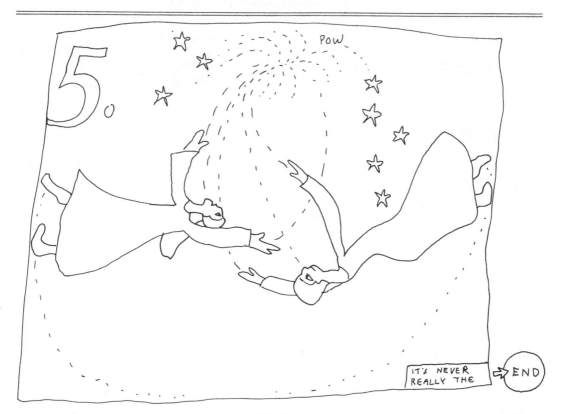

capture, circumstances or chance. If they endure, some magic within them which is reciprocal between the residents and the place, some graceful energy which has enabled all of us to share the secrets of the farm as well as the not so private transactions of day-to-day living among the teeming natives, has transpired. We call the dance we do "moving space." It is that quality of being able to lightly move through and around, what at first confronts the newcomer as turgid and threatening space, which gives the signal that this must be home, at least for a while. That signal, almost every time, is felt by the house and the new arrival, simultaneously. It happens infrequently but never with the slightest doubt or hesitation that a new place at the table must be set and room made for a new face.

But of those who have come and departed: Those other departures are the ones which occur when the magic does not happen. With as few scenes as possible they have been asked either one by one by those who wish their exit or by the group as a whole to leave, and the family, as it must, continues to grow without regret.

—RICHARD

·TUNNELING TO CALIFORNIA·
·AND BACK OR·
·PSYCHIC FARMING, PART II·

ERTAIN OF US came to the farm with some very set notions about work. We thought that work defined our existence and that people working together, sharing in the common tasks, blah blah blah, would more easily live together. Of course, having the foresight to make this initial assumption we also reserved the right to define work and to complain when it (and we were the only ones who knew what "it" meant) didn't get done.

The burden of the work fell to the few people who had some rudimentary skills or were clear in their heads about what they wanted to do. As I said, I was one of them. I fell in love with the forests, walked around with a guidebook, and soon learned to identify them all. I became skilled with the ax and chain saw, and learned to "read" the forest, to know which trees needed cutting and which trees should stand. On the other hand I didn't learn much about dealing with people, so woodcutting became my thing, just as Laurie became the carpenter and Michael worked with the cars, and the women, naturally, ended up in the kitchen.

I soon fell into a vicious cycle the creation of which was my own doing. The more I got into wood, the more time I spent doing it, leaving others to think that since I was so obviously into it I'd do whatever needed to be done. I, of course, wanted help from the others but didn't know how to ask them because asking would be coercive. So I waited for volunteers, while the others waited for me to ask their help. The more I worked alone, the more burdened I felt by responsibility; yet, also, I felt more important, as if the farm depended on my efforts. This led to more problems.

Feeling responsible about firewood affected my attitude toward other things. I was "man of the house" (probably all the males thought the same, it seems to be our accustomed way) and took it upon myself to oversee the whole farm operation and to try to do myself whatever I thought needed to be done. Whenever there was a vacuum in a work project, I rushed in to fill it. My high energy made it impossible for anyone else to assume responsibility and step into the breach. This soon drove me crazy, as it would anyone, as it did Laurie the carpenter, Ray the fund raiser, and Ellen and Connie, who thought the farm's financial burden necessitated their commuting to town to work. The farm soon became divided (at least in the eyes of the workers) between those who worked and those who lived off their work. The workers felt increasingly self-righteous and increasingly froze the others out of every possible task, convinced on that evidence that they were the only ones aware of the task and competent to do it.

It took me a trip to California to realize what was happening to me. This is one area in which I wish someone had taken me aside and told me what I was doing to myself and the farm. Probably if someone had (and Connie or Richard may have done so) I'd not have listened. Tunnel vision is a disease that usually has to run its course. I was a horse with blinders on, unable to see anything on either side, focusing always on the immediate tasks and the list that I carried inside my head entitled *"What has to be done."*

I went through the winter like that, adding gardening to woodcutting, devouring book after book on the subject, and establishing credentials as local authority. I really became involved with agriculture, and come spring, when I was first able to put my interest into practice, I realized that I wanted the farm to become a working farm. But also—and this was just as true— deep inside I felt that if I didn't do the garden nobody else would. And the cycle repeated itself. The more I did in the garden, the more I made it impossible for others to take an interest in it and the more my self-prophecy was fulfilled.

I go into this at length because it seems a common enough syndrome on every communal farm I've seen. A few high-energy people, no doubt success-oriented from childhood, monopolize all the work and then feel bitter because no one else seems to be helping. It's one of the great ironies of the farm that those of us who wanted to get away from specialized, success-oriented work identities fell right back into it, as if living on a commune farm was going to be our self-chosen career.

So I became, like Laurie the carpenter who couldn't see himself as simply one member of the family, Marty the gardener or Marty the woodsman; it was in these roles that I related to the farm. Where I once would bound out of bed anxious to get to the fields, I now found it difficult to sleep at night, counting, like sheep, each instance in which somebody didn't do something he or she should have done. I was very unhappy and thought many times of leaving, only to stay and do one last chore "for the sake of the farm."

At the end of the summer the woman with whom I was living and I split up (for mostly positive reasons) and now I had nothing to keep me at the farm. So come autumn I helped get in the winter's wood (if I didn't, who would, etc.) and then split to join a new commune that friends had started not too many miles away.

It took me six months to be able to return to the farm, as I guess I always knew I would. Most of the time was spent simply debriefing—getting all the accumulated bitterness and resentment out of my system and waiting for the farm to fall apart, as I was sure it must without my presence. It didn't, thank God for that. In fact, my leaving must have been a boon for the others, who suddenly found space for their own projects and for putting across their own private realities of what the farm should be like.

On the new commune I watched as the other people went through the same hassles we went through two years before. I thought our problems were exclusively ours and that there was an instantaneous solution to them. But there wasn't. Realizing that I couldn't go through the process of getting a commune together again, I got a drive-away car and went to visit Paul and Becky Johnson in New Mexico. I had a standing invitation to join their homesteading in the Southwest; I went there thinking I might stay. But somewhere on a backroad in Ohio farm country, near, I imagine, where Louis Bromfield rediscovered his roots at Malabar Farm, I knew I had to return to Total Loss Farm.

It was late autumn, the black soil was freshly turned or green with winter cover crops, the corn lay yellow in cribs, feed for the hogs, the land was wooded and rolling and reminded me of Vermont. Don Juan, the Yaqui man of wisdom, says that every person has one spot on earth that is his or hers and to which he or she must always return. There was no way of escaping it, my spot was Total Loss Farm. Yet, what I missed most about the farm was not the people but the land. I had said it a thousand times: it is the people and their relationships with one another that the commune is all about. But all I could think of was the land. Somehow I had missed the point.

New Mexico didn't appeal to me. It was great spending a month with the Johnsons but there were no trees. On New Year's Day, Ray, Schweid, Dale, Michael, and Dougie pulled up in a drive-away en route to San Francisco. God, it was good to see them. Ray and I spent one night talking about the farm; he, making it clear to me that I was welcome, or should I say "expected," back when I felt ready to come; me, implying that I would be back but not yet ready to make a public commitment to my friends. Then I joined their traveling road show to the Coast.

I spent about a month in the Bay area, stoned most of the time. Most days I hitchhiked about town, going wherever my drivers would take me. I felt free of any responsibilities. There was no future and I had finally transcended the past. I was no longer Marty the gardener or Marty the radical or Marty the writer. People who gave me rides never asked my name or what I did. But usually they turned me on. We either got on together or didn't, in which case I'd just hitch another ride. I discovered myself again or maybe for the first time. I realized that I had never been in a situation in which I had nothing to offer but my most naked existential self. But at heart I am an East Coastie. California living is just too easy. I felt it time to put some content into my newly created space. It was time to return home, to return to the farm, simply as *me* for better or for worse, for I had learned that this was and is what the farm is most about.

The past two years have been so good that I often fear something must be amiss in our lives; happiness isn't supposed to come this easy. There is a lot of space on the farm. The work situation is improving. We've all become aware of what needs or what we want to get done. So someone is always around to do it. Rarely does anyone feel a need to have to do something. Work is becoming like play. I'm finding more and more time to hang out, and learning to do many different things. We're not yet renaissance men or women skilled in many crafts, though that is a goal. But specialization is breaking down, and in many ways. Those of us who know the woods by its trees have come to understand its magic and those who understand best that the woods are magic know also that they are made up of maple, beech, and ash.

—MARTY

·AN ESSAY·
·IN·
·THE DEPRESSO·

ONE RELIC FROM OUR LINEAR PAST is the tendency to affix names to objects (ZsaZsa the tractor, Gladys the washer), as well as living creatures, spells of time (the Era of Ira's Accident, the Digestive Olympics, each one worthy of an epic). In these names the secrets of the tribe and its attendant myths are kept alive.

WHO'S SLEEPING IN THE IVY ROOM?

There was a small cramped room off the kitchen where no one especially wanted to live, despite the fact that it boasted a vent to the furnace and a door to shut, and the need for a place of warmth and solitude is as great in a Total Loss Household, as elsewhere. It was called the Ivy Room, for the walls were festooned with cheerless, bilious green leafy paper.

Each of us did time there before moving to more capacious lodgings. Often it was empty, a hideaway for occasional affairs of the heart. Thus, who's sleeping in the Ivy Room indicated much more than whose snoring rattled the wallboards. Someone had set up a blue fender as a headboard, and the decor took off from there.

There Elliot assembled his Bob Dylan Shrine, a homemade candle resting on a pedestal beneath a framed photograph, beside a dusty phonograph. He entertained Ray and Barf Barf on into the night, until he, Elliot, removed himself to graze among the freshman coeds in Boston, and Raymond took to globetrotting, and Barf Barf the dog, alas, gored his last deer and fell to the vengeance of the white hunters with their skimobiles and rifles.

Le Café Depresso *après midi dans*

Dale Evans bided many a lonely month in the Ivy Room with incense, Camels, and rapidograph, spinning out the world of hills and buildings of the farm, and the crosshatchings of the mind. There she tried to teach Verandah to draw a tree. Or passed the hours solving algebraic problems, in what looked like hieroglyphics.

Then Dan, her Man, came from the West and she split with him for the Coast. We blessed them both and waved our hankies as the ashram on wheels vanished from the driveway. "It's like carting off the barn. . . ."

With the knowledge that all things must pass, and that dwellers of the Ivy Room go first, Hugh swung the sledge, and it was Jericho. We started fires for weeks with wall dry lathe, and did not run across the insurance policy reputed to be hidden in the plaster, which when cashed in would have paid off the mortgage. Hugh propped up the shaky ceiling with a beam or two, and all sighed amidst the debris at the end of an era. The kitchen had doubled in size.

Everyone loves to hang out in the kitchen (even if they say they don't), especially in winter when one's sacred obligation consists merely of feeding others or being fed. The kitchen is the best place to do both, and to pass the time of day finishing novels, letters left too long unsent, or to scribble reminiscences like this.

The room lacked a name. It was, we fancied, a café. The Bonjour Tristesse? The Toujours Gezundtheit? No, the Depresso, said Jimmy. The Café Depresso, and it stuck to us as we to it. Soon a round table materialized from Marty's past, and a coat tree by Hugh's ingenuity. Then a checkers table; yellow wallpaper featuring strutting orange hens and hearts; a framed, lavishly illustrated Lord's Prayer; portraits of various madonnas and saints; a twenty-two pound black-finned tuna, sealed forever in commemorative plastic with plaque. Ellen macramed a lampshade like a wedding petticoat to spare the bleary eyes of the late-night shift.

Here Bob Payne locked wits with Stevie Diamond over nerve-wracking rounds of chess, and Hugh Beame joined hands in wrestling with Blanche Boyd of Mayday. Our cups ranneth over, we smoked and feasted, filled it with coffee chat. Here Luis read *African Genesis* to the fascination of all who joined one by one on rising and sat until noon hearing tales of how man evolved from the cave apes and the tree apes during a million years of foul weather.

Here the family dines when the numbers sink below ten in a style which might be described as Primitive Kitsch, to celebrate the decanting of Chateau Wizansky, Pete and Ellen's cider, Hugh's brews. Or Don will intone Gerard Manley Hopkins or Dylan Thomas from his vaulting chest, or Fritz recite epics from *The Spell of the Yukon*, by Robert W. Service. Here we witnessed the rise and fall of many a soufflé.

Especially in winter, six months of the year, folks from up and down the road might gather at noon to sip coffee and sample the output of the oven while waiting like vultures for the mail. And if the day offers slim pickings— *The Greenfield Ad-Viser, The World Tribune, The Lafayette Alumni News*, the *Tufts Criterion*, and so on—you can rifle through the mailbox where old letters are kept, to reread your favorites from the past three years.

Later in the day, Pete and Ellen might stretch a strudel across the table, or Alicia cut up a jaunty frock. On some freezing afternoon in January, the postman will deliver stacks of seed catalogs and all will gather at the De-presso for grandiose plans of a summer's toil and winter's feast.

—VERANDAH

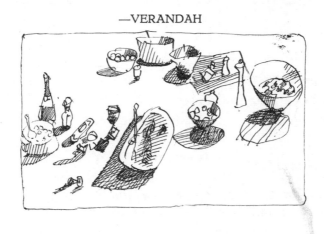

·BREAKFAST ON THE·
·SMALL FARM·

I AM USUALLY THE FIRST ONE UP for breakfast. If I am not the first one up for breakfast then Verandah is the first one up for breakfast or Pete is or Ellen is or Pete and Ellen are or Hugh is, but if Hugh is the first one up for breakfast then Pete, Ellen, Verandah, or I better not be far behind. For the first person up for breakfast in the morning—be he or she any one or two of among Pete, Verandah, Ellen, or myself—gets to feed the animals and milk the cow. Hugh neither feeds the animals nor milks the cow. He cuts kindling for the kitchen stove, brings in an armload of firewood and, if he beats Pete to it, makes hot chocolate which he calls ro-co-co. Joan also milks the cow and feeds the animals but never in the morning. She lives above the kitchen and never gets up until the people who follow the first person up for breakfast (who by this time is in the barn milking the cow) begin stomping around in the kitchen in preparation for the morning meal. However, Joannie's hacking cough is the first sound the person who is first up for breakfast hears upon entering the kitchen; and, when Joannie starts coughing, Pepper's initial appearance cannot be far behind.

Now I reside in a strategic location somewhere between the kitchen and the entrance to the barn. Verandah lives across the path but I don't know whether she appreciates my residence's strategic worth. Anyway, I've never told her (at least till now); she's never asked and probably doesn't care. But now that the cat is out of the bag, so to speak, all this has changed and the above paragraph about Verandah not knowing, not asking and/or not caring has become irrelevant to the matter at hand, which must be a great relief to all concerned. Actually, though, it's not the cats that would come out of the bag. They'd be coming out of my house, where they've recently taken up residence (or maybe it's their house where I've taken up residence) after being exiled from the main house for, rumor has it, shitting on the floor. If any animal came out of Verandah's house it would be Max, her dog. But that's her tale to tell or maybe it's his if he's talking.

The reason my house is strategically located is that I can lie in bed early in the morning and wait for Pete, Ellen, Pete and Ellen, or Verandah to come down the path carrying the milking bucket and the pig pail. Once Alicia accompanied Verandah to the barn to milk the cow and feed the animals. I knew it was her because she giggles. No one else giggles, though Verandah sometimes sings and I've been known to scat an occasional riff or two. Nevertheless, I can always hear whoever it is going down the path beside my house to feed the animals and milk the cow. Clump, clump, clump —I can hear their feet or his feet or her feet beating recklessly on the impassive earth. Whoever it is, is still asleep and sounds like a sleepwalking zombie (if you're familiar with the sound) walking the plank of an old pirate ship that has strayed into Vermont from a particularly obnoxious panel of an S. Clay Wilson comix cartoon, which is as mixed a metaphor as you'll find in this book (literary types being in charge). But, remember, I'm still in bed feigning sleep and will not be held responsible for either my metaphors (your choice—mixed or on the rocks) or for milking the cow and feeding the animals which is, to recapitulate (if you'll refer back into the text to paragraphs that may or may not now be obsolete), why my house is located in that strategic location, for I can wait in bed until I hear Pete, Verandah, Ellen, etc., walking past my house, milking bucket and pig pail in hand, toward the barn to milk the cow and feed the animals. Then, after a decent interval, I can climb out of bed, dress, and dash for the house, confident that Hugh has already gotten up, gathered kindling and stove wood, started a fire, put up some ro-co-co, and (whew!) begun BREAKFAST!

—MARTY

·VEGETABLE MATTERS·

AS WE WERE HEARING a draft of Marty's essay read aloud in the De-presso, it all came out so beautifully that I could only brush against one point. When he said—speaking of the mystic moment when he realized his connection with the farm and his love for this piece of land— that the earth wouldn't talk back, that's where I had to disagree. There was in fact a murmur of protest, and Alicia quoted, "The Tao does not speak, but it surely answers."

In the garden this summer there were those of us including Marty who quite literally spoke to the plants and the earth, and who were answered by the shiny purple eggplants, relentless tomatoes and peppers, brilliantly mottled beans, fat turnips and parsnips, sweet corn and pumpkins, nonstop broccoli and cauliflower, tender, prolific peas and snowpeas, popcorn, cucumbers, spaghetti squash, okra, celery, lettuce, spinach, chard and onions, red cabbage, green cabbage, winter cabbage and Brussels sprouts, carrots, beets, potatoes, winter squash and summer squash, fava beans, kidney beans, soy beans, green beans, black beans, and buckwheat. The vegetables flourished but I don't mean to imply it was ever a question of demand and response: it is a conversation.

Our part in the conversation was in preparing the ground, weeding out the old witchgrass roots, carrying compost, manure, and lime, rock and bone dust out to the rows, bringing water and special teas to encourage growth or discourage insects. We expressed our love of the domestic plants, as with the animals, by feeding them, and more intimately by grooming and by providing pleasant surroundings. Picking Japanese beetles off the soybeans, potato bugs off the eggplants, dusting cabbage worms at cabbage-family roots, and mashing cut worms were a few of the services we humbly performed for the vegetables. We committed murder a thousand times over (each insect leaving its slimy record on our fingers) for the loved ones. We

risked sunstroke and head staggers to see that they had shade, were coolly mulched with old hay from Maynard's barn, and protected but not crowded by tall weeds.

In turn, the garden provided us with a range of emotionally satisfying activities: righteous murder and pillage, compulsive orderliness, dreamy repetition, vigorous bending, swinging and carrying, tender thinning, companionship, and a few insights. Often in the middle of tending a row, I would look up to see before me the whole sprawling garden and the long summer. Then I'd remember that the only real order comes from the plants' ability to grow and from the weather's cycles. We did try to take part in both those factors, by good-vibing the vegetables and chanting, drumming, and dancing for rain; but those things we did because we felt them, not because we expected or demanded results. Time and again during the summer the desire to order and control yielded to the desire to nurture and to a sense of wonder at nature's abundance.

It was while we were waiting on the garden, waiting for the ground to dry out in some sections, then waiting for the vegetables to appear, that we turned to the food already growing wild. With the help of some pointers from Euell Gibbons and friends already on the bandwagon, we dined nightly on boiled milkweed with vinegar, dandelion greens, and fiddlehead ferns. Asparagus, escaped from former gardens and returned to the wilds of the peach orchard hill, we did not find until it had grown quite high, but a visiting gentle lady named Renée found a dinner's worth of tender stalks and showed us the places where they grew. Lamb's-quarters and tangy sorrel were the first greens to appear in the garden, and we ate them fresh for lunch each day from a salad bowl. Before the wild strawberries bore fruit, we picked some of their leaves, and those of wild raspberries, for making into tea in the winter. We dug up dandelion, chicory, and burdock roots, too, to bake and grind and brew into a drink some would compare to coffee. The first violets and red clover blossoms we dried and put away for soothing infusions in winter.

By the end of the summer the domestic plants regained ascendancy, except in the case of the mustard in the potato patch. Because we planted the spuds way up on the hill out of sight of the front yard, no one was particularly moved to visit them until wild mustard had made a yellow field of flowers above the limp potato vines. With mixed dismay and delight I saw that the blossoms themselves were alive with Italian bees from our new hive. I implored Marty and Joan not to weed the patch until the bees had had their fill, but the ungrateful wretches flew away from us after all; the mustard, which abounded in the garden as well, had no taste in leaves or seed; and the potato harvest was small indeed compared to previous years. Ah, the delicate balance, the many voices in that one great conversation.

In the early summer we live for the plants, though as this book attests, by winter we have shut them from our hearts and minds, locked their bodies in the deep freeze, and become preoccupied with the animal and human elements of the conversation. It's true that in the winter we live off the vegetables, but those plastic bags and glass jars, even the colorful steaming meals, are not the earth's answer to our exhortations. The active conversation is over with the summer: what's left is a record, sometimes works of art, in which dried kidney beans transmute themselves in a savory pot, in which tomatoes, peppers, and onions are born again in spaghetti sauce.

—ELLEN

·AGRICULTURE·

Certainly one of the happiest of men is the good farmer who lives close to the storm and the forest, the drought and the hail, who knows and understands well his kinfolk the beasts and the birds; whose whole life is determined by the realities, whose sense of beauty and poetry is born of the earth, whose satisfactions, whether in love or the production of a broad rich field, are direct and fundamental, vigorous, simple, profound and deeply satisfying.

—LOUIS BROMFIELD
From My Experience

WE'VE PLANTED FOUR GARDENS counting the first garden, which wasn't really a garden, just a few seeds of corn, peas, beans, and cucumbers planted in twenty-five-foot rows in front of the barn the first weekend—July 4th, 1968—that any of us spent on the farm. Peter Behr and Linda LeClair were mostly responsible for that planting. They tried to start a garden in the moine, which is the field where the garden is now, but it was too thick with weeds and brush and the sod couldn't be turned over by hand.

Our Vermont soil is still basically rich and fertile. Enough rain falls during the growing season to give plant life an irrepressible will to grow. If cleared land is not cultivated or mowed each summer it eventually returns to forests. Weeds come first, choking out the desired grasses. Then comes brush, followed by sumac and aspen which creep in from around the edges. These "weed trees" give the forest its foothold in the meadow, and permanent stands of hardwood and hemlock and pine follow close behind. When we bought the farm all of our cleared land, about twelve acres in all, was being encroached upon by forest. Our first task, in addition to breaking sod for the garden, was to beat back the forest advancing on our fields and to get our hay and pasture land back into production.

During the nineteenth century, Vermont was mostly pasture. Stone fences that crisscross each other in even the most dense forests are testimonials to the efforts of our predecessors to clear the land and mark off boundaries for the pastures where sheep and cattle grazed in abundance. The small farms, first the ones like ours, set deep in the hills, have gradually been abandoned and the woodland has taken over. This history is beginning to repeat itself in the richer valley lands below. Small farms like ours and like the half dozen working dairy farms that have gone on the auction block in our town since we moved here have no place in American agriculture.

The first garden was small, but the crops came up and that gave us cheer. By harvest time, however, Peter and Linda and many of the people who had spent the first summer on the farm had left and we were down to the dozen or so people who, with a few later additions, would come to be the family. Peter is now homesteading in British Columbia near Steve and Janet Marx, Columbia friends who also spent the first summer on the farm. Linda visited once or twice the first year and then dropped from sight. Walnut Acres still sends us its catalog addressed to her, c/o the farm.

The first autumn we bought a 1949 Ford 8N tractor (named ZsaZsa) with a front end loader that never worked and a double moldboard plow. Later, with Michael of the Lohnson Pasture, we bought an old disk harrow that Maynard delivered to the farm on his truck, saying it once belonged to Forrest Franklin and was bought at the Franklin auction by a man from Hardrain who was now selling it back to us. We also bought a used cutter bar for the tractor which enabled us to mow the fields and upgrade the hay.

Old ZsaZsa was as fickle as her namesake and gave us much grief. On her first drive home she ran Michael off the road and into a tree. The Streeters of Branderston, who sold it to us, apologized profusely and fixed the faulty steering mechanism for free, but the pattern was set. Michael and Harry rebuilt the engine one winter only to have it blow up again the next autumn. A faulty air filter probably ruined the engine both times; the inflated cost of experience comes hard even at the best of times.

We are now half-owners of a 1963 British-made Ford 2000 Diesel tractor which turns over sod like a speedboat skimming across water, leaving long evenly plowed double furrows in its wake. What a pleasure! With the 2000 we'll start turning over portions of our hay field, which at best consists of orchard grass with a smattering of clover, and reseed with a grass-legume mixture of clover or alfalfa and brome and timothy. The tractor is jointly owned with Harry, a neighbor, who shares our agricultural ambitions. Last summer, Maynard gave us two nearby hay fields to maintain and with Ralph Rhodes, another neighboring farmer, we crop the fields and split the hay. The tractor is also used to prepare the gardens at the Lohnson Pasture and Mayday Farm, neighboring communes. It's a real community asset.

Many of us would like a team of workhorses in addition to or in replacement of the tractor. At least we talk about it a lot. The tractor burns gas, shatters the silence, and gives (or used to give) grief. Horses burn hay and give manure. But hay is still in short supply and until we get our hay fields and pastures in full production (for which the tractor is a necessity) workhorses are out. Still, it would be nice to have a horse-drawn wagon to take up the logging roads across Mt. Muste to visit our friends at Mayday. Alas!

When we started, no one knew much about gardening, organic or otherwise. Our initial instinct, I believe, was to farm organically in order to keep ourselves out of the commercial economy. We didn't want to spend money on fertilizer and pesticides when we could utilize the organic wastes we produced at home. Yet, not everyone was in agreement that this was possible. Ira of Gonamute was the only one on any of the communal farms who had ever farmed before. The previous summer he cultivated a patch of corn in Virginia and this made him an expert. Ira believed, because U.S. Department of Agriculture pamphlets said so, that chemical farming was the way *real* farmers did things. But Ira didn't really believe his own arguments. He's now growing organic grains on a large communal farm in Willet, New York, which, in part, is an offshoot of the Wellden Workers communal farm near us.

The second garden, in the newly plowed and disked moine, was about an acre in size and produced fairly well, though Rosemary the goat spent a number of pleasant mornings nibbling on the broccoli and eating the onion tops. An autumn garden of root crops, planted in July, did especially well and proved that we had learned something from earlier mistakes. Yet, doing this first major garden project drained us of most of our energy and we couldn't put together an adequate root cellar for the winter. Most of the root vegetables—carrots, turnips, rutabagas, potatoes, and parsnips—froze in the barn. And an old freezer, which we had been given as a gift, failed early in the winter.

The third garden, almost double the size of the previous garden, was a resounding success. Our neighbors from Mayday Farm, who had just moved to the land, dined regularly from it as did other neighbors on our road. The potatoes, which kept in the new root cellar right into June, and the winter squash, mostly Table Queen, kept about the same length of time. The corn, two thousand row feet of it, mostly Seneca Chief and Butter and Sugar, gave us one hundred quarts to freeze and we ate it fresh off the cob almost every night from early August to October. Tomatoes caused a shortage of canning jars, green beans filled the freezer, and everyone got tired of zucchini. The failures were the carrots, which rotted in storage, and the cabbage, which didn't keep because we grew the wrong kind.

Our fourth garden was almost three acres in size. Again the corn filled our freezer and our tummies. In one row of Seneca Chief we dug in extra compost and got three full-sized ears per plant. We grew about five hundred row feet each of eggplant and pepper, despite assurances from everyone that these warm-weather plants wouldn't produce this far north, and got a fair harvest, especially from the peppers. Our tomatoes, as usual, got out of hand; we couldn't can or eat them fast enough. The broccoli came in so fast we had to stop freezing it to keep space for later crops and the right variety of cabbage, Danish Ballhead, has kept well in the root cellar all winter. The surprises were New Zealand spinach, which was so prolific it completely overran the Chinese cabbage; and the edible sugar pea, which is more prolific than the sweet pea and easier to harvest because it is eaten pod and all. We grew many kinds of beans, most with great success, including the fava, soldier, French horticultural, kidney, green pole, and bush and a variety called Caswell, which we got from Gus Dodge in Portsmouth, New Hampshire and from which we are developing seed.

The fourth garden was not a total success, but we learned something from each failure. We planted the potatoes in a poor place, waited weeks after planting for rain, fought off potato bugs with rotenone and then lost what there was of the crop to late blight. Yet, we planted a small part of the potato patch under a thick hay mulch (as suggested by Ruth Stout) and ignored it until harvest. They grew prolifically, two and three times the height of the other sickly vines, gave us no trouble with either blight or insects, and provided us with enough potatoes to last into winter. We also learned about the importance of carefully planned successive plantings when most of our lettuce headed at the same time.

We've experimented with many different kinds of mulch. When hay was not available we've used sawdust, newspaper, and black plastic. We grew a few eggplants under a clear plastic mulch which absorbed the heat and gave us our best plants. We use the thinnest plastic mulch available and buy it in thousand-foot rows from Ward's, cutting it to size at home. It seems to last three years and does well on crops that prefer warm soil. We'd mulch the entire garden with hay if we had enough; but we don't. Before spring planting we might offer to clean nearby haylofts in exchange for rotting hay.

Insect pests have never been a big problem in our garden, though now that the word is out, that the moine is back under cultivation, they seem to be on the increase. Each season we stock the garden with ladybugs and praying mantis eggs. This year we'll add green lacewings and possibly experiment with such biological controls as the microscopic Trichogramma wasp. The minor insect problems we've had are flea beetles on the eggplants, against which we've used wood ash and rotenone (an organic dust); potato bugs, controlled by rotenone; cabbage worms, which we handpick; cabbage maggot and Japanese beetles.

The Japanese beetles appear late in the season and feast on the bean foliage. They've come too late to do damage to the harvest and we've limited their number by slapping them between our hands. But they are on an area-wide increase and next year, perhaps, we'll inoculate the soil with the milky spore disease which is said to destroy the grubs. The cabbage maggots attacked the roots of our early cabbage plants last spring and we had to dig up every one and spread wood ash around the roots. It seemed to work.

From experience, we've learned what the organic people have always maintained, that healthy soil makes for healthy plants. One example is the potatoes planted under mulch which resisted both insects and disease. But we've seen in other parts of the garden how pests will attack weak, sickly looking plants and leave the vigorous specimens alone. Now I think most of our effort is going toward building up the soil. Having lots of animals, of course, is a necessity for large-scale organic gardening. The bedding for the goat goes right on the asparagus and strawberry beds as a permanent mulch. In the autumn, we collect all the manure from the hens, horse, and cow (not much, since they spend most of their time at pasture) and spread it on that portion of the garden where the earliest spring crops will grow. This year, Pete and I took the truck to the city and filled it with bags of leaves which we dumped on this same plot in a six-inch layer and then plowed and disked it and the manure under. This section of the garden is now ready to be

seeded in the spring, as soon as the ground is sufficiently warm and dry to germinate seeds.

The winter's accumulation of manure, amounting to many tons, is spread in the spring as soon as the ground is solid enough to support the tractor. Lacking a manure spreader, we have to spread it by hand, a time-consuming job. Maybe we'll come up with an old spreader for this year. We can never get too much manure, however, so in the spring we're out scouring the neighborhood for the stuff. Manure is our basic fertilizer, but in itself it is not enough. This autumn we bought eight tons of rock phosphate through a local cooperative and with Ralph Rhodes's lime spreader broadcast it on the garden and the hay fields. We also use all the wood ash we can find. In the autumn, we sow a cover crop of winter rye on the entire garden, excepting the early plot, and disk or plow it under in the spring, along with the manure.

Last year, we started to rotate a green manure crop into the garden. In spring we planted millet, which grew very thickly. In early August, when the millet had reached a lush, green stage, we disked it in and planted buckwheat in the trash. This was disked under in September and the winter rye broadcast in its place. By this time, the soil had become deeply textured, like a sponge, beautiful to handle, and teeming with life. That is how we'd like all our soil to be; full of organic matter in various stages of decay, live with earthworms and microorganisms, sweet to smell, and rich to touch. We prefer to disk our cover crops rather than to plow; though best of all would be a chisel plow that mixes up the soil more than a foot in depth instead of turning it over in a thin, compact, sandwiched layer as the moldboard does.

We've always had compost piles of different shapes and sizes, but the size of our garden is such that sheet composting might be better. Our compost piles have been framed by sumac poles or spread out in long windrows. Either way, they are difficult to turn the three or four times necessary to hasten the composting process. Residue from the garden (especially corn stalks) and kitchen wastes go into the compost in alternating layers with manure, weeds, and other green matter. This winter we're throwing the kitchen wastes right into the manure pile. I poked around in it this morning before writing this essay and even though the temperature is near zero the pile is smoking hot and the wastes are starting to break down.

I think we still have a long way to go before we bring our soil up to a high level of fertility. We need more manure and must do more cover crop-

ping. Sowing a legume into the green manure would aid in restoring nitro-
gen to the soil, and gathering many more truckloads of autumn leaves each
winter will aid the process. Still, our garden soil is better than it was when
we first turned it over three years ago, despite the three heavy vegetable
crops we've taken from it.

Most of our harvest goes into our two freezers, canning jars, and the
root cellar. A lot is given away to friends. This year we started to sell some
of our vegetables to local organic outlets in a sporadic and haphazard manner. We sold enough to meet all the expenses of the garden, which included
the rock phosphate, seed, some lime, one bag of bone meal used to give the
tomato and eggplant transplants an extra dose of phosphorous, and the
wear on the tractor. We could easily grow more vegetables if we could find
a convenient way of marketing them. One idea is to work with a city-based
food conspiracy cooperative and grow exclusively for them. We'd rather
produce for a cooperative than for a retail outlet because health food and
organic food stores are outrageously expensive.

The garden is just one interdependent part of our agriculture. Grains
are our biggest barrier to self-sufficient farming. Last year we grew less
than an acre of buckwheat for harvest. We cut it with an old-fashioned
cradle Tom Hannan had in his barn, stood it up in shocks to dry, and ended
up feeding most of it to the animals for want of a means of threshing. Grains
also demand more land than we have and are more costly to grow than hay.
Last year, we dried corn for the first time and it worked out very well. Hugh
made a needle from a spike on his anvil and we strung the ears from the
barn rafters and this freed us from the cost of buying corn meal. Our corn
bread, made from our own Seneca Chief sweet corn, is the sweetest and
tastiest we've ever had, the meal being much sweeter than that available in
stores.

I don't know if we'll ever become a self-sufficient farm. Louis Bromfield, whose books on Malabar Farm are a tremendous source of wisdom
and inspiration, suggests that self-sufficient farming involves too much
equipment and is too expensive. But he was farming on a scale that necessitated heavy equipment. We hope to make do with old secondhand implements salvaged from the junk.

Our animals and garden form the basis of our agriculture. This past
autumn we were given care of a one-hundred-tree apple orchard, which
we'll use mainly for cider. We've a peach orchard on our own land as well
as apple, pear, plum trees, and many kinds of berries. We're experimenting

with apricot and nut trees and starting a vineyard. Eventually, we'll have maple products and honey (we had one hive but the bees swarmed—we lost them). Our long-range plans include a fish pond and more livestock to increase the protein in our diet. It may take a few years, but I'm sure it'll happen.

I think we have proved that a small farm, like our own—the kind of farm that has been written off by policy makers as having no place in the system of large-scale commercial, industrial farming—has an important place in society. Not only can it sustain a dozen or so people on a diet that is nutritionally far superior than that of most Americans, regardless of affluence, but it is a good life as well. What is exhausting work for a small family of four becomes a game for a communal family of twelve. Our farm stands rooted to the earth against the surface trends of agricultural history. Absentee owners, corporate farmers, real estate speculators, agri-businessmen, and development specialists creep toward our hill grasping at the borders of our land. But they belong to a present that has already become obsolete. We've gone back to our roots, discovered the past, and inherited a future.

—MARTY

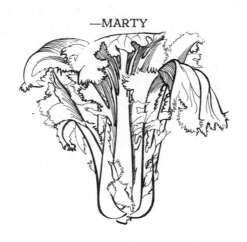

HUGH BEAME AT HIS BARROW

·THE BARROW WRIGHT·

WHEN I FIRST CAME HERE there was no wheelbarrow. There had been one. Its wooden parts having rotted away, only the iron wheel and a few struts and bolts remained to give mute testimony to the former existence of a valuable machine. Perhaps Forrest had trundled things about in it years before our arrival on the scene and gradually abandoned it as its dilapidated pieces began to tell more and more about its advancing years. To look at what remained of those pieces of white oak, I'd say that probably his father had used it for years before that.

With this vision before me I put the wheel away, seeing a resurrection. Years passed; the wheel refound under a pile of other such visions prompted me to fulfill the old dream.

My grandfather made a wheelbarrow. He made it of wood and nails. It was green on the outside and gray where the load lay. I used it doing chores for my folks, which was seldom if I could help it. I remember the creak that marked every full turn of the wheel. The sides of this barrow were fitted so that they could be removed to ease unloading or perhaps to make easier some awkward load. With this memory as model I began the reconstruction.

A frame of seasoned ash poles was pegged and lashed together. Seasoned till dry because green wood would shrink and loosen the lashings. Two stout poles formed both the handles at one end, and on the other the arms that held the wheel between them, two socket holes having been augered out to hold the axle ends. Holes were made, too, for the struts which were inserted and then lashed strongly between and separating these two poles. The struts, two in number, held the handles a comfortable distance apart. In the front, this distance was dictated by the wheel axle being about one foot. Legs too, hole and peg, are lashed on with cross-braces and many a strength-giving triangle both between them and the front of the frame. A frame to hold the upright front of the body was constructed in a like manner but in such a way as to leave a slot on either side, between the outlying strut and the slats that make the front of the barrow.

The body, ash slats riven from a log with the froe, consists of the floor and the front pieces, lashed on permanently. The sides, two slats apiece joined by short pieces of pole, fit easily into the slots in the front of the body and holes bored toward the rear that hold a short extension of one of the poles that holds the side slats together. All the lashings are protected with pitch. These poles with their lashings give the barrow a marvelous flexibility coupled with a strength that makes this barrow a marvel in the heaviest of chores. Altogether, it seems to me to have the look of an old German biplane. I was even tempted to add some iron crosses. Standing out in all weather it has already seen a cheap metal thing called by the same name go to its grave, from where I doubt if it will ever be resurrected. So far, it's needed no repairs. And if any troubles do develop, why it will be like helping an injured comrade.

—HUGH

·COPING WITH CANNING·

I WAS KIDNAPPED from a sunny Gonamute porch step one day when the summer was young by Verandah, who had come for help in the removal of three recalcitrant porcupine quills from Max's elegant nose. She brought me to the farm, I was caught by the magic, and have stayed ever since. When I came it was the time of gathering wild things, berries and pea pods, the first food of the garden. On my first afternoon Verandah, Pepper, and I climbed up the peach orchard hill to pick wild strawberries, which many of us prefer to the more florid cultivated variety. On the way up I received the ritual instruction not to look back till I reached the top, and I was indeed rewarded with an astounding view of hills, greenly wooded in the foreground, blue in the distance. The next day we were peasants of the Golden Age, or maybe Kajamunya, moving slow across a field, broad-casting buckwheat, the ladies holding the grain in their skirts.

I marveled at the proportions of the garden, but little expected the extent of its bounty—in some ways we spent the late months of the summer as slaves to its abundance. I remember waging wars of attrition against tomato plants which never seemed to give up but clamored to be canned every time you approached them. And I hated canning. Standing in front of a wood-burning stove, steam rising in my face, getting my fingers burned on the hottest of days when all I could bear to wear was an apron. But the days were long and there was always time to walk down the dappled road to the beaver pond or to lie in a hammock and watch the sun cross the sky and the pollen hang heavy on the goldenrod.

And now in winter there is sense to all of that. I was amazed at the activity because I had been accustomed to thinking of summer as a time of sitting in the sun doing nothing; but no, winter is the celebration of the year, when all you need to do is be and eat the harvest and keep warm.

Some ways to make canning easier:

Tomatoes: When you are using plum or other small tomatoes, instead of peeling each one and canning it whole, you can just heat the tomatoes in

a pan and mash them down. You don't need to add any water, but have to stir a whole lot until it's all mushy. This can be canned when the tomato pulp, juice, and skins are well-integrated, or you can heat it down until it makes a paste (and maybe this will be so thick you can freeze it instead). These tomatoes can be used in vegetable stews or soup.

Eggplants: Eggplant requires a horrifically long processing time if canned alone, but if it's mixed with an acid vegetable like tomatoes this can be reduced to a regular ten minutes. Verandah and I made a crude ratatouille by cooking chopped up eggplant, zucchini, pepper, tomato, and onion in butter and garlic, and then freezing it. This can be made up later into a winter ratatat, adding more tomatoes and onion, and maybe cabbage or lentils or whatever is around to make it more interesting.

Fruit sauce: None of us were particularly eager to preserve with sugar this year. Instead we made fruit sauce of the less than perfect peaches and pears. These we cut but didn't peel and then simmered for a short time either alone, which is nice, or with honey, apples, nuts, raisins, etc. It is canned like applesauce, for ten minutes. The sauce makes a splendid breakfast with wheat germ, Familia and yogurt, and maybe maple syrup, which is the sweetness of winter.

—JOAN

·DYEING·
·IS AN ART LIKE ANY OTHER·

THESE DAYS you have to take your epiphanies where you can find them, and if that means goldenrods, rotten peach leaves, or butternut hulls, so be it. The best part is the tangible souvenirs, in the form of incredibly soft, delicate, and organic colors, which remain from that walk through a field of flowers or the late summer woods. The following is a brief how-to-do aimed at sharing a little of my own delight in nature, and from nature through the exploration of an ancient craft, that of dyeing with natural dyes.

The following recipes are all for wool. Linen, cotton, and silk are more complicated when it comes to dyeing, and I have no experience with these fabrics. Also, the dyes I've used have been for the wool I've spun myself, heavy and coarse, largely to be woven into rugs. The end result of such thick, bumpy yarn in soft organic colors is a pebbled, earth texture which feels good to the feet.

Wool, like any material, must first be mordanted before the dye will adhere properly and forevermore. Clean, damp wool which has been washed in a mild soap is placed in a warm solution of four gallons of water in which three ounces of alum and one ounce of cream of tartar have been dissolved. The temperature of the solution is then gradually raised and the wool simmered at around 200° for an hour, after which, without further rinsing, it may be dyed. Those who are really into the subtleties of natural dyes may use other mordants, such as iron sulphate, which will affect as well as fix the dyes, although alum is the most common and accessible mordant.

The general procedure in preparing a natural dye demands that an often large quantity of vegetable matter (such as half a bushel) be chopped or mashed up, soaked overnight in water, and finally boiled to produce a dye liquid which can then be strained. The damp mordanted wool is then placed in this liquid and boiled until the desired color is reached. Such colors could only come from the earth, for they are soft, muted, and whisper and sigh rather than buzz. Cochineal and indigo, dyes endemic to the Orient and therefore store-bought imports, are the only natural dyes I know of, outside of the purple obtained from certain Mediterranean shellfish, which will give a truly bright color.

Shades of yellow and orange are among the easiest colors to obtain from the dye plants of North America. Goldenrod, which literally covers the fields in late summer, will produce several rich shades of yellow when mordanted with alum, and a more orange shade when mordanted with potassium dichromate. The paperlike outer skins of brown onions will produce deep copper tones when a sufficient quantity is boiled, and yellow shades from smaller amounts of skins. Also, peach leaves will produce a remarkably unique shade of brilliant, clear, light yellow, depending upon one's dedication to the production of natural dyes: a bushel or so of peach leaves is shredded into a large pot, water covering the leaves, and a lid is placed upon the pot. The entire mixture is allowed to stand for about five days in a warm spot until the leaves are something of a foul and fetid mess.

To make things worse, the pot is then boiled for about an hour, and the resulting liquid strained for the dye bath. The color, however, is out of sight.

It is nearly impossible to obtain clear, deep shades of either blue or green from the plants of North America. Blueberries and elderberries are about the best bet, although wild grapes also will provide shades of gray-blues. (Rosemary, our lately beloved and departed goat, did manage to dye herself a brilliant purple after eating the makings for wild grape delight.) I've found, however, that colors obtained from berries fade rather quickly if exposed to too much sunlight. By way of experimentation I've obtained something like a grayish forest-green color by allowing the juice of elder-berries to ferment in an open glass container left in a cool dark place. The juice turned from purple to dark gray, which then dyed green on alum-mordanted wool. This same dye used on chrome-mordanted wool produced a deep, rich earth brown (chrome-mordant being essentially orange, orange and green mixed produce brown).

A remarkably delicate salmon-pinkish-orange may be obtained from the common yellow and red late spring flowers known as the Indian paint-brush. A strong dye color requires about two large brown shopping bags full of these flowers, which should then be crushed and left overnight in enough water to cover them, before boiling. Following the same general procedures, a yellow or buff can be obtained from marigolds; gray-green from one-half pound of bayberry leaves; tan from still green butternut hulls; and red from the fresh roots (eight ounces) of the bloodroot flowering plant, or from the spokelike roots of the lady's bedstraw plant.

Well, that's just for starters. There's an almost endless variety of shades that can be obtained, depending upon how interested one is in that great spectrum in the sky.

—CONNIE

·HATS MADE OF BOREDOM·

A CROCHET HOOK MAY BE USED AS A TOOTHPICK, or in lieu of a chopstick to bind up a head of hair. When time looms long and finds one empty-handed, it is often a relief to let down the hair and take up the hook. An afternoon of going around in circles will create a hat. Time gives way to matter. It is no effort and requires little patience to delight family and friends with jaunty or bizarre berets or sombreros.

My mother taught me to crochet when I was quite young. I fashioned a hat with a hole in back for the scrawny pony tail which hung down to my waist. By the time the hat was completed, I had bobbed off my hair. Last winter, after remastering the chain stitch and the single and double crochet, I set about making hats for the entire household, the final counting coming to near twenty. Each one was the last. Most were inspired by the beret, and executed in whatever hues of yarn were available, in whatever combinations they inspired. It was hard to believe that a garment fashioned from much madness would please the eye and warm the mind.

One year later, the hats have traveled to the far corners of the globe atop the heads of many loved ones. Schweid's was used as a centerpiece for the Christmas table on an island off Spain. Cousin Ken's was traded with a small boy in Sao Paulo, Brazil, where the weather never sinks below boiling. Raymond keeps his in his suitcase in Vancouver, where he waits for the slow boat to China, and maybe Michael has his in Oregon. Jimmy says he wears his in Maine where the winters are much harder than they are here. Maybe Connie hangs hers on a cactus plant down in Arizona. Some went to Gonamute, and others were lost amidst the squashes and flotsam from spring cleaning up in the living room loft.

No one wears them this year. They were a fad, a flash in the pan, the school colors, or freshman beanies from the winter of '70 to '71. Hugh says it never gets cold enough to need his. Joan has promised to get married in hers. Ellen says hers looks better on Luis. Marty prefers an Indian headband. Bobby confessed that his gave him a rash. Pete washed his and it shrank, so we'll save it for the baby. Besides, he borrows the lavender night

taking a constitutional:
three ladies
in hats
made of boredom,
djellavas,
& tractors
(felts & rubbers
from Sam's
army-navy store)
hit the sno-mobile
trails through the hills

cap I made for Alicia. Fritz assures me someone nice must be sporting his, which, I recollect, was one of the largest. It could have served as a toilet seat cover, had we a toilet.

For one day, it was my crowning glory, so to speak, when all present donned their hats and we drove into Brookstowne to take in a movie. What a rakish bunch, I thought.

Sometimes I picture the world flat-faced as a pizza pan and slippery, on which all of our loved ones, among everyone else's loved ones, careen around on the ice, arms outstretched, as if it were the outhouse path, trying not to lose their grip, their centers, their balance. I know where my loved ones are. I can pick them out at a glance, for their bright and woolly heads.

To make a hat, knot together two ends of yarn and take three chain stitches. Then go back to the first stitch and make six or eight single crochets in the hole to form a circle. Continue around and around, increasing as much as you have to in order to make the crown lie flat. This might mean two stitches in each hole. When you tire of this, begin double crochets, increasing accordingly, or change the yarn you use, until it's large enough to cover the skull of the one to be fit. Then begin to decrease the hat in size by taking one stitch in two holes at intervals, evenly spaced around the circle. Finish by a row or two of single stitches which will keep the hat tight on the head in the face of gale winds. And there you have it.

The same principle can be used for concocting all sorts of accessories, pot holders, pocketbooks, pouches, lap rugs. One needn't be a shut-in or an invalid to while away a fortnight or a year.

This year, however, the hot head has been replaced by the warm heart. Three hot-water bottles hang on the wall of the Depresso ready for use. They are filled before bedtime with boiling water and wrapped in towels, sometimes held on the lap in rockers for hours, in which event they often grow disagreeably tepid and must be refilled.

Last winter, when I laid aside my hook, Marty and I took to sawing down trees above the peach orchard, in an effort to push the forest back to the rock wall. I wrote thirty pages of a novel. Ray Mungo moved his headquarters to New York. We dug up parsnips as the snows receded and spring, so long in coming, was upon us.

—VERANDAH

·RITUALS·

WE NEVER consciously initiated ceremonies and rituals on the farm. They just happened, and still do. In moments of serious retrospection I often find myself hunting down the reasons and sources of ritual behavior with an eye to discovering how it came to be that the whole world at various times and seasons ceases in the midst of whatever they are about, and celebrates a moment or an event or person with prayer or play. I have no conclusions to offer as yet, other than the guess that there is a passion in all of us to come together with one another, and reaffirm our love, and to move space in such a way that there is room in the crowded hours of our lives to forget time and circumstance, and dance in celebration of the moment.

Our first realization that ritual was a part of farm life centered around food, and with my cloudy understanding of ages past I knew that there, too, it was the planting and harvesting of food which ignited spirits. Even in the first lean winter of living here the hours of dusk set in motion some crazy energy in the kitchen which caught up the whole house in the animated preparation of food. And when the turmoil died away, the steaming results beckoned all of us to sit down together at the dinner table to eat and discover one another.

It was in the midst of scraping knives and forks and jawing music that we revealed to one another our histories, ambitions, and dreams. We found out then we were all, every last one of us, crazy for food. I guess it was then, too, that we realized how important it was that this place become a farm so that we could be close to what we ate, and have what we wanted always at hand. If we were unduly poor and loved eggplant it was obvious we would grow eggplant and freeze eggplant and eat eggplant out of season.

The garden beckoned, and in the spring, after the frequently bizarre experience of being cloistered in the grips of our first Vermont winter, we came together to plant our desires and appetites for food. Discovering then how tightly our lives would be placed in the fickle palms of the elements, we began to sing and dance and pray that the sun would shine, and the rain fall. We found our enthusiasm and spirit for the dance and the chant, and it was not long before the whole house, even after the garden had been harvested and canned and frozen, often shook with the pulse of drums and

dancing feet. It is a tradition here to dance as often as possible, and every-one who lives here, even the most awkward and self-conscious, has learned how the body is eager to relax, and wants to move to the rhythm of a drum.

On the first of May, and if we are lucky the spring will show its petti-coats, and in the early autumn when the moon turns to gold and the harvest is in, we open our hearts and bounty to ourselves and friends and family to celebrate the luck and satisfaction of food. And when our wine is un-corked, or there is a birthday or a first of anything to celebrate, or a new animal has arrived, or an old one has been slaughtered, or because the joy of being together moves us, we open the larders and crowd the tables with food and drink, and dance and sing and pray, often till the sun rises over the barn.

One of the more merry celebrations of the past has evolved into tra-dition. On a freezing winter's day, Connie came home from her studies dragged by the promise of an evening's devotion to studious occupation. She decided to declare "Syrian Night," and went to work in the kitchen preparing choomis and flatbreads, etc. Pete, I think it was, knew that the heavy operation in the kitchen would need suitable and joyous music. Searching through the endless piles of a communal record collection, he discovered a lost record which Laurie, who had studied anthropology at college, had purchased many years before in an attempt to understand the spirit of the East. The record cover, printed with a gaudy painting of some new-age harem dancers, featured the title "The Magic Carpet." Pete cour-ageously put the record on, and lo, the mysterious music of the East wafted through the house, beckoning everyone's attention.

Unable to resist, Connie, glad to sneak away from the heat of the Home Comfort, began to dance Salome's seven veils around the kitchen, and the whole house was immediately primed for celebration. The Retsina was uncorked, and everyone moved to the living room dance floor; the fes-tivities, even before dinner, had outrageously begun. It was then that we discovered "Ali Baba," the one song which drew the entire house to tears and laughter and furious dancing. We played the song over and over, and when dinner was set on the table, and we sat sweatily down to eat, toasts to "Ali Baba" and ourselves were raucously shouted.

The spirit of that evening endures and, every now and then, the "Ali Baba" music, mysteriously put on the record player to break tension or create spirit, sends us all into fits of dancing and reminiscence. That Christmas, Raymond, caught up in the spirit of the dance, sat in the Green Room all Christmas Eve sewing djellabas so we could dress for the occasion.

—RICHARD

·CHOOMIS AND CHAPATI·

Choomis is a necessary ingredient for any "Ali Baba" night. Sometimes we call it "macro-tuna fish." The traditional method of eating it is with flat pieces of bread called chapati. To make choomis, you need:

1 cup chickpeas
½ lb. sesame seeds
juice of two lemons
4 cloves garlic
salt to taste
dash of paprika
oil (sesame or peanut)

Soak chickpeas overnight. Next day, cook them till they're tender, drain, saving the water for soup stock or bread.

Put chickpeas, sesame seeds, and peeled garlic cloves through a food grinder or grain mill. I've tried other methods, but this one works best. Add lemon juice, salt, paprika, and enough oil to make it the consistency of dryish peanut butter.

To make Chapati, mix one tsp. salt for each cup of flour (whole wheat and cornmeal mixed is nice).
Add a little cold water at a time to make a stiff dough.
Knead on board till smooth.
Shape into flat, thin rounds.
Cook on top of stove in lightly oiled frying pan or on a griddle.

·THE DJELLABA STORY·

Djellabas were once rare and exotic garments possessed by the very few of us who traveled to Morocco or who knew someone who had been there. Authentic ones seem to be mostly striped and made of camel's hair. They have an air about them of dung and good hashish, which they retain long after they've left their native land.

Total Loss djellabas are quite different from these. They're mostly made of wool or acrylics or cotton, even of silk. They are not rare. Last year, while the craze was at its peak, any stranger who might happen to wander up our hill would mistake the farm for a monastery, one or two hooded figures always being in view. They are easy to make, great to wear, over your clothes to go for a visit, or over your skin right from bed to dash to the outhouse. Ideally, you should have two, one made from a heavy Army-Navy store blanket and one of some lightweight stuff for summer.

After just one lesson, on Christmas Eve, Raymond cut out and sewed up three blankets into djellabas, in time to hand them out for presents the next morning. They are that simple to make. Try it yourself.

—PEPPER

To Make a Djellaba

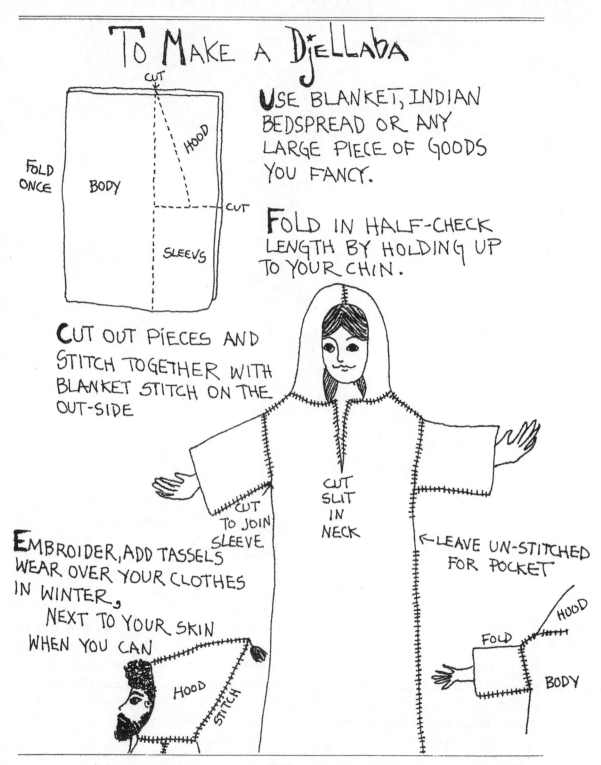

USE BLANKET, INDIAN BEDSPREAD OR ANY LARGE PIECE OF GOODS YOU FANCY.

FOLD IN HALF-CHECK LENGTH BY HOLDING UP TO YOUR CHIN.

CUT OUT PIECES AND STITCH TOGETHER WITH BLANKET STITCH ON THE OUT-SIDE

EMBROIDER, ADD TASSELS WEAR OVER YOUR CLOTHES IN WINTER, NEXT TO YOUR SKIN WHEN YOU CAN

CUT

HOOD

FOLD ONCE

BODY

CUT

SLEEVS

CUT SLIT IN NECK

CUT TO JOIN SLEEVE

←LEAVE UN-STITCHED FOR POCKET

HOOD

STITCH

FOLD

HOOD

BODY

·EMPTY POCKETS MAKE· ·THE MOST NOISE·

INDEED, there were mornings during the summer when Pepper and I were sun-stir-and-love-crazed enough to crawl naked on all fours through the corn patch, weeding the rows. Our delirious laughter grew louder as the stalks stretched higher and hid us from workmen passing down the road in trucks to Don's and Evelyn's. Characters were assassinated with the renegade plants beneath our vengeful hands. Our tongues were little kinder, but it was all in jest or fever, and the corn prospered.

One afternoon over coffee, our closest neighbor, Alison, remarked that she could hear from her house quite clearly every oath or confidence uttered in the garden. Somehow we had thought that the scrubby hedge of sumac and poplar saplings lining the moine provided a boundary to the ear as well as the eye. It was not so. We chuckled.

◆　◆　◆　◆

There are few secrets here. Our laundry flaps on the revolving line until the elements have had their way: spun, bleached, shrunk, and buffeted by winds. A pair of Dale's socks, securely knotted to the rope in 1969, a party dress of Diana's abandoned in the heat of flight, briefs and bedsheets, burlap bags, hand towels, T-shirts, unclaimed and unflagging. Only Pepper conscientiously collects her clothing from the front lines before it goes stiff and rigor mortis sets in.

◆　◆　◆　◆

From the haystack by Pete's spice garden beneath The Apple Tree (known to us as the Party Tree), which stands part way up the orchard hill, lying in the haystack which bore the perfect imprint of my back (the stack dismantled with a pitchfork for mulch on the strawberries), dozing in the hay in fragrance of September, I heard arpeggios on air and applause of leaves above my head. More clearly, steel string plucked and strummed wafted to me, it seemed, from nowhere across the valley. Each afternoon I would lie there when the day grew too sweaty for harvesting or canning, and always the music would arrest me from imaginings. And often a voice, a descant with words that were lost in leavetaking.

It got so I could hear that music wherever the day took me. Making my way across the marsh balancing a bushel of tomatoes on my head, or picking beans and drying rose hips from the cow pasture, or pickling beans.

Autumn light is like cider. The evening sun dangles in the sky for hours, then drops suddenly as a windfall. I made my way up the Bloom Highway following my feet.

◆　◆　◆　◆

Following my bare feet in September up the dirt road that leads over Mt. Muste, past Myron's house where bread was unmistakably baking in the oven, and past the stone foundation where I picked out a dozen whole bricks, down the bed of a waterfall and across the pine woods to Sugar Pond, where I waded over a concrete dam to a jutting rock where I cooled my feet and kitchen-dazed brain. Hawks and herons winged about. Max nosed through the pine needles for clues. I rummaged through my pockets for a match. There were beer cans on the pebbled floor of the pond.

And back over the hill, I stopped to gather blackberries from the thorny bushes beside the hunting camp. Max ran off the road to chase Myron's black kittens.

◆ ◆ ◆ ◆

He was standing by Myron's mailbox, smiling at the window of the envelope which held his unemployment check, his ticket to ride. Tall, bare-armed, black-haired, skinny, and rosy with the first blush of one who is new in the smogless air. He had hands long and crooked as if put together from pipe cleaners.

We walked down to the picnic grove to lounge under a linden tree.

◆ ◆ ◆ ◆

A huge green gallon bottle of the Brandy of Napoleon, dusty and unopened for twenty years, amber in the glass, and amber again in the mind, which rested in the brine like a pickled egg. October chill is first felt in the elbows. November makes the hair stand up on end.

He kicked the door shut, loaded from waist to chin with logs for the Ashley. He was endlessly fond of Max, who parked his faithless chin on the young man's knee waiting to be scratched and fondled. A guitar stretched across his lap like a mermaid. He placed his empty glass on an end table and played his fill.

◆ ◆ ◆ ◆

"Some in rags and some in jags, and some in velvet gowns." Nooks and crannies, rocks and boughs, mudflats and snowfields, hours, eras, seasons, and kingdoms. Everyone has his favorite, I no less than others. It took a year to feel myself more or less than a trespasser here. To share this space three years hence was a luxury.

From the autumnal equinox to the winter solstice and on after New Year, we left our imprint on the landscape and our boots by the stove. I had promised him pummeling blizzards with winds that knocked you over like a bowling pin. Spells of winds to ground you on a couch. But aside from the downy snow of Thanksgiving, there was little freeze to give a person pause. Especially when he's passing through season and kingdom and the time of our lives, to the Tropics, to the Coast, or elsewhere.

◆ ◆ ◆ ◆

When Hans Castorp, ("life's delicate child"), arrived for a visit on the Magic Mountain, intending to stay for three weeks, he was informed

that the smallest measure of reckoned time was a month, but for the seven minutes required to chart a fever. Sequestered on the hill with moist lungs, moribund vehicles, the earth, a sheet of ice lumpy as cobblestones, it is a simple trick, or an inevitable hazard of life here, to find the mind and body free from the dictates of the calendar. Time dilates and contracts in the eye of the beholder. If the eyes of the beholden are tuned to each other, then the landscape is theirs to share for the duration of their vision. The fidelity of friends or lovers can be measured only in terms of fine tune. When walking at night we see with the feet.

◆　◆　◆　◆

There is seemingly no end to the curiosities of heat and cold and their effect on the human heart. Time is weather here more than elsewhere, and weather is the mingling of heat and cold, wet and dry. Ice is water fixed in time. Since ice is my element, slipping and sliding are my means of locomotion. Treading on ice leaves no mark, unless it is a bruise on the pedestrian.

Who can say why some ease off this hill and others cling for dear life? Or why the last stretch of road before the flatlands holds for some the terror of walking the plank, while for others it is the gateway to liberation, or the threshold of dream?

◆　◆　◆　◆

Early after milking, I am turning the morning cream in the churn, crank, and paddle. The front door opens, welcoming a wedge of frosty air and the young man whose eyes today are full of exit: images of aqualungs and porpoises, palm trees. I am aware that the cream will clot soon into butter, gathered in an instant when the turning is hard and then over, and that the butter, no matter how much is churned at a sitting, will be gone by nightfall. Tomorrow someone going through the same motions will draw from it conclusions of his own.

◆　◆　◆　◆

Not to be spellbound by fossils, footfalls, vestiges, echoes, or absences. The larder's full, and that's no metaphor.

—VERANDAH

·CHRISTMAS DAY·

Christmas day, my twenty-ninth. In three days I'm thirty.

The day before Christmas I had nowhere to go that I wanted to go to, except the farm, whose invitation I was glad of, & uneasy about, too. Marty & KK. But KK was in Princeton, I liked folks at the farm, liked Marty, & know the farm as a place I can have my own space in without being crowded. As it got dark, I drove over.

I arrived a half hour before the case of cold duck & champagne. Verandah had promised Joannie a case of cold duck when her "ship" came in & this was the day it came, as an advance on Verandah's book of poems. The farm folks don't "celebrate Christmas" exactly, but we were sure celebrating something before very long. Everyone a little into their own heads but together with each other, too. At first I felt awkward with Marty, there were things to say, but we were each uptight, & it wasn't right yet. Besides, it wasn't public fare & the cold duck was & we all drank. & drank: bottles popping, glasses fizzing, spilling over, & in the clear glasses were little upside-down rose-tinted portraits of us all. Something was coming together, we knew it, but we didn't give it a name.

Alicia & Verandah & Joannie put on Arab folk-dance music & danced in & out of the kitchen while Pete rigged up a hookah from a gallon Alamaden bottle, using a cork, a hot-water-bottle tube, & a douching attachment. *Let grass enter the houses and the hearts of my people shall rejoice!* When it came around to me, I looked at the attachment for a second, we laughed, and I ventilated myself, then went to dance. No one was there so I danced alone in the room and realized in a minute or two I was standing there with my hands on an upright beam, smiling at it, talking with it. It didn't seem to mind one way or the other.

Then I had to piss so I went to the outhouse by the barn—wind roaring, pulling at my clothes, the whole bald hilltop threatening to tear loose like a shingle & sail off into the stars—& I stood in that little refuge peeing & singing back at the wind loud as I could. Coming back, it's maybe twenty or thirty yards from the barn to the house, & I got lost. Didn't matter except I had no coat & the wind made it bitter cold. I sat in the snow between the barn & the spice garden, looking at my muddy boots, thinking how I wld freeze if I passed out but scary as that was I was running deeper, grooving on the wind & stars & the tightfrozen ice & loose cold mud. I suddenly realized I had my hands in up to the wrists. I was sinking? No. Just sitting there with my hands in the mud. Stayed there don't know how long, then my body was getting up by itself with a fuckyou attitude toward my spirit, which enjoyed sitting in the cold stream of the wind. Up it was, eyes taking a bead on the houselights, then I slipped, whirled around toward the garden again, flat on my face in the snow, laughing but wondering if I could get back. So I stood up—after a little talk with my spirit—& whirled & whirled, on purpose, to shake the whirlies, then headed back for the house fast.

Next thing I knew I was sitting outside somewhere throwing up. Realized I hadn't eaten all day. Not much came. Enuf. I was OK, cold, & weak, & laughing, riding some kind of freaking mustang I cldn't guide or control but knew I cld stay on top of so long as I gave it its head & gave myself my own head, body riding wild over a cluttered frozen turf. The hooves found their way thru this night by the illuminations of starlight and grace. O Everready!

It was cold. I was cold. What if I throw up my whole body now & it's there in the snow like a newborn babe & nobody knows it's there? I wanted to. Newborn. Looking in its sac like a bull's heart, with arms & legs. A tadpole. Forming and reforming, auras pulsing and shining, appearing and disappearing. Everybody's here sooner or later. It feels like dying but it's being born. And always the three camel drivers arrive in time. Bearing gifts it's difficult to recognize, gifts just the same. Where was I?

I lifted up my head and looked around: this windblown shoulder of the earth, the frail lit house, hair on my head the wind brightens with ice, eyes singing with vision—this tiny spot of the earth is all there is, island in the void, wind chipping its edges & wearing it away while no one else knows at this particular instant & nothing to do if they did know except what they are doing inside now. Dancing as friends, talking & laughing as friends, the celebration together of our individual lives; is there anything more we can do for each other, is there?

I love them all & want them warm in my arms & safe forever living like this now, drunk & high & bright-eyed & beautifully young in their dream of their lives becoming true. Together with each other, friends friends friends trying at last & becoming: then I felt something growing huge & changing, myself & not myself or anything I knew before, hovering above the house like invisible girders of pure will to fend off wind & let the rain thru & light thru & snow thru but not this particular wind, not this time, wolfwind shrieking to blow down the house & blow out the lights there. And it held, I thot, letting thru just enuf to let the folks know they were on a journey now, threatened by a storm, but not enuf to wreck things.

& the next thing I knew legs, legs I memorized the pants of so I'd know who helped me (Pete it was, widewale brown cords), & a faraway voice saying O no O no & my head down low, smiling a smile & cldn't raise up high enuf to show him, but I held up a hand to say howdy I'm OK, just drunk. So he went off & I got up & made it to the front door, where I cldn't get the door open. I sat on the step until more legs came & told me where a room was I cld rest in, told me friendly, & I made a still space in my mind where I wrote it down like a Navajo sand painting on a stretch of spreadout sand & said Thankyoufriend thankyou. The legs went off & in a while I got up & got thru the door & laid on something in the right room & started to sleep, cold still but knowing it was OK now. Pete put a blanket on me as I disappeared.

How long it was I don't know, but I saw Joannie drift past looking like I'd felt earlier. She crashed just out of sight. Stared at the ceiling a minute, then knew I wanted stove heat so I went on into the kitchen feeling OK now, but knowing I looked like the coyote after roadrunner had pulled a good number on him. & lucky lucky a chair free. I sat in it & was warm and dark before I realized my eyes were closing by themselves. I was still nodding. In & out, but mostly there, with my ears. New people. One a big fat round fellow looking like Jonathan Winters. He had come to read poems & a story. He read a few short poems, then Hopkins' "The virgin compared to the air we breathe," which I cldn't follow, having a hard time enuf just breathing air, no less comparing it to anything. I only caught the music, not the words, but his reading of that poem set us up to hear "A Child's Christmas in Wales" & he read it well, close to Thomas' own Caedmon reading.

& "I said some words to the close and holy darkness and then I slept."

Then he left, funny fellow he was, & I got clear enuf to see everyone was sleepy now & tired. I ate some of the meatballs & red sauce. Joannie came back in I gave her my chair because she looked cold & wobbly. We were all talking & then some folks came by & one was a singer & played guitar & was good & trying to put the make on Verandah, but not getting far. They sang together & made good music of it. By the time they left, Pete & Ellen were gone, Alicia was gone, Hugh was gone, Marty was gone, leaving me & Joannie & the jeweler who lives across the road, & Verandah. Then the jeweler left, Joannie went to bed, & it was me & Verandah sitting at the stove, & both too tired to talk. The electricity went off. After a few minutes' dark she lit a lamp. We looked at each other once, too tired, smiled, & went off to our beds.

I lay awake to hear the wind, the flapping of the plastic put up for storm windows. It becomes the flapping of the canvas sails. *Long John Silver is at the end of the spit of land, his makeshift sailboat lodged on the shore as he pushes at it, one-armed, bright-eyed, the righteous crew of Jim's saviors running up the beach toward the two of them & still distant but clos-*

ing the gap. Long John doesn't ask Jim for help but his eyes appeal. Jim throws his shoulder at the bow & shoves; weeping, he shoves & shoves & the keel comes free & the small boat moves into the surf. Long John clambers in, raises the sail with his one deft arm, turns to Jim, & nods, "Aye, Jim, you're a fine lad," & busies himself with catching the wind as Jim stands hip-deep in water, his rescuers over his shoulder approaching now. He is crying. "Long John, Long John Silver, take me with you!" John looks back & grins & has the wind now, ducks. The first volley of musketfire splatters the water around his boat.

The electric lights come on, I wake up,—*I wanted to take you with me, Jim; I couldn't. I know you couldn't take me with you, Long John, but I wanted you to, I love you—* & I'm hungry. I get up, put the lights out, light a candle & eat a grapefruit, then to bed again, wishing a while Kathryn were with me, & as I start to sleep she is a green parrot on my shoulder. I sleep as warm & cozy as ever a fellow cld hope to, in the hold of a Christmas Eve.

—BILL

TAKING THE HORIZONTAL

A LESSON LEARNED HERE, so basic, it embarrasses the page: one might mold the planet to fit his comfort, or mold his comforts to the planet. A lovely woman named Pip left me a chaise longue worthy of Elizabeth Barrett Browning, a barge for Cleopatra, of flowered and buttoned velveteen, bursting with entrails of excess stuffing and recoiling springs which greet the weary body with their tender hooks. Ankles, feet, and toes of the sphinx or chimera; hollows and convexities which contort the sleeper, reader, or sprawler into compromising postures. I have surrendered my form to the shape of this couch, filled it with pillows which require constant attention. In somewhat the same manner, I have come to rest inside my skin: the psyche frayed and haywire in a sturdy frame, awkwardly upholstered, partial to elegance of a humble sort, possessed of an endless need to recline. When a wind is up, I wrap my knees in the fur cape I wore in the first photograph of the first foray we made to this farm: seven of us looking *très* California, and glazed, as if we had some inkling of the outcome.

I have barely left the couch for days but to barter time with the elements. Wind chill against woodblock. An armload of split logs (for traction down the treacherous slope to my house) dropped in a clatter on the floor, and tossed in the lid of the stove, purchases an afternoon or evening of repose, to stretch and sigh as in a dog dream on a braided rug; to chisel away at my latest epic (They'll never say this one is Confessional); to sip my Christmas sherry (wish it were the Brandy of Napoleon, thanking God it is not water) while it lasts. To cast about on a raft of wind, of afternoon.

I keep a set of words to hoard or herd in a box that Evann gave me. "Tangerine, the evening sun, Images abandoned, like spinsters, God's spiders." One year, I cut apart some Yeats, Eliot, and others, and stored them in a box shaped like a pagoda, which still intimates cedar boughs and Havana cigars. Some see it as an oracle, a way to mend and weave the mind. Poems tend to find themselves in the random dark.

A neighbor engaged me in conversation one morning. I was home alone. We sat in rockers with our feet upon the bar atop the cook stove. Black birch was burning. The coffee perked. What did I have to say to my brothers and sisters on farms across New England: what greetings, tidings, hints, and visions?

Assume nothing, only this: four years on this hill and twenty-two in the flatlands reveal again, call it what you will: mortality, frangibility, "the rag and bone shop of the heart." It's you and the void again, you and the void on the IRT, the MTA, in Macy's, by the ocean, on the telephone, on voyages from and returning to your dearest home, or dozing in your rocker.

Once from the pine woods with a toboggan load of dry kitchen wood, I emerged into a Brueghel pastorale. Our pack of huskies (deceased or dispersed this year) ran rampant on the hill. It was mud season, and in the valley Marty and Bob, dressed in minute and colorful plaids, carried a tremendous hoop of black sap hose to the sugarbush. The men were tiny, bent to their task and making slow and steady progress.

The hoop: sometimes it seemed a serpent, a mirror, then a frame. Suddenly it was perfectly empty, yet teeming: a cyclone of space. A void. I had to laugh. Laughter like the aftermath of an ice storm, as the vision flew apart. For Bob and Marty inched along with eternity, innocent of their burden.

*   *   *   *

The cow has an itch.
She wriggles against a barbed wire fence.
I say
It pays to be thick skinned.

The dog has indigestion.
His heart's a spiny pear
Transfixed on a trellis of ribs.

*   *   *   *

Pete says the west wind weaves, drifts, and binds our dreams. The sleeping mind of everything alive on the farm is a sitting room, a hive, a silo, or cauldron. Pete ran to my door one not yet morning two years ago, knocked on my door in a fright. I woke from wheeling my father in a bathchair along a boardwalk. Pete had lost his father only weeks before. I pushed the bathchair gently down my ladder, unlatched the door, fanned the fire, and put up tea for three or four (had he carried his father on his back?). My father grew gray, eerie, and translucent, and vanished through the stovepipe, before Pete, now rocking where my father sat, my father's quilt around his shoulders, found his first words. "I can hardly breathe," he rasped. Constriction of the chest. Grief unwept.

That winter Pete stopped the Horse Clock galloping in the Green Room at six minutes past four, and gathered everything he knew to write his elegy. He typed an overture, a prelude. I curled on the couch and scribbled a counterpoint, above the root cellar where days are stored in leaves and sawdust with pears and apples until they compost into dreams. Burnt-Toast-with-Marmite-Pete.

Once I fell in love with his double. It wasn't actually his double, it was his cousin, because Pete has more cousins than a camel driver, cousins to stir and steal the hearts of lonely winter beasts. Or perchance Pete has no cousins whatever, but shapes and faces tailored to our dreams.

I woke with worn-out shoes. Pete walked me down to the beaver pond where we swim in summer. It was twenty below zero. Pete made his mouth into an O, the way it trembles slightly before eloquence. Did someone come? Was that you? We traded hats. The dog has eaten mine. My shoes are full of holes. Did I dance?

But only frozen O's came out. He made his mouth into the smile that looks like a birchbark canoe with red trim.

◆　◆　◆　◆

Richard says that love is blighted here. I say the fruit is sparse, sweet, hard, and mottled as the Seckel pears we stored in jars with brandy in the summer of '68. One man cherished my mind, yet longed to embrace another here. So closely fused by time we are. Joan says, why can't we bide as one being, she and I, and never be sundered by a fickle man's heart? Love is sealed in quarts on the pantry walls.

Vinegar is bracing. Green beans are tender. Garlic serves to ward off wens and worms. When you crave a taste to make you squint, dill beans will do. Make enough to last a month or two, and next year you'll make a closetful.

Wash all utensils and leave them where they won't get dirty. The warming oven of a wood stove is a perfect autoclave. If you've bought the beans in a market, wash them too. Otherwise, inspect them to make sure they are not gritty, and are relatively similar in size. Some people pick off the stems, but this seems a foolish waste of time.

Brine for pickles is made of water and vinegar in equal parts for a start. Experiment to find the proper strength for your taste. You can always add more of anything as you go along, and use leftover brine to pickle other vegetables or eggs. I use white vinegar and I like strong brine.

Stuff quart jars with beans until they are packed tight.

Add chopped green peppers, onions, garlic, dill weed, mustard seed, black pepper, a dash of soy sauce.

In a saucepan combine water, vinegar, and salt. Bring to a boil.

Funnel brine into jars to cover. Seal immediately and store until the snow flies, or until the craving hits.

Into the cozy quiet of an evening chat in the chicken house comes a droning din. Is the teapot boiling? No. Is it the mare snorting, or the wind, the racial memory of Gestapo in the dooryard about to knock? No, it is the hellicrs, the chain saws on treadmills, the snorkels, the frogmen, the bane of winter, in short, the ski-doo, not 23, but the latest claptrap of the American mind: the snowmobile, careening through the darkness, promising broken limbs, instant blindness, sudden deafness, and downright fear to the pedestrian.

In our four winters on the glass hill, the skimobile population has dwarfed that of the ambulating set. Nothing can set one's teeth on edge like the onslaught of the packs advancing, as he pauses in the midst of a constitutional to observe the migration of Orion across the cloudless winter sky.

Some of our dearest neighbors in Massachusetts, however, arrive astride the dread machines from time to time, and the pleasure of their company abates even the most righteous indignation, and gives one pause to wonder.

—VERANDAH

·THE BURNING OF·
·THE LIBRARY AT KAJAMUNYA·

N AN EVENING LONG AGO, when the stars fluttered like night birds over Kajamunya, a young man and his maiden strolled aimlessly through the streets of the capital. Anyone who saw them pass would smile and immediately know that the two were helplessly and joyfully in love. Cartogrenga, the young man, could be seen animatedly gesturing and defining space with his hands while talking rapidly to the young woman at his side, whose attention seemed to be glued to every word. If one had listened to the conversation, he would have heard the mention of strange and exotic places, and of the dreams of travel and adventure which passed between the two. One would have also noticed the great skill and knowledge with which Cartogrenga described the routes of passage from Kajamunya to anywhere on earth, for it was apparent that he must be apprentice to the wise and ancient Gleana, the court cartographer. Indeed it was so. And the young woman at his side whom Cartogrenga was so intent on pleasing would be the beautiful Fiona, born out of the brief but happy marriage of Borimini, chief architect of the realm, to the only woman he had ever really loved, Denina, who died so tragically at the birth of her daughter, and so ended the whimsical and flighty designer's only attempt to settle, and change his ways.

As the couple approached the National Library, Cartogrenga suggested that Fiona return with him to the labyrinthine stacks from which he had earlier surfaced, aborting his studies, in order to meet her by the fountain which adorned the palace courtyard. There he would show Fiona his work on the renowned Kajamunyan map collection, and their dreams of the evening could be charted.

The library loomed before them like a great mural painted in air. The towers and terraces and secret passageways were the pride of Borimini and

the young
borimini
dreaming
of the
national
library

all of Kajamunya, for it was here that all of the tales and mysteries and knowledge of Kajamunya were housed. Every Kajamunyan had wiled away studious and happy hours in pursuit of history or entertainment behind the bronze bas-relief doors. For it was a tradition of Kajamunya that all children, upon reaching the age of five, were taken to the library to browse and discover its treasures. And the library was of such comfort, and its collection so appealing and imaginatively arranged, that the child was immediately enamored and remained so till the end of his days.

At least one day of the week of all Kajamunyans was spent in the library, whether to read or contemplate, and there were rooms for each purpose, or to add one's own memoirs or fantasies or wisdom to the constantly growing collection. The loving pursuits and labors which the library inspired had become the national pastime of Kajamunya and, of course, the library, too, had become the most conducive place for lovers' trysts, and meetings of friends and family. Indeed the library was the most friendly and convenient spot in all of Kajamunya, and much—we will never know how much—of the history and fable which was housed there had occurred within its very walls.

Cartogrenga and Fiona had settled in the great walnut-paneled maproom on the lowest level of the building. Their conversation had not lost one jot of its former intensity, and Cartogrenga was now hastily pulling maps from their leather bindings in an attempt to reveal his present work to Fiona, who beamed with pride at the skill of her lover. The subject of conversation turned from geography to love with the slightest innuendo, and it was not long before one hand of Cartogrenga turned the pages, while the other lovingly held Fiona's delicate palm.

As the evening wore on, the subject of lands which had been discovered and lost arose, and Cartogrenga found it necessary that the couple move from the great maproom to the adjoining anteroom which housed the ancient maps that pictured the earth as flat or square or egg-shaped, and delineated continents now lost or forgotten. The small room, which had long ago been one of the busiest in the library, had now fallen out of use and was now used for storing the outdated geography of the Kajamunyan forefathers. Cartogrenga took a candle, and led Fiona within. There the two thrilled to the dreamy ignorance of the past, and forgot themselves in the darkened room where history beckoned.

But, alas, caught up in their adventure, and so pleased to travel together through a latitude which knows no bounds, the lovers moved closer until Cartogrenga reached out to embrace Fiona on the divan where they sat. In the tumult of their embrace, the candle which Cartogrenga had so cautiously placed on the table beside them (which held a bust of Galvinto, Kajamunya's most noted geographer) fell to the dusty floor and initiated the moment which was to be Kajamunya's greatest tragedy and loss. For, blissfully ignorant of the candle's fall, Cartogrenga was finally betrothing his heart to Fiona. It was only when the floor, which held scraps of dried parchment and dust, began to blaze, that the two realized that their passion had ignited more than their love for one another.

Faced now by a growing sea of flames, Cartogrenga, horror-stricken, knew that time had rebuffed them, and that their fates would tragically be sealed in one another's arms if their exit were not immediate. Smashing the leaded window above the couch, Cartogrenga lifted Fiona to safety and, looking back helplessly one last time at the flames which were now lashing at his life's work, exited himself through the window. Dazed, the couple ran to the minaret which guarded the west wall of the building and, climbing the winding staircase with the fury of fear and remorse, reached the upper balcony and tolled the bell, which only infrequently before had raised panic and summoning in the hearts of Kajamunyans.

Roused from sleep by the doleful bell, all of Kajamunya covered themselves against the chill of night and gathered by the library, where now the windows, like the eyes of nocturnal tigers, blazed with light. And there, making his way through the crowd which had silently and efficiently begun to fetch water from the fountains which ringed the library, was the old Borimini in his stunning crimson cape. Silently he moved toward the building, coming as close as the heat of history and fable aflame would allow. The tears streamed from his eyes which, though smarting from smoke and grown tired with seeing, were still as radiant as when as a young gallant the architect had conceived his dream to build the library in the shape of things which do not exist. Borimini watched as the damaging flames, which had burst through the roof of the east end, were doused by his comrades. He promised then to begin the reconstruction as soon as the wind and work blew away the cinders.

By dawn, with all of Kajamunya—king and courtier and tradesman—working through the night, which was once so starry but now obscured by the billowing smoke which hung over the mountaintop, the flames were conquered. Borimini was the first to enter the building. With customary reverence, the assembled Kajamunyans waited without while the tearful Borimini

walked through the halls which now held the ashes of so much he had lived through, as well as the joys and sorrows of the past which he had sought to protect. As he walked on, examining what remained and what had burned, jumbled bits and pieces of Kajamunyan history and story which he had learned with his heart as a child and as a man echoed through his ears. He took relief in knowing that much would be remembered and recorded once again, and that the flames which struck the library in a youthful moment of embrace could never damage the spirit and familiarity which compelled all of Kajamunya to weave their lore and work into a picturesque tapestry. It would hang always in the souls of Kajamunyans, as well as once again in the halls and rooms of the National Library.

Reappearing at the great front doors on which the architect himself had engraved tableaux of the exodus which brought his people to the mountain, Borimini wiped the tears and smuts from his eyes, and asked all who were gathered in the courtyard to begin then and there to gather up the charred remnants. He promised that within the fortnight the plans for reconstruction would be drawn. Trembling, he told them they had lost little, and that indeed if they searched their dreams, and lit their nightly fires and shared at dinner the stories of their passing days, as was their habit, they had lost nothing. The lyric chant, which had appeared many years before at the laying of the library's foundation, passed through the entire assemblage. They began to dance to its moving rhythm, hand in hand, around the library, entering one by one to begin their work.

Borimini departed to find the lovers, and begin to draw his plans. He found Cartogrenga and Fiona curled in sleep around each other, at the base of the minaret. Gently waking them, and peering into their frightened and shame-filled eyes, he promised them then that even though they had courted and ignited disaster in their passion, it was far better that love and not enmity or violence, had kindled the library into flame. He commissioned Cartogrenga to lead a group of scholars to appraise what maps and geography had been lost, and to refurbish the collection—a lifetime calling of which Cartogrenga had only dreamed. Borimini also requested of the couple that they marry on the very day the library would once again open its doors to Kajamunya. Fiona, decorously holding back her tears and gratitude, kissed her aging father, and promised to fulfill his request.

Borimini returned home. He asked that he not be disturbed for three days, neither for food nor company. On the evening of the third day, Fiona came to her father's house with food and news. Her knocks unanswered, she entered. In the study she found the architect reclining on his couch. Thinking to wake him, she kneeled to whisper in the earring-studded ear. The smiling Borimini never moved nor woke, and on the oaken worktable, where it seemed as if some furious hurricane had struck, neatly piled at one end were the plans for the reconstruction, and for a new wing, which was the most spirited and elaborate structure the architect had ever conceived. Borimini is buried there beneath the marble floor. A fountain, in the image of a dream about to be born, marks the grave.

—RICHARD

·LETTERS FROM RAY MUNGO·

San Francisco, California
December 1, 1971 (Full Moon, Gemini)

Dear farm folk,

   Out of the general insanity, chaos, and happy accident of my life came a new, brilliant, and unmistakable glow, and a certain direction. Now I know who I am, what I'm doing, and why. I know too much! And I'm going to Japan, certainly, by the turn of the new year. Paul Williams is going with me, and a third person, a lady, who will be revealed to us before the Japanese pulp boat grinds out of Georgia Straight. Until then, I'll live in Seattle at Cathy and Lazarus' place. Good company, good food and dope, no hardship, no misery. No more me.

I don't know when I'll see you again, only that I will see you again.

It's time I owned up to some heavy confessions. I left the farm last Christmas, nearly a year gone now; although I returned for portions of February, March, and April, my real identity departed before the end of December. At the time I left, I was both very deeply in love and very close to mad.

I'd never been in love before, and I didn't realize that it would strip me of everything I owned, but it did. The only important thing in life, for me, was to be near and with the one I loved, everything else was gone. I felt completely vulnerable for the first time in my life. And I fell down hard. Whew.

It's the greatest story never told, and I don't guess I can tell any of you what love is, you know that already. I believe the farm was built on love, and love has nurtured it. For me, the love among us farm folk was of a pure, innocent sort, like the love children feel. Sweet youth served us, we posed in meadows green. Body-love, sex, grown-up love with overtones of pain, reluctance, irony, and loneliness: these things exist for me only in the world outside our farm. And I need these things. At the farm, I slept alone, but for rare and beautiful interludes with Ellen and Linda. Here in the world again, I sleep with others and they keep me awake.

Somehow, we all of us maintained the gentlest and most subtle understanding of each other, and many others than me slept privately too. Such delicate, actually exquisite, self-imposed celibacy is the mark of almost all conscious religious communities. Ah, we never started a religious community, just a hippie farm, but that's what we turned into. Much merit!

Much virtue. We worked the land and suffered the cold winters, used no more than a small allotment of electricity, lived on no money or less, did not pollute the air or water any more than absolutely necesary, fed ourselves and buried our shit. We are Earth-people, living not just in harmony but actual union with the planet under our feet.

The farm is the only home I've ever had in this world. In the months since I left, I've merely put up in ports for the night, never finding a place I wanted to settle 'cause they were all inferior to the place I *had* settled in

Vermont—and fled Paradise. In Miami, Florida I was 21st Century Man in suburban home with swimming pool and abjectly miserable; I'd sit in semi-lotus position on the rug for four hours bolt upright until the physical pain screamed out the psychic. We got to Costa Rica on some burn-scheme free airplane tickets, and next I lived in the tropical rain forest and met with the dead. No kidding. Then a roachy hotel in Panama and a big earthquake— I was scared shitless. A cabin in snowy Nova Scotia for the vernal equinox: looking East. A gilded cage of a Village apartment, with girl, in bad New York City. Cocaine, cocaine. Beautiful cabin on Pacific Ocean, San Francisco opium dens, now the Pacific Northwest, now the Orient! My feet are roller skates, I'm a bum.

I did the impossible. I lost Total Loss Farm. I grew up.

But, as grown-ups are only older versions of the children they were, I am only a product, like any can of maple syrup or peach, of the farm. Ding-dong, I lose still, and have no roots to hold me earthbound. Zoom zoom I'm on the moon, and I love it. The truth is I want it all, I want to live everything, die everything, be everybody, go everywhere, I want it all. The farm's standing motto, "The Best of Everything," stays. Earth-people are the richest of all, but some flowers only bloom on the moon, within the vast desolation.

And now I'm going around the world, always in motion, always uncomfortable, traveling hard. I been doin' some. And the farm is a mythological kingdom I have dreamed, a delicious and loving universe to which I aspire as I make my Way through the cold and bitchy World!

I dreamed it was December, people were thinkin' about Christmas and schemin' gifts to give, it snowed some and all the stoves roared at night, all the cars coughed in the morning, and we all had high thick boots. Warm apple cider in teacups from the stove. A little cinnamon on top. An unceasing scurry of early-winter energy in the living room, with Ashley ablaze. Wood chippings on the rug.

Or May, and the green warm morning made the ground ooze with mud and new grass, the earth squished and breathed, and all the creatures in God's technicolor jungle paradise garden of eden came crawling, swimming, flying, running, and walking around. The fabulous warmth of the sun brushes away all the dead karma of the long winter, windows fly open, the very earth is our heaven.

The golden day in September, timeless, spaceless, when I sat in the graveyard all afternoon propped against a slate marker commemorating the remains of Captain Packer. A fresh red and golden peach, juicy and sensual in every detail.

A long summer's incredibly green afternoon, naked cross-legged under the Chief Peach Tree, watching the mountains melt on acid. "Striving to understand. . . . It's all the same!"

And good food to eat, not just your regular nutritional diet but a real gourmet dinner of fruits of our earth, and milk of cows, meat of pigs, eggs of chickens, it's all there like a cross between a Salvation Army soup kitchen and some impeccably high-quality seafood restaurant on the waterfront in Boston. Little more curry, I think.

And wonderfully personable animals, cows, goats, horses, chickens, pigs, ducks, dogs, cats, you can talk to and get to know. Many many laughs in a single day, many zany adventures, and colorful characters around. An unceasing consciousness of cold. An overwhelming wave of wholesome, peaceful thoughts and moods. A cosmically inspired chain of events leading to a mind-blowing conclusion, *change*. Change is our only constant.

We have to be strong and honest now. People out here in the world expect it of us, they patiently listen to us and support our modest endeavor and bumming, and they deserve a good show. I am no longer paranoid about American empire crumbling economy crashing population turning to heroin and lobotomy—people are just simple and they want some Light and so do we and we all get together in the new age and light up the darkest night.

And nurse infants by the stove in the kitchen.

It is too good to be true. Yet it is real.

Salem, Oregon
December 3, 1971

Some of you may experience the land as hard reality—for you it is not a "dream-farm of the soul" but an actual collection of hills and trees, cows and tractors. Collecting maple sap drop by drop from trees promotes such a real-istic view, hence the laconic nature of the natives. And it's not soft country, like the steep valleys of Costa Rica, but hard and enduring land which'll clearly outlive us all. All in all, we are in danger of experiencing the land as real. But the lesson, as always, is that nothing is real, and the farm is in truth an outgrowth of fantasy-consciousness. New York City may be a stone drag, but in Vermont everybody acts like they don't care, and they should not when they're given the *incredible freedom* to construct

a whole new, imagined universe to live in. So we've made just an old farm into a whole World to our liking.

And the whole world wants a piece of our world now—everybody wants the changes we've been going through already, and everything out here has changed. Principally, the United States has gone off on a Total Loss Bender, the dollar's just a piece of sweaty paper and the war in Vietnam lost. Mr. Food Stamp outsizes Mr. Buck in supermarket cartoon displays. Junkies everywhere. We're living in a second-class nation at last. Lovely mystics and ancient religious practice return to fill our leisure and ease our pain—zazen is dying in Japan, flourishing in America, and Indian music, Ali Akbar Khan, Ravi Shankar, et. al., moved to California. Astrology is our national "understanding," and god lives in each of us.

It's a Brave Soul Village of a world we've made—like the village of freaks near Mt. Siskiyou in Free State of Jefferson who were "brave souls" to the natives—when they arrived in 1968—and we got to love it and suffer its awful tortures, because it's our home. Ladies and gents of the universe, the youth in us is at your service!

It's a powerful mythology for what's just cow-milkin' and teeth-brushing; it seems we're simply living when we're really carrying the responsibility for leading a giant motorcade into the Promised Land, the new age.

But all we can do is simply be and simply see.

I'm a fool and justly diagnosed as a self-destructive and messianic character—but I'm out here losing my way to heaven, spreading the word and spirit far and wide, finding the same great energy in the forest and sea, but suckling the great tit of the cities for its people, who are more important —critically wounded as they are in the battle of coping—to me now. How many frightened people's hands I've held! How many tears, too, for their pitiful lives in glass and steel! How many nights and days more for me before peace ends it! I'm not dead yet.

There will be no end of the world. It's already happened.

Tear the planet to divots under my heels, I can never escape your love. It follows me everywhere, like my gone innocence, I carry it with me.

And the new age will be an end to separation and regret.

Love,
—RAYMOND

·MORE RECIPES·

The pumpkin recipe was inspired by Mrs. Fred Tenney; the squash by Mrs. Carlyle Gabaree; both in *The Vermont Cookbook*. Neither lady will recognize the result.

·PUMPKIN PIE·
(Makes three pies)
2 tablespoons flour
2 tablespoons corn meal
1 cup honey
4 eggs
2 tablespoons butter
4 tablespoons molasses
2 teaspoons cinnamon
1 teaspoon cloves
1 teaspoon nutmeg
1 teaspoon salt
5 cups pumpkin
5 to 6 cups cream or milk

New England Sugar Pie Pumpkins are the only pumpkin worth eating. Its flesh is fullest and most sweet. Slice it into small sections and pressure cook it till the rind separates from the flesh. (Roast the seeds to chew on or give seeds and pulp to the animals). Mash the pumpkin through a collander and spread thinly on a pancake iron till all the moisture is out. The pumpkin should be a rich orange color, fine in texture, and non-stringy. Now mix all the dry ingredients together, then the molasses, honey, and eggs. When these are all blended, stir in the pumpkin and finally the cream. Six cups makes a lighter pie. Five cups is more like a pudding. Pour into pie shells and bake about 50 minutes at 350-400 degrees. Pie is done when the top thickens.

·SQUASH PIE·

(Makes three pies)

Any winter squash is good, though Hubbards should be the last of the season to be used.

    1   cup corn meal
    ½   cup ground wheat berries (if available)
    3   teaspoons ginger
    2½   teaspoons salt
    5   teaspoons cinnamon
    4   eggs
    1   tablespoon molasses
    2   cups maple syrup (or honey)
    6½   cups squash
    5   cups cream or milk

Prepare the squash as you would the pumpkin in the above pumpkin pie recipe. Any winter squash is good, though Acorn squash should be the first used, Hubbard the last. Mix together dry ingredients, then syrup and molasses, then eggs, squash and cream. Amount of cream can be adjusted to suit desired thickness. Pour into pie shells (single crust per pie) and bake about 50 minutes at 350-400°. Pie is done when top thickens.

·TEMPURA·

"Your farm reflects the tempura of the times."
—Marjorie Himel

Tempura means "deep fried." It is most easily done in a wok. A Japanese-American friend of ours, Harlin Himel, taught us how to make tempura, but I've never been able to duplicate his exact method. For one thing, he used only chop-sticks to handle the vegetables and arranged the finished delicacies as though they were flowers. A beautiful ritual to see.

Fill the wok with four to six inches of oil (sesame is best) or lard.

Batter: 1 cup wholewheat flour,
or ⅔ cup wholewheat plus ⅓ cup rice flour
¼ teaspoon salt
1 cup cold water
1 beaten egg

Mix all ingredients together but don't stir them too much. Lumps don't matter. Keep it cold and don't make it in advance. Dip the veggies into the batter one at a time and then into the oil. The oil should be hot enough so the vegetables will float. Brown on one side, then gently turn and brown on the other. Drain on paper and keep hot until served.

Just about anything tastes great tempura-ed. Try things like carrots (in long thin slices), cucumbers, zucchini, mushrooms, snowpeas, broccoli, turnips, smelts, chicken (cut up), shrimp.

Tempura takes patience. It's a long slow process best undertaken with love and time. Lots of both! Sometimes you can't help feeling like a short-order cook in a greasy spoon, so only attempt it when you're really feeling

good. It's such beautiful food to look at and really delicious to eat. It's well worth the effort.

Serve with brown rice. Have several bowls of sauce available. The tempura is dipped into the sauce and then eaten.

Sauce: simmer and serve hot:
- ½ cup tamari
- 3 tablespoons wine or beer
- ½ teaspoon ground ginger
- ½ cup water

·V.'S GOLDEN RELISH·

6 lbs. golden pear tomatoes quartered
6 lbs. yellow cooking apples cored and sliced (skins on)
1 lb. box golden raisins
3 large fresh onions cut in rings
6 sliced green peppers
2 cups cider vinegar
Cinnamon, cumin, mustard seed, cloves, tumeric and honey to taste (2 cups)
2 cloves mashed garlic

Simmer apples in vinegar until soft.
Add onions, peppers, raisins, tomatoes and honey.
Add spices, stir and simmer for twenty minutes.
Correct seasoning to taste.
Pour into pint or quart canning jars and process like tomatoes.

·PEPPER'S PICKLES·

16 large cukes sliced
1 dozen medium white onions
4 tablespoons celery seeds
4 tablespoons mustard seeds
12 cups cider vinegar
8 cups honey or maple syrup
4 tablespoons salt
1 good sized cauliflower, cut into small pieces

Combine all the ingredients in a large pot
Cook until the syrup clears
Pack into clean jars and seal
Makes eight quarts.

·ICKLED PEGS·

Got extra eggs? We do. I pickle them. They're great and keep for as long as. A recipe with numerous variations. Beet juice makes them Violet; ginger, Brown. Last time I hard-boiled fifteen eggs. I barely squeezed them into a wide mouthed canning jar, along with lots of garlic, carrots, onions or what ever. I filled the spaces twixt the eggs with a mixture which amounted to: A cup of cider vinegar, a half cup of soy sauce, ginger, dill seed, salt and what you like in picklings. Set in the cellar for a week or so. They are a delight even to those who had disdained the thought of them. My father first turned me on to these. Great with a home brew.

·ONION RINGS AND YOGURT·

ONION RINGS: One night when we were having fish and cole slaw I remembered that I had read in an Oregon "Poor Students Cookbook" a secret for perfect onion rings. It was to use Aunt Jemima Buttermilk Pancake mix for batter and fry the rings in peanut oil. Having neither of those ingredients I approximated a pancake batter with white flour, oil, milk (perhaps yogurt) and eggs. Also a little salt, baking powder and sesame seeds which I love. I made sure the oil was very hot. The onion rings were all perfect, from first to last, approaching the Howard Johnson's ideal.

YOGURT: I made a lot of yogurt that didn't gel, time after time, and finally correcting every mistake I thought I was making came up with these hints (and some very good yogurt).

1. Yes, bother to scald the milk and let it cool until it feels the same temperature or slightly cooler than your finger.

2. Mix one tablespoon of *Dannon* yogurt with each quart of milk, mixing a small amount together first. We use canning jars.

3. Make do with the utensils you have. The yogurt containers should be able to nest in water to their tops somewhere warm not hot.

4. Let them sit in *lukewarm* not hot water for 8 to 12 hours. I've made the best yogurt in the kitchen on a winter night as the stove fire was going out. If the temperature is too hot at any point it destroys the culture. If it's too cold for it to grow, you can always gradually make its water bath warmer. Keep the pot covered, but not each jar.

5. If you have been making yogurt and someone else sets out a pan of milk or cream to sour and separate, they will probably get a yogurt product too (without even trying!) because of the bacteria in the air. Cottage cheese or cream cheese can still be made by hanging up the gelled mass and letting the whey drip out. It will be particularly delicious as well.

·RECIPES FROM THE TOWN HOUSE·

I'm Margot and I live with David and Baby Ben of the Bright Eyes in the Total Loss Town House which sits in a green part of the city. I'm sister to Pete and David is brother to Richard. We live in the city because David once had a big, trying, important job and we became the Town House. We talk a lot about leaving but we don't. It's inertia maybe or maybe it's just too nice being the Town House. Almost every time someone knocks on the welcome sign on our front door three floors up, it's the smiling faces of our country cousins with a dog and a sack of fresh veggies and lots of good news about the harvest or someone's book. But . . . before we can sit and chat over a cup of oolong, they head straight for the shower. It's the best shower in three states and that's what the Total Loss Town House is about. It's the place to come when you're weary of crowds and when you badly need a shower where the water runs strong and when you'd just like to do nothing. Everyone knows where the towels are kept.

This all means that many times a dinner planned for two miraculously grows to feed eight. No cookbook tells how to do that. Town House cooking, like Farm cooking, is done with the wits, but includes a few specialties de la maison as well.

Aunt Jameelie Haddad taught me how to make stuffed grape leaves, Syrian style. They're good to serve when you have one pound of hamburger and suddenly six people are in your kitchen, hungry. I always keep a jar of grape leaves on the shelf. You can mix up the stuffing and then subdivide. Once nine people who didn't know each other were in my kitchen. I set them to rolling grape leaves and by the time the meal reached the table, everyone was friends.

·STUFFED GRAPELEAVES· ·SYRIAN STYLE·

1   jar of processed vine leaves, or
     30-40 fresh grape leaves (pick young tender ones
     if you can)
1   pound hamburger or chopped lamb
1   cup white long grain rice
1   large onion, chopped
1   can tomato paste
½ stick soft butter or rendered butter
Salt and pepper
Red pepper and thyme (optional)

1. Before you proceed, you must find the right cooking vessel. I use a 6 quart pot with either a dinner plate or a 9 inch baking tin that just fits inside, weighted down with mugs filled with water. The object is to weight the rolls with something flat so they don't float away.

2. Soak the rice for ten minutes and drain.

3. Rinse the leaves well if you use processed ones. Save torn leaves and tiny ones to line the bottom of the pot. If you use fresh leaves, pour boil-

ing water over them and let them soak for about a minute and drain.

4. Mix meat, rice, onions, tomato paste, butter, salt, and pepper in large bowl with your hands.

5. Roll leaves thusly. Place them vein side up. Put about a finger's width of stuffing across the widest part of the leaf. Roll tightly from the bottom up. No need to tuck the ends in.

6. Line the bottom of the pot with the discarded leaves. Pack the rolls in closely in layers going in alternate directions. Weight down with plate or tin. Fill with water up to level of weight. Simmer over low heat for 45-60 minutes. Taste after 45 minutes. Fresh leaves take a little longer than processed.

7. Serve with lemon and/or yogurt. Good hot or cold and great for picknicking. Can be cooked and frozen. Can be heated wrapped in foil or in a covered baking dish in a low oven.

When David and I were on Isla Mujeres in Mexico we met Luis, an expatriate Italian who had a beautiful wooden sailboat painted yellow. Just after we left the island he took an outboard motor from the harbor and headed for Cuba. He took us to his hut for lunch one day and made us

·SICILIAN PEASANT STEW·

The proportions simply do not matter.
Bacon or smoked ham
Onions
Potatoes
Tomatoes
Water
Eggs
Dill weed
Salt and pepper

Saute the bacon or ham and when enough fat has been rendered, toss in some coarsely chopped onion. When the onion begins to get soft, add potatoes, unpeeled and cut julienne. Let this cook up till the potatoes are a little brown and add some tomatoes in chunks. When the tomatoes begin to break a little add water to make a stew-like consistency. Add lots of salt and lots of black pepper and about a tablespoon of dill weed. When the potatoes are tender, break a couple of eggs into a little water. Beat lightly and throw in the stew, stirring constantly. Serve hot.

·PUMPKIN BREAD·

¾ cup white sugar
½ cup brown sugar
½ cup salad oil
2 eggs, beaten
1½ cups mashed pumpkin (boiled fresh or canned)

Beat all of the above together. Then sift the following together and add:

1 cup white flour
¾ cup whole wheat flour
1 tsp. baking soda
1 tsp. salt
½ tsp. nutmeg
½ tsp. allspice
½ tsp. cinnamon
¼ tsp. ground cloves
¼ tsp. ginger
¼ tsp. mace
⅓ cup chopped pecans or walnuts
½ cup raisins and/or chopped dates, candied orange
    peel, or other dried fruit

Pour into well-greased pan. A loaf pan is nice and a bundt mold is beautiful. A 9x5x3 loaf pan takes about one hour, the mold a little less. Bake at 350° till cake springs back when pressed with a finger. DO NOT OPEN THE OVEN FOR THE FIRST 30 MINUTES. Don't ask why: I've never tried it. The warning was enough for me.

·TRINIDADIAN RIVER CURRY·

We first ate this curry under the bamboos on a riverbank in the Lupinot Valley and it now appears regularly on the Town House menu. We swam in the river while our Indian friends prepared the meal. The chicken and vegetables washed and chilled in the river as we swam. Puna made a rock fireplace and set a huge pot of rice to boil. When that was ready, he wrapped the rice in banana leaves, keeping it perfectly hot till the rest of the food was cooked. Meanwhile the chicken and vegetables were marinating in curry and pepper. He heated some oil in the big pot and threw in a handful of brown sugar. When this was starting to burn, he browned the chicken, minus the vegetables. When the chicken was golden, he added more curry and the vegetables and some of the rum we were drinking as we watched. His brother cut bamboo sections and split them for dishes. Someone else came down from their mud hut with warm Dhal Pooris. It was a perfect feast, with singing and dancing on the riverbank, far into the night. The recipe, adapted for other climes, follows:

    1 chicken, cut in small pieces
    3 or 4 cloves garlic
    3 tbsp. madras curry powder *
    Lots of black pepper
    1 tsp. salt

Fresh or dried hot peppers to taste
2 large tomatoes, cut up
Parsley, about 8 sprigs
1 tsp. thyme
5 or 6 scallions
Fresh coriander (optional)
3 tbsp. oil
3 tbsp. brown sugar
2 tbsp. brandy or rum
Water

Wash the chicken. Put in large bowl with garlic, 1 tbsp. of the curry, the pepper, salt, hot pepper, tomatoes, parsley, thyme, scallions, etc. Heat the brown sugar in the oil. When it just begins to burn, throw in the chicken, without the vegetables. After the chicken has browned, add vegetables, the rest of the curry, and the rum. Cover and simmer slowly about ½ hour. Check from time to time to make sure there is enough liquid. If not, add a little water. Serve when chicken is tender.

* Note: you must use Madras curry powder, available in most international food stores.

·QUICK BATIKS·

(These aren't edible, but they're done on the stove)
You will need:
Crayons with a high pigment content
Paraffin
A muffin tin or small pans

A roaster or large baking pan
Any old watercolor brushes
Cold water dye in a dark color
An iron
Paper towels or other absorbent paper
Cotton cloth (I use men's handkerchiefs from the five-and-ten.
    They're cheap and they're already hemmed.)

Set the muffin tin over simmering water in the roaster. Melt 3 or 4 crayons of each color you want to use with about a half inch cube of parafin. Start painting on your piece of cloth. I do a sketch first. You must work quickly and it helps to know exactly where you're going to put your color. Be sure the color soaks through the fabric. Leave spaces where you want a dark outline or a dark area. You don't have to clean the brush between colors; just wipe it off while it's still wet. When you're finished laying on the wax, crinkle the cloth slightly and dip it in a cold dark dye bath to fill in the crinkles and the areas you've left white. Then place the cloth between sheets of absorbent paper and iron to remove the surface wax. If you use rice paper or the like, you can get a lovely print on the paper.

·EPILOGUE·

The letter which follows, dated Turners Falls, Massachusetts, March 23, 1945, was discovered in the walls of our house shortly after attention had shifted from writing *Home Comfort* to making home improvements.

It seemed a warm omen as well as a testimony to the confidence and good-living which our cookstove could inspire then as now. The letter is addressed to "Rosie", the farmer lady who sold us the farm. We include excerpts.

We are going to sell our Home Comfort Range. Raymond's father is moving, and we are going to get his stove. Raymond remembered that you once wanted one so he said to write to you and give you first chance. Here it is! He wants thirty-five dollars for it. We haven't used it since we have been here but it is in good shape and has been stored under cover—most of the time in the back room. We hated to part with it. It might come in handy. Let us know if you want it and we will save it until you can get down. Otherwise he is going to put an ad in the Recorder and get rid of it. . . .

I forgot to say the stove is a grey and white enameled one with a warming oven over the top. I don't believe you have ever been to our house, so you don't remember seeing it here. It has a reservoir that can be placed either on the fire-box end or the back. The fire-box is all newly lined. It is supposed to be able to burn either wood or coal but the coal was the reason we had to get new lining. We are burning oil and coal in our old stove. It is a Crawford. We put it in to try out the oil and it is very satisfactory in this house. We are going to get rid of it as soon as we can get a heating stove and we can't get a new one as long as they are rationed. Of course, you probably have a new one of your own by now. . . .

The authors would like to acknowledge their thanks to and confidence in Jeffrey Weiss, of N.A.L., who as much as anyone helped to make this book possible, and to express their gratefulness to Don & Evelyn McLean, Chris Rohm, Tom and Alison Hannan, & Phil Spencer, for help in the production of this book. And their special thanks to Margot and David Wizansky for their contribution and frequent shelter.

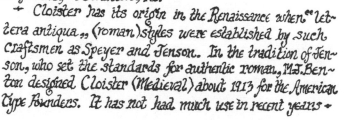

Douglas Parker, at Total Loss Farm, designed this book. It was illustrated by members of the community, and set in 12 point Cloister Old Style by Dix Type-Setting Co. of Syracuse, New York, printed by The Bloomsburg Craftsmen, Bloomsburg, Pa., and bound by the Haddon Craftsmen, in Scranton, Pa.

→ Cloister has its origin in the Renaissance when "lettera antiqua" (roman) styles were established by such craftsmen as Speyer and Jenson. In the tradition of Jenson, who set the standards for authentic roman, M.F. Benton designed Cloister (Medieval) about 1913 for the American Type Founders. It has not had much use in recent years →